# Sales, Marketing, and Continuous Improvement

## Six Best Practices to Achieve Revenue Growth and Increase Customer Loyalty

Daniel M. Stowell

Jossey-Bass Publishers • San Francisco

Substantial discounts on bulk quantities of Jossey-Bass books are available to corporations, professional associations, and other organizations. For details and discount information, contact the special sales department at Jossey-Bass Inc., Publishers (415) 433–1740; Fax (800) 605–2665.

For sales outside the United States, please contact your local Simon & Schuster International Office.

Jossey-Bass Web address: http://www.josseybass.com

Manufactured in the United States of America on Lyons Falls Pathfinder Tradebook. This paper is acid-free and 100 percent totally chlorine-free.

**Library of Congress Cataloging-in-Publication Data**

Stowell, Daniel M.
    Sales, marketing, and continuous improvement : six best practices to achieve revenue growth and increase customer loyalty / Daniel M. Stowell. — 1st ed.
        p. cm. — (The Jossey-Bass business & management series)
    Includes bibliographical references and index.
    Contents: The six best practices — Manage for change — Listen to customers — Focus process — Use teams — Practice an open organization culture — Apply technology — Making it happen — Conclusion.
    ISBN 0–7879–0857–6
    1. Corporate culture.  2. Selling.  3. Marketing.  4. Work groups.
5. Customer relations.  6. Organizational change.  I. Title.
II. Series.
HD58.7.S755    1997
658.8—dc21                                                    96–45846

FIRST EDITION
*HB Printing*   10  9  8  7  6  5  4  3  2  1

The Jossey-Bass
Business & Management Series

# Contents

| | | |
|---|---|---:|
| | Preface | ix |
| | The Author | xvii |
| **1** | The Six Best Practices | 1 |
| **2** | Manage for Change | 24 |
| **3** | Listen to Customers | 52 |
| **4** | Focus on Process | 93 |
| **5** | Use Teams | 134 |
| **6** | Practice an Open Organization Culture | 175 |
| **7** | Apply Technology | 214 |
| **8** | Making It Happen | 252 |
| **9** | Conclusion | 270 |
| | References | 275 |
| | Index | 277 |

*To Cindy Hunt*
*For her loving and continuous support*

# Preface

Over the past fifteen years, business organizations have experienced a virtual revolution. They have faced increasing customer demands, cost pressures, and global competition. The survivors have responded with a variety of practices. They are focusing more on their customers, implementing quality management, benchmarking world-class companies, and reengineering their major processes. They are examining their corporate cultures, changing their management styles, organizing themselves into teams, and empowering their people. Finally, they are applying the latest technology in almost every area.

However, two vital business functions have lagged behind in adopting change. In many companies, sales and marketing are not participating in the improvement process at all. Even when they do participate, they often fail to take full advantage of the new management practices and improvement techniques. The prevailing attitude among many sales and marketing executives and managers is that all these changes are important in the other parts of the organization, but they do not apply to sales and marketing.

As always, there are exceptions. The leading companies have applied these practices in sales and marketing and achieved outstanding results. This book tells you what these companies have done and how they did it.

## The Foundations of This Book

Although dozens of books and articles have been written about current improvement practices, few have focused on how these practices apply specifically to sales and marketing. Those that have describe a single practice, such as quality management, and present a theoretical view of how to use it. This book takes a very different approach. It presents the real experiences of dozens of leading companies, identifies their best practices, and describes how they use these practices in their sales and marketing functions.

I have been fortunate enough to have experienced many of these practices during my career at IBM and in my consulting practice. However, my work did not begin that way. When I joined IBM in 1961, the company sold its hardware and later its software products the only way it knew how, through face-to-face sales. That is the way it was until 1978, when the company's Data Processing Division awakened to the idea that there might be other, more effective and efficient ways to sell selected products. Management decided to check out this idea with what it called the Alternate Channels Marketing Test. One element of the test was a pilot program to sell application software using direct marketing techniques.

At the time, I had just accepted a job to help establish a new department. Our mission was to support application software sales in the western half of the United States. My manager, Bob Blair, had the eastern half. Just as we began to recruit IBMers for our new operation, the division assigned us the alternate channel test for software. It was a job we were not prepared to handle. Our new staff was made up of people with recent field sales experience, and none was familiar with direct response marketing techniques. To compound the management challenge, they were all in remote locations, one in each of the fourteen regional sales offices.

It became immediately apparent that we could not accomplish the goals of the test using existing knowledge and traditional management methods. Without knowing that we were using the team approach that is in fashion today, we developed a process and conducted the test using consensus management. We retained an advertising and marketing consultant, James W. Holland, and built a campaign around the process that customers used to make software buying decisions. We called the program Software Direct.

The test results were outstanding. Fourteen percent of the customers responded to the first mailing, and their response to later mailings was even higher. The Direct Marketing Association (DMA) recognized the program with its ECHO award for excellence in direct marketing. The team clearly demonstrated that IBM could sell software using direct response marketing. We could never have achieved the same results using traditional sales methods.

The Software Direct program made a lasting impression on me. It was my first experience using a team approach to solve problems and implement a new marketing process. In this situation, that approach was clearly more effective than IBM's traditional "command and control" style of management.

Later I trained and facilitated quality improvement teams in branch offices dedicated to selling software. Then I led a headquarters team that analyzed and improved the software sales training process. Both activities reinforced for me the effectiveness of teams and demonstrated the power of team problem solving and process improvement. For the eight months before I took early retirement from IBM and began a consulting business, I worked full time in the business unit's quality department. Again, I had the opportunity to experience firsthand the power of the quality improvement techniques.

Today, as a consultant, I help companies apply quality techniques to sales and marketing. Originally, I intended this book to report the experiences of real companies in using these new practices. Then, as I began interviews with my own clients and prospects and the Malcolm Baldrige National Quality Award winners, it became apparent that the leading companies were using more than just the quality techniques to improve their sales and marketing processes. As a result, the objectives for this book multiplied. *Sales, Marketing, and Continuous Improvement*

- Identifies and describes the best practices for improving sales and marketing
- Reports specific examples of how companies applied the best practices
- Supports the design and implementation of an improvement process in sales and marketing
- Shows how sales and marketing contribute to an organization-wide improvement process

More than sixty companies have contributed directly to this book. They all willingly shared their experiences and results, their successes and failures. In addition, I searched the general business, sales and marketing, technology, and quality literature; attended seminars and workshops; and networked with over fifty other consultants.

The organizations I interviewed represent virtually every industry, from high-tech computer and electronics companies to basic manufacturing, from small software developers to major communications giants, from banks and insurance companies to distributors and consumer products firms. Their sizes range from the giant General Motors to a small software value-added remarketer (a list of the companies that contributed appears at the end of this Preface). The interview subjects came from almost every level in their organizations. They included company and division presidents and middle and first-line managers and supervisors. They represented many functional areas including general management, sales, marketing, quality, and human resources.

Many of the supporting examples in this book come from well-known companies, highly rated by their customers, valued by Wall Street, and recognized by the business press. Other illustrations are from companies equally successful but less well known. Still other examples come from companies that may not be as highly regarded or successful or that may have regressed in their improvement activities since they shared their stories. This does not diminish the value of their ideas. Their stories are included because they are good examples of the best practices in use. Remember, there are many contributors to business success. Effective use of improvement techniques is just one of them.

In most cases, the companies are identified by name. When they were willing to share their bottom-line results, those are included as well. However, many of the companies considered that information confidential. Others just did not do an effective job of measuring their bottom-line results.

In exchange for the companies' input, I agreed to share the research findings with them. These presentations of the research findings not only benefited the companies but identified subjects likely to be of greatest interest to readers of this book. At the conclusion of each feedback presentation, I asked what parts of the research were of greatest interest to the people I interviewed and what they wanted to learn more about. Moreover I was able to observe each company's progress since the initial interview, a period that frequently amounted to a year or more. Some companies had continued their improvement, others had faltered, and a few had even slipped backwards. Learning what had happened over time and why was also an important addition to the content of this book.

## Organization of This Book

From the research, I identified six best practices employed by the leading companies. In Chapter One, you will discover what these practices are and learn some basic concepts and definitions. Chapters Two through Seven describe each of the practices in detail, show specifically how each one applies to sales and marketing, and provide examples of how companies are using them.

The research also made clear that there is no one best way to implement the six best practices. Because every organization, organization culture, and organizational circumstance or situation is different, each company must choose its own approach. Thus Chapter Eight suggests a process for creating and implementing an action plan to implement the six best practices and instill a culture of continuous improvement.

## Audience

This book is intended to give executives and managers with responsibility for sales and marketing practical assistance in using the six best practices to improve their functions. Internal and external consultants, academics, and graduate students in sales, marketing, quality, and organization development will also benefit from its insights, research among real companies, and many examples.

## Acknowledgments

I want to recognize and thank the people who made this book possible. First on the list are the people who contributed the most to the book's content. They are the more than sixty people from organizations across the United States and Canada who took valuable time out of their busy schedules to share their experience and knowledge, their ideas and insights. As Wheelabrator sales executive Tom Warren said, "I don't have the time to do this, but I will, because it is so important." Over 90 percent of the companies I contacted agreed to be interviewed.

Thanks also go to the editors who have contributed to this book. Hollis Barnhart, then an acquisition editor at Quality Resources, first asked if I would be interested in writing a book, and it was her persistence that finally got me started. Beth Anderson, former senior editor at Lexington Books, bought my book proposal and gave me the support, editorial advice, and counsel that got me through the first few chapters. I know it was not easy. After the book was assigned to Jossey-Bass, editors Larry Alexander, Byron Schneider, and Judith Hibbard guided it through the remainder of the publishing cycle. Elspeth MacHattie added her many copyediting skills, keeping me honest on spelling and grammar, and tying up all of the loose ends. My thanks go to them for their efforts in bringing the book to completion.

I also appreciate the efforts of the seven academic and marketing professionals who reviewed the first draft of the manuscript. They provided a reality check, and their comments and suggestions were invaluable. Thanks also go to my many colleagues in consulting. Some helped identify the companies described in the book or provided examples of their own. Others reviewed parts of the book and provided feedback. All have been supportive throughout my journey.

My final and greatest thank-you goes to my partner, Cindy Hunt. She fills many positions of responsibility in my consulting firm. In addition to being a top-flight consultant, she is also the facilities manager, information systems department, and corporate nutritionist. Most of all, she was here every day to support me through the highs and lows of the creative process.

This book is the result of the efforts of all of these people and many more. I sincerely appreciate everyone's contribution.

*Southbury, Connecticut*         D. M. STOWELL
*December 1996*

# Contributing Companies

The following companies were interviewed for this book (Baldrige Quality Award winners are marked with an asterisk):

3M
AccuRate, Inc.
ADC Telecommunications, Inc.
AlliedSignal Inc.
Amica Mutual Insurance
  Company
AT&T*
Attachmate Corporation
  (formerly Digital Commu-
  nications Associates, Inc.)
Barnett Securities, Inc.
Bausch & Lomb Inc.
BOC Gasses
Cadillac Motor Car Division*
Calgon Corporation
California & Hawaiian Sugar
  Company
Century Furniture Industries
Champion International
  Corporation
Digital Equipment Corporation
DSSI
DuraTemp Corporation
Eastman Chemical Company*
Elf Atochem North America,
  Inc.
Ethyl Corporation
Federal Express Corporation*
Foseco, Inc.
General Electric Capital
  Corporation
General Electric Company
Globe Metallurgical, Inc.*

GTE Corporation
Heublein, Inc.
Hewlett Packard Company
IBM Corporation*
ITT Fluid Transmission
  Corporation
Kimberly Clark Corporation
Marlow Industries, Inc.*
Medicus Systems Corporation
Motorola, Inc.
The Mutual Life Insurance
  Company of New York
NeuroDimension, Inc.
NeXT Computer, Inc.
NYNEX Corporation
Park Place Motorcars
People's Bank
Pitney Bowes Inc.
Secura Insurance Companies
Square D Company
Steelcase, Inc.
Texaco, Inc.
Texas Instruments, Inc.*
TransCanada Gas Services, Ltd.
The Travelers Companies
Ungerman Bass Networks, Inc.
Unisys Corporation
Westinghouse Electric
  Corporation
The Wheelabrator
  Corporation
Xerox Corporation*
Zytec Corporation*

The following companies also provided information for this book.

The Alexander Group, Inc.
Bain & Company
Bank of Oklahoma
Coopers & Lybrand, L.L.P.
The Dartnell Corporation
Ernst & Young, L.L.P.
Harte-Hanks Direct Marketing
Holox, Ltd.
Interstate Battery System of America, Inc.
ITT Hartford Group, Inc.
James River Corporation
The Juran Institute
Kaiser Permanente
Labatt Breweries Alberta
The Larry Weber Group
Marriott International, Inc.

MCI Telecommunications Corporation
Northrop Grumman Norden Systems, Inc.
Ogilvy & Mather Direct Response, Inc.
OSRAM SYLVANIA, Inc.
Oxford Health Plans, Inc.
The Paradyne Corporation
Solectron Corporation*
Stew Leonard's
Sun Microsystems of Canada, Inc.
Susanna Opper & Associates
Systems Sales Support Company
USAA
World Color, Inc.

# The Author

**Dan Stowell** is founder and president of D. M. Stowell & Company, a professional services firm providing consulting, training, facilitation, research, and project management in the area of sales, marketing, and quality. He has led organization-wide improvement initiatives and business process redesign efforts and is a recognized authority in the application of quality improvement techniques to sales and marketing.

Stowell's practice draws on twenty-six years of experience with the IBM Corporation, where he held significant management positions in sales, marketing, and quality improvement and was responsible for developing and driving the quality improvement process in a 6,000–person business unit. In other assignments, he created and managed many innovative sales and marketing programs. Stowell has contributed to such publications as *Quality Progress* and *Quality Digest,* and he is an active member of the American Marketing Association and the American Society for Quality Control. He is also a member of the ASQC's Quality Management Division Council and is responsible for developing marketing programs for the division.

# Chapter One

# | **The Six Best Practices**

Organizations today are facing the most rapidly changing business environment in their history, and there is no end in sight. To survive and grow, they are responding in a variety of ways. They are increasing their customer focus, cutting costs, slashing layers of management, making decisions more quickly, and improving product and service quality. In many companies, however, the sales and marketing functions have not kept pace with the rest of the organization in these efforts. These companies are now looking for ways to include these two vital business functions in their companywide improvement efforts and to accelerate the rate of change in those functions.

## The Drivers of Change

Several factors are driving the need for change in the sales and marketing functions. Customer demand leads the list. Customers are changing the way they make their buying decisions and acquire products and services, and they expect their suppliers to align with the new ways they want to do business. They want fewer points of contact with their suppliers, and they want each contact to add value. Many customers are reducing the number of their suppliers to improve quality and reduce cost. They are also entering into longer-term supplier contracts and partnerships.

Change in sales and marketing is also being driven by the improvement efforts that are already reshaping other parts of the organization. Companies are using quality management, employee teams, process management, reengineering, and benchmarking to increase their effectiveness and cut costs. The sales and marketing organizations are a vital part of many of the key cross-functional business processes that companies slate for improvement. Although many sales and marketing departments have successfully avoided these change efforts in the past, their active participation is a virtual requirement for company success. The improvement process cannot be companywide without including sales and marketing.

In addition, both sales and marketing are important sources of customer information. In most companies, marketing is responsible for customer satisfaction surveys and market research. Salespeople are in direct contact with customers daily. Input from both of these sources is a vital part of any improvement process.

Sales and marketing also represent a significant part of every organization's budget. Their combined costs average about 15 percent of revenue and range well above 30 percent in many companies. With today's emphasis on increasing growth rates on one hand and controlling costs on the other, organizations continue to seek ways to increase salesforce productivity and make the marketing budget go further.

Competitors are part of this picture as well, and they are not letting up the pressure. The best of them already understand and are responding to changing customer demands. They are taking advantage of the best improvement techniques to reinvent themselves, and they are applying the latest technology to increase their effectiveness and productivity. In these companies, sales and marketing are already an integral part of the companywide improvement efforts.

## How Organizations Respond

With all these factors confronting them, how are sales and marketing organizations responding? The answer is mixed. Some remain on the sidelines. A few of these are in a complete state of denial while others just hope the problems will go away so they can continue with business as usual. A few organizations that have yet to take action realize they should but for a variety of reasons have not. For some, the reason is fear of change. Others lack understanding of the improvement techniques and technology available or do not believe they apply to sales or marketing. Yet others are so caught up in the day-to-day press of business that they have not taken the time to consider the potential for change.

Many companies have taken some kind of action but have yet to experience notable success. Some tried a new practice once, failed, and walked away. Their failure reinforced their underlying belief that the improvement process does not work in sales and marketing. Those organizations are back to square one. Other companies have tried improvement practices but have yet to reach the full potential of their efforts. Some lacked the necessary commitment to the improvement process. Others were not able to master the skills necessary to manage a change effort. Reorganizations, management turnovers, and mergers and acquisitions have also taken their toll on attempts to improve sales and marketing functions.

As always, there are exceptions. They are the leading companies, the role models. They have made change work for them across their organizations, including their sales and marketing functions. They are the companies with high customer loyalty and employee satisfaction, strong growth and profits, and an increase in shareholder wealth. In some of these organizations, the sales or marketing functions have led the improvement efforts.

Now stop and consider where your own organization falls on the continuum. Is it still denying that a problem exists or hoping the problem will go away? Does it remain on the sidelines waiting to get into the game? Has it tried and failed or met with limited success in its efforts to improve? Has it been successful but wants to continue the improvement journey by learning more about what other companies are doing and how they do it? If the answer to any of these questions is yes, this book can help. According to author, speaker, and trainer Anthony Robbins, "Success leaves clues," and it is this book's challenge to find those clues, to identify the practices that made these companies successful, and to share them with you. That is what this book is all about (Robbins, 1986, p. 26).

*Sales, Marketing, and Continuous Improvement* is based on a survey of companies from across the United States and Canada. (A list of contributors appears at the end of the Preface.) Over five dozen organizations participated through face-to-face interviews; others participated by mail and telephone. A literature review rounded out the search for best practices. All the companies that participated have taken some action to improve, and in some cases they have virtually reinvented the way they sell and market their products and services. Many are well known for their improvement efforts and for their sales and marketing practices.

An analysis of the survey results revealed six best practices used by these companies to improve their sales and marketing functions:

- Manage for change
- Listen to customers
- Focus on process
- Use teams
- Practice an open organization culture
- Apply technology

Certainly not every company has adopted all six, and in some cases the practices have not been adopted companywide. However, there is a relationship between high performance and the use of these practices.

## The Eastman Chemical Company Story

The following story of one of these high-performing organizations, Eastman Chemical Company, offers an introductory illustration of the six best practices.

### Company History

Eastman Chemical's headquarters and home of two-thirds of the company's 18,000 employees is in Kingsport, Tennessee, a small community of about 50,000 located in the scenic Great Smoky Mountains. The company's roots go back to 1920, when George Eastman purchased a partially completed wood distillation plant in Kingsport to provide methanol for the Eastman Kodak Company. Over time, Eastman expanded its product line, grew its customer base, and moved into international markets. Today the company is a world leader in the development, manufacture, and sale of a wide variety of chemicals, fibers, and plastics. Its products are used in coatings, food and consumer packaging, appliances, electronic components, cosmetics, toys, eyeglasses, brushes, and medical devices, among others. As the company's product line expanded, several new plants were brought on-line around the United States, and Eastman opened its first off-shore manufacturing facility, in England, in the late 1960s. To serve its growing international markets, Eastman also opened sales offices around the world, and by 1992, the company had thirty international sales locations.

Up to the late 1970s, Eastman was an industry leader in product quality. However, Eastman's customers were becoming more quality conscious, and the company's competitors were improving their own product quality. Eastman began to lose market share in a major product line, and the members of senior management realized that they had to take action. For a few years, they practiced Management by Objectives (MBO), one of the popular management techniques of the time. According to several Eastman people I interviewed, this management technique resulted in a "flavor of the year" approach.

In the late 1970s and early 1980s, Eastman's senior managers recognized that MBO was not getting the results they wanted. After carefully considering the alternatives, they decided to make a companywide commitment to a quality management process. They resisted the idea of adopting a canned approach and instead proceeded to develop their own management system, one that would build on the company's unique culture and strengths. The company then formed a high-level management team to accomplish the task.

The team studied the well-known quality gurus Deming, Juran, and Crosby and the ideas of management consultant Aubry C. Daniels. Daniels's contribution was Performance Management, an "approach to managing people at work that relies on positive reinforcement as the major way to maximizing performance" (Daniels, 1989, p. 4). The result of senior management's commitment and the team's efforts was a management process that lives at Eastman Chemical to this day. Of course, the company continually reviews the quality management process and has revised its "Quality Policy" twice to reflect the changing needs of the company and its stakeholders. However, the fundamental approach is still in place.

One of the first steps in Eastman Chemical's new quality management process was to establish better relationships with its customers. The company began to conduct customer satisfaction surveys to identify areas for improvement. It also invited customers into the plants for the first time. This campaign, called Customers and Us, was successful and evolved into Quality Partnerships with several of the company's key customers. By listening to customers, Eastman identified specific ways to improve its products and services. As product and service quality went up, customer satisfaction increased, and the company's financial performance improved. Improvements were not limited to product quality alone. When customers asked Eastman to adopt new ways of doing business, the company responded with new, innovative services as well.

One of the first customer requirements Eastman identified was the use of electronic data interchange (EDI). This technology provided a standard way for trading partners to exchange information electronically. It enabled Eastman's customers to submit orders and the company to respond with order confirmations, shipping notices, and invoices. EDI reduced data entry costs, improved accuracy, and made communication faster between Eastman and the customers who were ready to use the technology. Although EDI is in common use today, it was on the leading edge in the early 1980s when Eastman adopted it.

Eastman's Worldwide Sales Division was a player in the improvement process from the beginning. According to V. A. Robbins, Jr., the division's coordinator of quality management, "Worldwide Sales started by identifying our trade customers, our internal customers, our inputs, outputs, processes, and suppliers. We developed a list of Key Result Areas as well as a mission statement for Worldwide Sales."

## Eastman Employee Satisfaction

Employee satisfaction is important to Eastman. In 1989, the company established a process to survey employees. It also conducts employee focus groups. The Worldwide Sales Division uses input from both these sources to identify opportunities for improving employee satisfaction. According to Robbins, "Eastman believes that you cannot satisfy customers until you have satisfied employees."

## Eastman Makes International Business Easy

In late 1989, Earnie Davenport became president and CEO of Eastman Chemical Company, and the senior management team revisited the company's vision for the year 2000. Recognizing the need to increase international business in order to meet the company's growth targets, team members set an objective to grow international sales from the current 20 percent of the business to 50 percent by the year 2000.

Eastman faced a challenge in reaching this goal, however. Surveys showed the satisfaction of international customers was far behind that of U.S. customers in several critical areas. According to George O. Trabue, Jr., former Eastman president of Worldwide Sales, the company was "experiencing what seemed to be an exponential increase in the complications and difficulties associated with growing international business." Eastman's marketing managers understood the problems, and they could easily have used them as an excuse for not meeting the growth target. They chose a different path.

Trabue describes the next step: "One of our internal quality consultants kept suggesting that the thing to do was 'retreat'; not retreat from the situation but retreat to a workshop to deal with this growing need and the opportunity associated with internal business process and international customer satisfaction." Even with the customer data in hand, it was not easy to convince the international marketing management team to commit to a three-day working retreat to tackle the problem. However, today Trabue says, "I [now] realize that those three days were only a tiny portion of the commitment that would be required to overcome the paradigms we had and to bring about the needed improvements."

Eastman's Worldwide Sales management team did conduct that three-day workshop. Trabue recalls:

> At the workshop, we studied our process of doing international business. It became painfully evident that something significant had to be done to simplify the process and to make it work smoothly for our customers. When we mapped it out, it covered the walls of our entire working room. The Allies freed Europe during World War II with fewer charts and maps than we had stuck on the wall. We began to see and feel what our international customers had to go through to do business with us. As one member of the team said, "You know, an overseas customer would have to be desperate for product to go through all this." The management team arrived at a consensus that could best be described as a need to "Make International Business Easy" (or MIBE as we called it) for

our customers. The concept of "being easy to do business with" caught on from the moment the phrase was first formulated and became the theme of our efforts from that time on.

To make MIBE happen, many groups throughout the company and around the world would have to be involved. Many people would have to help in the areas of responding to the customers, acknowledging orders, managing credit, scheduling, determining product availability, delivering product, making sales contracts, and all the other aspects of doing international business. Problems would have to be addressed at more than thirty international locations. And there was another challenge. Many of the people who would have to take part did not report through the sales division. The management team had to develop a way to include these groups, to make sure they understood the need and how they could participate. Everyone had to be motivated to help solve some very difficult process problems.

From the workshop emerged the first details of the action plan. It would be based on voluntary participation of groups from the Worldwide Sales Division and all the support functions, such as finance, distribution, and technical service. In other words, the management team designed MIBE to be a "want to," not a "have to," effort. The company would recognize and reward people for each step in the process: for attending presentations to learn about MIBE, for selecting a project, for forming a team and linking-in, and for completing their project.

### Announcing MIBE

In 1989 and 1990, more than one hundred kickoff presentations were held with groups in the field who had the potential to make an impact on international business processes. Each meeting covered answers to these four questions:

- What did Eastman need to accomplish to make international business easy?
- Why was it important to do this to grow sales?
- How was the international marketing team going to support the process?
- What help was needed from the functional teams all around the world?

"In the kickoff meetings," said Trabue, "we explained to each group exactly what they would have to do to become part of the process. We asked them to help by forming teams and selecting projects to make international business easy. The teams were to find ways to improve the process, measure progress on improvements, reinforce those who helped with their project, and share their results with international marketing. Then the improvements could be merchandised to customers and replicated in other areas of the world."

Unlike many past efforts, this effort set no deadlines for reporting back and selecting a project. Instead, each team was asked to spend time determining how they could help make international business easy for customers and then to let the sales management team know what they came up with. Team participation was based on a team's understanding of the need and on their desire to be part of the effort.

### Linking-In

Once a team selected a project, their next step was to "link-in" to the MIBE process, making senior management aware of the team's commitment and the project chosen. When a team linked-in, managers held a ceremony to welcome the team to the MIBE effort and to thank team members for their participation. If the team was located in Kingsport, team members, team managers, and other managers from various levels met at an MIBE display outside the worldwide sales offices. On the display, they placed a team photograph and a photograph of a communications satellite on which the team had recorded the project name. Team members described their project and plans, photographs were taken, refreshments served, and MIBE tokens given out. For teams in the international sales offices, local managers held a similar ceremony and sent the photographs to Kingsport to be added to the display. Over the next two years, approximately 150 teams linked-in to the MIBE effort.

### Training and Support

Eastman's improvement process integrated the principles of statistical methods and the behavioral sciences. To provide the teams with the skills they needed, Eastman conducted three-day workshops in all international sales offices. Having a common improvement process facilitated communications within teams and between teams around the world. Eastman also supported the teams with trained facilitators.

### Communicating the Results

The international marketing function provided scoreboards to make progress visible to the teams and help them share their progress with others. The scoreboards tracked three measurements: the number of link-ins or projects that teams started each quarter, the number of completed projects (including a list of each project's benefits and improvements), and customer satisfaction as determined by Eastman surveys. In addition, frequent newsletters communicated progress and results. The company's worldwide electronic mail (e-mail) system provided a fast and effective way for the teams to share information among themselves and keep international marketing management informed.

### MIBE Results

Here are some examples from individual improvement teams of MIBE results:

- Order problems reduced from sixty-one in 1989 to thirty-two in 1990 to thirteen in 1991.
- Delivery time dropped from forty-five days to fourteen days.
- Invoice time decreased from seventeen hours to eight hours.
- Orders delayed for pricing problems reduced from six per month to zero per month for ten consecutive months.
- Technical service phone response to customers within forty-eight hours increased from 76 percent to 90 percent.
- Time to complete a technical service laboratory study reduced from 15.6 days to 9.6. days.
- On-time pricing requests to customers increased from 40 percent to 90 percent.
- Customer satisfaction with the distribution, handling, and ordering of Eastman literature improved from 24 percent to 96 percent.

In total, teams worked on more than 150 projects. As a result of the improvements they made, customer satisfaction increased from 55 percent ranking Eastman as their number one or preferred supplier at the end of 1987 to about 75 percent. Over the same time period, international sales increased from 20 percent to 30 percent of total sales.

### Celebrating Success

With results like these, it was time to take time off and celebrate, and celebrate they did. Eastman held an international business festival that gathered more than one hundred teams from around the world to celebrate progress and share improvement ideas with each other. The festival also helped build further interest in the MIBE process.

## Making Eastman the Preferred Supplier

MIBE had clearly met its objectives. International customers had rated Eastman Chemical Company at about the same level as had U.S. customers. George Trabue commented:

> It was obvious that we needed to expand the process to a wider scope to impact more customers and to get even more Eastman people involved. We updated the process to meet these objectives. All Eastman employees were invited to get on board the MEPS Express, an acronym for "Making Eastman the Preferred Supplier" to our customers. This supports the message of Eastman's strategic intent or vision: "To Be the World's Preferred Chemical Company."
>
> By any measure, MIBE had been a total success. If 150 teams involving 1,000 people could create the differences that they did, we were confident that involving all 18,000 employees with what we hoped would be over 500 projects would drive even greater results. Thus, we could make the transition from MIBE to the new process . . . Making Eastman the Preferred Supplier. We set a goal in 1992 to have ninety-two teams linked-in to the MEPS process.

Within a year, Eastman had almost double that number of teams in place.

MEPS continues the tradition begun by MIBE at Eastman. To celebrate its success, in 1995 the company held a second major festival at which teams shared their experiences and ideas and were recognized for their contributions.

## Eastman Applies Technology

Technology has played an important role for Eastman's sales and marketing functions. In addition to using EDI and e-mail, the company has established a database of customer satisfaction information, implemented salesforce automation, and recently started using the Internet for sales and customer support. The customer database includes information from customer satisfaction surveys, the complaint-handling process, customer partnerships, and sales call reports. V. A. Robbins reports that these data are "available companywide." More than two hundred people use the database "on a regular basis," and "the information helps them decide what is important from a customer perspective." Then they build their business plans based on customer input.

Eastman's sales division is already into the second generation of a salesforce automation system. Salespeople around the world access e-mail through the latest laptop computers and modems. They can review messages, enter responses, and transmit them back at their convenience. They can also access the companywide software system that tracks the production process from raw materials and inventory through production control and order status. A simple inquiry gives salespeople the status of their customers' orders. The ability to access data and to communicate with locations around the world is especially important to a global salesforce that operates in so many different time zones. Of course, Eastman's salespeople also have stand-alone computing capability. Their laptops are equipped with a suite of software for word processing, spreadsheets, and presentations. The latest in sales literature is available electronically and can be printed out whenever a sales person needs it.

The Internet is the most rapidly growing tool for sales and marketing, and Eastman is already taking advantage of it. The company's World Wide Web site (http://www.eastman.com) provides customers and prospects with information on the company, its products, and the markets it serves. The web site also includes the company's "Quality Policy" and announces current employment opportunities.

As mentioned earlier, Eastman also offers customer support through the Internet. For example, customers can now talk to Eastman's technical service representatives over the Internet. And Eastman listens to customers through the Internet as well. The web site includes an electronic customer survey that asks site visitors what they think of the web site information and asks for their ideas on how to improve it.

Eastman continues to look for ways to use technology to improve sales processes. The company currently has a project underway to design the salesforce of the future, looking at all the latest technology and how it will affect the way Eastman and its salesforce support the company's customers.

## Eastman Chemical's Results

All these activities are fine, but how is the company performing? The answer is very well. Since Eastman Chemical was spun off from Eastman Kodak in 1994, revenues have grown by 18 percent and operating earnings are up by 31 percent. By the end of 1995, 37 percent of the company's revenues were coming from international customers. This puts Eastman Chemical right on track toward its objective of 50 percent by the year 2000. The value of company stock had increased by 33 percent by the end of 1995. The company has received its share of national recognition as well. In the fall of 1993, Eastman's quality management process earned the company a Malcolm Baldrige National Quality Award in the large manufacturing category. Eastman's salesforce was rated number one in its industry by *Sales and Marketing Management* at the magazine's 1994 Power Selling Conference.

## The Six Best Practices

As its results show, the Eastman Chemical Company is a winner by almost any measure. The company also provides an excellent example of the six best practices for improving sales and marketing, as follows.

## Manage for Change

Change did not just happen at Eastman. It came as a direct result of commitment by senior management and the sales and marketing organizations. Managers' commitment was backed up by their leadership and direct involvement in the improvement process. Recall how the management team in worldwide sales met for three days just to define and document what the company's international customers had to go through to acquire Eastman products. As the saying goes, "they walked their talk." They ignored the traditional command and control approach to management as well. Instead they practiced leadership by establishing a vision and a direction: first, the Make International Business Easy process, and later the Making Eastman the Preferred Supplier process. They asked everyone who could help to do so. They provided training and support and gave people feedback on their progress. Each time the teams took a step, management provided positive recognition for their accomplishment and contribution.

## Listen to Customers

The second best practice is listening to customers. Eastman does this through a collection of methods including its customer satisfaction surveys, complaint-handling process, customer partnerships, and call reports and through its recently added external surveys and web site. This combination of methods gets Eastman the customer information it needs.

## Focus on Process

Processes are the way things get done. At Eastman, the sales and marketing management team personally defined the processes that international customers had to follow to get the company's products. To "make international business easy," Eastman teams had to improve those processes, making them more user-friendly for customers. By focusing on process, teams made improvements that resulted in faster responses, fewer defects, and improved customer satisfaction.

## Use Teams

Eastman used teams to organize and carry out the improvement effort. Some of these teams existed within the sales division; others were cross-functional. There were teams at all levels, from teams of sales and administrative people in the worldwide sales offices to the senior management team in company headquarters.

## Practice an Open Organization Culture

The term *open organization culture* describes an organization that is flexible and responsive, one that eliminates internal barriers and tries new ideas. At Eastman the people looked beyond their own jobs and departments and took a broad cross-functional view. The improvement teams shared their progress and their ideas. The company made customer satisfaction data available to anyone who needed them. Management empowered team members to take informed action, to measure their results, and to learn and improve continuously. All these actions typify an organization with an open culture.

## Apply Technology

The Eastman story also illustrates the sixth best practice, the application of technology. At Eastman it began with the use of EDI to improve the speed and accuracy of information exchange with customers and e-mail to improve communication within the company. Eastman also created a customer information database, automated sales processes, and established a site on the World Wide Web. This technology enabled sales and marketing to improve existing processes and do things previously thought to be impractical or even impossible.

## The Missing Management Practice

Notice that one of the most popular management practices of the last decade is conspicuous by its absence at Eastman: downsizing. Many companies have employed downsizing: some out of necessity, others because it is fashionable with Wall Street analysts. In the past five years, the Fortune 500 companies have reduced their employee population from over 16 million to fewer than 11 million. However, for most, downsizing has not met their expectations of increased productivity and profits. Moreover, it has resulted in a significant loss of valuable knowledge, experience, and employee loyalty.

During the same five-year period in which the Fortune 500 was shedding five million people, Eastman managed its employment process and maintained its employment level at just under 18,000. Eastman has chosen to increase profits through customer focus, growth, and productivity gains. Clearly, for most companies, downsizing is not one of the best practices for improving sales and marketing.

## Best Practices Conclusion

There they are, the six best practices used by leading companies to improve their sales and marketing processes. At first glance, the list may seem to be a blinding flash of the obvious. After all, these items appear on virtually everyone's list of today's best practices for improving quality, customer satisfaction, and productivity. The list parallels the results of the 1991 U.S. General Accounting Office study of companies that won or were leading contenders in the first three years of the Malcolm Baldrige National Quality Award competition. These six best practices are the same practices that companies have successfully applied in virtually every other department or function.

And that is just the point. These practices are as effective in sales and marketing as they are in every other part of the organization.

Some experts think their potential in sales and marketing is even greater. One of these experts is John Lawrence, currently a consulting partner in Xerox Business Services. Speaking about the potential for improvement in sales and marketing, he says, "I see even greater opportunity in sales and marketing than I saw in manufacturing in terms of the impact on the bottom line." Lawrence speaks from experience. He has held quality management positions in sales and marketing as well as manufacturing and engineering at Xerox.

Another key point is that most of these practices are not new or unproven. Most have been around for many years, and they have stood the test of time. When Tom Watson, Sr., was in charge of sales at National Cash Register, he called his sales managers together once a week to look for new ideas to improve the sales process. That was in 1903. Many of the statistical techniques used in quality management are based on the work of Walter A. Shewhart, an engineer at Bell Laboratories. He first published them in a two-page memo in 1924. In 1938, Alex Osborn invented brainstorming as a way to generate creative new ideas for his advertising agency clients. Although Michael Hammer and James Champy (1993) made "reengineering" popular in the early 1990s, the concept of creating new processes from scratch is hardly new. American Airlines developed the Sabre System in the early 1960s, and it represented a totally new way to process airline reservations.

All of the six best practices are tried and proven. It is only their acceptance in sales and marketing that has lagged behind in many companies.

## Basic Concepts

Each of the next six chapters describes a single best practice and shows how it applies to the sales and marketing functions. Before examining the best practices, however, we need to define several concepts upon which the best practices are founded.

## Quality: The Objective of the Best Practices

At the heart of improving sales and marketing is the concept of quality. Yet quality has never had a commonly accepted definition. Almost every company has its own characterizations as does every consultant or quality guru, but most definitions can be derived from Figure 1.1. Just take one term from column A, one from column B, and one from column C, and you will have someone's definition of quality. Notice, however, that any definition created from Figure 1.1 will be customer centered. For the purposes of this book, I define *quality* as *meeting customer wants and needs,* or more succinctly, *meeting customer requirements.*

Meeting customer requirements is the objective of the six best practices. Companies improve or reengineer their sales and marketing processes to produce output that better meets customer requirements. Benchmarking identifies world-class products, services, and practices against which to measure a company's own. Technology is applied to improve current processes and to make possible

**Figure 1.1. The Definition of Quality.**

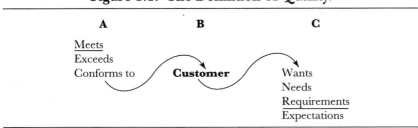

new ways to sell and market, ways that were previously not possible. All are done to meet customer requirements.

Not all companies have chosen a customer focus for their improvement efforts. Some view their efforts as ways to reduce costs and increase profits. Most leading companies reject this idea, however. The leaders believe reduced costs are a step toward meeting the customer requirement for greater value and that increased profits are a measurement of how effectively and efficiently they are meeting their customers' requirements.

## Customers

If the objective is to meet customer requirements, then the term customers must be defined before they can be identified. A *customer* is anyone who receives and must be satisfied with the work product or output of a process. The primary customer of sales and marketing is the person or group making or influencing the buying decision for a product or service. Note that the customers of sales and marketing may or may not be the end users or consumers of the product or service.

Although decision makers and influencers receive the majority of the output of sales and marketing processes, they are not the only customers. There are many people and groups within every company who also receive the output from that company's sales and marketing functions. In one client seminar, a salesperson in a small plastics firm identified internal customers in order entry, product design, manufacturing, shipping, customer service, sales management, marketing, billing, and accounts receivable.

## The Product of Sales and Marketing

If decision makers and influencers are the primary customers of sales and marketing, what is the output or product that they receive? Most sales and marketing people will answer that it is the product or service of the company. For our purposes, however, it is not. It is more useful to think of the *product* of sales and marketing as information! For external customers, the information concerns the company's products or services, terms and conditions, delivery, price, and so on. The internal customers may receive information in the form of customer orders, requirements, or complaints. Thinking of the product of sales and marketing as information makes it possible for teams to identify, analyze, and improve processes.

## Sales and Marketing Missions

Sales and marketing have different missions.

### Sales

Most sales executives and managers still view their salespeople as knights in shining armor, riding forth to slay the competitive dragon, or maybe a reluctant customer or two. Ask them to define the purpose or mission of sales, and they will quickly respond with answers like "closing orders," "booking business," or "getting ink on the contract." Although these are purposes for most sales organizations, they rarely reflect the complete sales mission or include everything salespeople spend their time doing. Without an understanding of the complete sales job, it is difficult to improve it. That complete understanding is also necessary in order to hire, train, motivate, evaluate, and compensate the salesforce effectively.

The Eastman Chemical Company Worldwide Sales Division's mission statement, for example, is "To sell Eastman Chemical Company products, to enhance customer satisfaction by building long-term relationships and to provide sales and market information to other internal Eastman units." The first element, selling products, does reflect the most commonly accepted purpose of sales. The second and third elements, however, enhancing customer satisfaction and building long-term relationships, involve much more than the traditional sales activities. They require that the salespeople provide added value to the customer in a variety of ways. The fourth element, providing sales and market information to internal units, recognizes the sales activities that serve internal customers.

The Dartnell Corporation in Chicago is a well-known publisher of sales-related training and motivational materials. It also surveys salespeople to find out how they are compensated and how they spend their time. Dartnell's surveys reveal that, on average, salespeople spend about half of their time in non-selling-related activities. Failing to examine and improve these activities is also to ignore significant areas of potential improvement.

### Marketing

Defining the mission of marketing is even more difficult than it is for sales. In most companies, the two functions share the mission of delivering information to customer decision makers and influencers. The sales department generally does this through face-to-face contact. The marketing department does it through advertising, direct mail, catalogues, telemarketing, and trade shows. However, in most companies, marketing owns other functions such as market research, market identification and segmentation, new product development, and sales support. Before a company begins an improvement process in marketing, it is important that it have a clear understanding of its marketing function's complete mission.

## Business Processes: How Things Get Done

A formal definition of a *process* is "Any activity or group of activities that takes input, adds value to it and produces an output that goes to an internal or external customer" (Harrington, 1991, p. 9). Business processes include all of the people, equipment, procedures, and information involved in creating the process output. They exist in every facet of a business and are the way most things get done. The Eastman Chemical Company story has already shown the value of identifying and improving business processes.

Sales and marketing professionals often reject the idea that they follow defined processes and that improvement techniques apply to what they do. They support the idea of process improvement in other parts of the organization but are often heard to say: "What we do here is an art, not a science or a process. We're creative and never do things the same way twice." But is that really the case?

While Jack Caffey was quality manager for the North American Field Operations unit at Hewlett Packard, he often faced that attitude as he worked with field sales managers. "We don't have processes out here," they would say. In response to that, Caffey asked them to describe how they train a salesperson new to the job. The sales managers would then relate the steps through which the salesperson goes to identify leads, qualify prospects, write proposals, and close orders. At that point, Caffey would point out that those steps constitute a process and that like virtually all processes they are subject to definition, measurement, analysis, and improvement.

Consider the processes in sales. We have already noted the traditional selling activities, such as identifying leads, qualifying prospects, writing proposals, and closing orders. In many companies, salespeople also enter the orders, make changes, and solve problems. They account for their time and expenses, complete sales forecasts, and report their activities. Sales mangers are also involved in processes such as hiring, training, coaching, and evaluating their salespeople.

There are even more processes in the marketing function. Marketing people develop advertising campaigns and create direct mail pieces, flyers, brochures, and press releases. They do market research, gather customer requirements, provide input to product development, launch new products, design incentive programs for salespeople and customers, and maybe even measure the effectiveness of their own activities. All of these activities can be improved to make them more effective and efficient and to reduce or eliminate the errors or defects they might produce.

## Defects in Sales and Marketing

Eliminating errors or defects is one of the primary objectives of process improvement. If we define quality as meeting customer requirements, then a *defect* is anything that does not meet those requirements. Defects are relatively easy to recognize in manufactured products, and the current quality focus has reduced them to an all-time low in most product categories. In services, eliminating defects is more difficult. Greater human involvement and less precise standards make measuring services tougher and improving service quality a greater challenge. As a result, customer satisfaction is generally higher for manufactured goods than it is for services.

The sales and marketing functions are not immune to defects either, and theirs potentially have much greater visibility and impact than those of other functions. In sales, defects usually occur at the customer level. They begin with little things like misspelling words in letters and proposals or not returning telephone calls promptly. Failing to respond to customer requirements in an RFP, recommending the wrong solution, or incorrectly entering an order are more significant. Unfortunately, very few sales management systems track defects, and most salespeople are not compensated, recognized, or rewarded for how few errors they make.

Defects in marketing tend to be the most visible. Recently, an invitation to visit a trade show booth arrived in my office. That is good trade show strategy except that this invitation arrived with postage due. Two more beautifully designed and expensive invitations arrived almost two weeks after the same show concluded. Someone in each of those companies decided to save money by sending the invitations by bulk mail. On a broader scale, advertisements that offend a particular ethnic or gender group are clearly defects. Other defects include the highly visible promotional schemes that have inadvertently declared so many winners that if fulfilled, would have bankrupted the companies. When marketing produces a defect, it is frequently expensive to correct and highly visible to the public.

## Influences on the Buying Decision

Customers are influenced to buy a product or service or to establish a long-term supplier partnership by a number of factors, many of which go far beyond the direct efforts of sales and marketing. Consider the results of Eastman's MIBE effort. Some of them came directly from improvements in the sales processes, such as reducing order entry problems, responding faster to pricing requests, and increasing customer satisfaction with the ordering and distribution of literature. Other results came by reducing order problems, shortening delivery times, and responding faster to technical service requests. All these changes worked together to increase Eastman's international customer satisfaction by 15 to 20 percentage points.

Even the best sales pitch or ad campaign may not be able overcome poor product quality, late delivery, billing errors, or a failure to respond to an inquiry or complaint call. Moreover, many companies sell or support their products and services through trading partners such as independent agents, distributors, dealers, franchisees, retailers, or brokers. Customer experiences with these third parties also influence customer decisions to purchase.

Although this book focuses primarily on the sales and marketing functions, the entire company and its distribution partners must be involved in the improvement processes described in the following chapters if the company is to increase customer satisfaction and loyalty and ensure long-term profitable growth.

## Conclusion

The six best practices introduced in this chapter should come as no surprise to anyone. Most are not all that new, and all have been proven in their use in many business functions. However, as the Eastman Chemical Company example shows, they can be just as effective in sales and marketing as in any other area of the business.

Key to implementing these practices is the idea that the product of sales and marketing is information and that both of these critical business functions do have processes. Improving these processes can lead to improved quality and productivity, higher customer satisfaction and loyalty, and increased revenue and profit.

# Chapter Two

# | **Manage for Change**

Most meaningful change begins with commitment. Just ask anyone who has tried to lose weight, stop smoking, or improve his or her golf swing. All these personal change efforts require a strong and lasting commitment. The same is true in organizational change, where all levels of management must make the commitment to improve. After they commit, they have to support the effort with effective leadership skills and good management practices. That applies whether the organization plans to make change through continuous improvement, a complete restructuring, or better yet, some combination of the two.

Organizations with successful improvement processes have reached another conclusion as well. Improvement must be part of the day-to-day management process. People's Bank in Connecticut was one of the early adopters of quality improvement in the banking industry. According to People's first vice president, Pat Manion, "There is such a temptation to look at quality as a separate issue." At People's, management learned that making the improvement process something apart from the day-to-day way of doing work just was not effective. As TSS's vice president, technical support, Marianne Crew notes, "Quality processes are not something separate. They are the way you run your business."

Implementing an improvement process and using quality management principles are not intuitively obvious things to do. Hewlett Packard's Jack Caffey notes that "people can see a hint of ways to improve their business results, but they are not quite sure how to lead the effort." In this chapter, we will address that issue. We will begin with the most important element of managing for change: management commitment. We will also examine the leadership skills and management practices that support commitment. Because old management paradigms die hard, we will conclude with some ideas on how to overcome management resistance to an improvement process.

## Why Management Commitment Is So Important

The gurus of improvement are generally a contentious lot. Each has his or her own ideas about which approach is most effective or where a company should begin its improvement efforts. However, there is one point on which they all agree. Long-term improvement requires top management commitment. Without that commitment, major change efforts wither and die. That is not to say that pockets of change at lower organizational levels are not possible. They are, but they are difficult to start and even harder to sustain. For that reason, this chapter expands its focus beyond commitment in the sales and marketing functions and discusses commitment by the organization's top management as well.

Several research projects have verified the requirement for top management commitment. One of the first was the U.S. General Accounting Office's 1991 study of the early Malcolm Baldrige National Quality Award contestants. That study found that the winners and finalists in the competition had better employee relations, improved operating procedures, greater customer satisfaction, and increased financial performance. The study also identified six characteristics that set the finalists apart from the rest of the field. Management leadership was the second item on that list.

Two years after the GAO study, two quality professionals, Chuck Ramirez and Timothy Loney (1993), surveyed companies that had received the Baldrige Quality Award during its first four years. They also surveyed a group of quality consultants. Their objective was to identify the importance of various quality activities, and the results were clear. Top management commitment headed the list. According to Ramirez and Loney, "The Baldrige award winners and quality consultant respondents have clearly articulated the critical nature of senior management commitment to the success of a quality process." They go on to say, "Not only is commitment essential, but so is management participation through support activities such as setting policy, creating a vision and being involved in the strategic quality plans" (p. 39). Of the top ten items on Ramirez and Loney's list, seven were related to management. On the bottom of the list were three of the old favorite quality techniques, statistical process control, cost of quality, and zero defects attitude. Tom Peters (1985) may have put it best in his book *A Passion for Excellence* when he said, "The heart of quality is not technique. It is commitment by management to its people and product—stretching over a period of decades and lived with persistence and passion" (p. 118). This is not to diminish the value of the tools and techniques. It simply places the importance where it belongs, on management. In *Thriving on Chaos*, Peters (1987) went on to say, "Most quality programs fail for one of two reasons: They have system without passion or passion without system. You must have both" (p. 74).

The International Quality Study (1992) also confirms the requirement for top management commitment. The American Quality Foundation and Ernst & Young conducted this survey of companies in the automotive, computer, banking, and health care industries in Canada, Germany, Japan, and the United States. The companies are divided into three categories—lower, medium, and higher performance—based on their profitability, productivity, and quality. According to Ernst & Young's H. James Harrington, principal international quality advisor, the latest analysis of the company's growing database of information reveals that there are only three universal best practices that produce results in every country and industry and in companies at all levels of performance. They are top management commitment, work simplification, and cycle time reduction. The other practices studied are helpful only in certain situations.

The results of my research for this book are consistent with the findings of these more extensive and formal studies. Of the five dozen companies that I interviewed, none achieved significant and long-lasting improvement without top management commitment. Many of the people interviewed communicated the need for management commitment with an almost missionary zeal. Some had tried to make significant changes without commitment from the top levels of their organization, but most of these had experienced frustration and disappointment.

Without the commitment and active participation of the senior management team, midlevel managers, supervisors, and employees respond to the improvement process just as they have to every other management technique that the organization has tried. They listen to the hollow words of their leaders, sigh, and utter that famous phrase, "And this too shall pass."

Clearly the senior management of the company must provide leadership for the improvement initiative. But for the improvement process to work, that commitment must extend to the managers of each business function, including sales and marketing. Gary Hessenauer is a former corporate area manager for General Electric. In that position, he was responsible for making major changes in sales operations. Hessenauer emphasizes that "you need commitment and passion by your leaders and your managers to make it all happen."

Getting commitment from managers in sales, marketing, and other business functions does not relieve top management of its responsibility, however. That cannot be delegated. According to Peter J. Zummo, former vice president of marketing at Travelers Insurance Asset Management and Pension Services, "The Travelers quality process lacked direction until the senior executives determined that it was a management process and that for it to work, they had to take an active role." At People's Bank, the senior executives got the quality process started, then tried to delegate it to a quality executive. That did not work, and the quality process was reinvigorated only when a council of senior executives was reinstituted to lead the effort.

To be effective, management's commitment must be focused on the areas critical to the success of the business. These are usually the areas most important to customers. From a companywide standpoint, the critical success factors may be product quality, on-time delivery, customer service, product innovation, or being the low-cost product or service provider. In sales, the critical factors may be salespeople who know their products, understand the customers' business, or have problem-solving skills. Whatever the critical areas, the commitment to improving them must be consistent and enduring, and it is management's job to keep that focus. When James L. Barksdale was chief operations officer at Federal Express, he said of the job of the executive, "The main thing is to make sure the main thing stays the main thing."

Management's commitment and participation in the improvement process is not important just because management carries the banner and leads the charge. Its importance is also about power and influence. Management owns the business processes that produce the organization's output. As process owners, managers are responsible for how well those processes function. Management controls the resources, the head count, and dollars that are needed to make change. Management also has the most influence on the organization's culture. Managers have the power to reward and punish. They decide who gets recognition, pay increases, and promotions. Senior-level managers also have the power to overcome the internal barriers to change. No matter how much people in the lower levels of the organization recognize the need to improve, without the support of top management, that improvement is difficult if not impossible.

## The Role of Managers: Leadership

After executives and managers recognize the need for continuous improvement and the importance of their commitment, their next step is to identify their own role in the improvement process. That role is one of both leadership and management. Leadership has been characterized as doing the right things; management as doing things right. Both are important. Tom Peters stated the need for both passion and system in the improvement process. Leadership provides the passion; management, the system. To look further at leadership, we begin with vision, the first element of leadership.

### Develop a Vision

Many attempts have been made to identify the qualities that set successful business leaders apart. Although results vary, most of the lists of qualities include a common theme: successful leaders have a compelling vision of the future. Burt Nanus begins his book *Visionary Leadership* (1992) with this statement: "There is no more powerful engine driving an organization toward excellence and long range success than an attractive, and achievable vision of the future, widely shared" (p. 3). Educator and author Warren Bennis agrees that the first quality of the business leader is a guiding vision. In an interview for *Fortune,* for example, Bennis said, "All of the leaders I know have a strongly defined sense of purpose. And when you have an organization where the people are aligned behind a clearly defined vision or purpose, you get a powerful organization" (Loeb, 1994, p. 241).

The management literature abounds with stories of visionary business leaders, people like Mary Kay Ashe, Bill Gates, Michael Eisner, Ted Turner, and Sam Walton. Clearly it is easier for managers to commit to a compelling vision of the future than to a directive from above. But do visions have to be companywide, or can a business function such as sales or marketing have a vision?

The answer is obvious. Of course a business function can have its own vision as long as it supports or at least does not conflict with the company's overall vision. At General Electric, Chairman Jack Welch has a vision of a boundaryless organization, one with a single face to the customer. Gary Hessenauer explains how GE's Western Area went about coordinating the sales and support activities of the company's many businesses: "The focus was on establishing a vision, creating a need, identifying what had to be done, and sustaining the activity so that we were able to implement it and make it happen and then measure it." GE's Western Area vision clearly supports the company's corporate vision.

Century Furniture in Hickory, North Carolina, has established its own vision in sales. According to Dave Leffler, senior vice president of sales, his department wants to be a "world-class" salesforce. To accomplish this, the salespeople are listening to the company's customers, the furniture dealers, to determine what "a world-class salesforce" means to them and how Century can achieve that vision.

## Walk the Talk

The executives and managers that lead successful improvement efforts do more than just create a vision. They live it. In the business vernacular, they "walk their talk." Leading the improvement process means listening to customers, employees, and associates. When training in improvement techniques is required, the leaders attend the first classes themselves. Then they kick off subsequent training sessions, demonstrating their commitment to the vision by the way they spend their time. They are congruent in their actions and decisions as well.

A manager in an international beverage distributor related how *not* to lead an improvement effort. The company had a visible and highly promoted customer-oriented quality process. However, when someone used the terminology of the quality process in talking to an executive, he responded, "What, you working on that? It's surprising that you've got time to do that." That message to the employees condemned the company's improvement efforts.

One way for executives to walk their talk is to use the quality tools themselves. That communicates the message that the improvement process is really important. Take Federal Express for example. There, vice presidents head "root cause teams" to focus on the issues that negatively affect the company's Service Quality Index, a measure of what their customers think of company service. At Motorola, a sales quality council is made up of five vice presidents, one from each of five divisions. They work together to decide what sales quality is and how to improve it.

One of the most convincing examples of an executive who made the quality process part of his own job is Bernie Sergesketter. Before his 1994 retirement, Sergesketter was vice president of sales in AT&T's central region. With more than one thousand people in his organization, he was responsible for marketing AT&T's long distance services (voice, data, image, and video) in medium and large accounts. When the quality process was rolled out at AT&T, he recognized its value in a sales organization. He also realized that he had to lead the effort personally. What better way to lead it than to apply the quality principles in his own job?

He stepped back and looked at what executives do. He decided that they attend meetings, talk on the telephone, and write letters. On the basis of this quick analysis, he developed his own personal quality checklist. Here are some of the items on Sergesketter's list:

*Meetings*

- Begin meetings on time.
- Have relevant meeting materials on time.

*Telephone Calls*

- Answer the phone in two rings.
- Return calls the same or next business day.
- Voice mail to 5:00 P.M. cleared the same day.

*Letters*

- Respond in five business days.
- Only one edit per letter.

In April 1990, Sergesketter put his personal quality process to work. Each time he failed to meet his personal standard, he counted it as a defect. He kept a copy of the checklist handy, and marked it each time a defect occurred. At the end of the first month, he tallied the total number of defects. He found he had accumulated almost one hundred.

By the end of the year, his monthly tally of defects was down to less than ten per month. The surprise was the effect this had on his personal time. He had freed up over an hour a day. In addition, people were no longer waiting as long for answers to phone calls and correspondence. His secretary retyped letters only once. Other people attending meetings were not kept waiting.

Soon, many of the members of Sergesketter's management team were keeping their own personal quality checklists. They did not copy his, however; instead they developed lists of their own, focusing on improving areas that fit their own jobs and personal habits. One colleague lost twenty pounds when he began counting each time he ate something with a high fat content.

More important than the time saved in the executive offices of AT&T's central region was the leadership Sergesketter showed. It demonstrated his commitment to the quality process, and it showed how easily the improvement techniques could be applied to any job (see also Sergesketter and Roberts, 1993). Even after retiring from AT&T, Sergesketter maintains his personal quality checklist.

Like Bernie Sergesketter, many of the executives and managers mentioned in this book have shifted away from the traditional command and control management model. They recognize that it is based on the one-hundred-year-old assumptions made by Frederick Taylor when he developed his theories of scientific management. A century ago, workers were uneducated and unskilled, and managers and supervisors knew how to do the jobs better than the workers. They decided what the workers needed to do and how they should do it. They directed employees to carry out specific tasks and then put controls in place to ensure that the employees got the assignments done.

In 1960, my own management training began in a course on principles of management. There I was taught that the functions of a manager were to plan, organize, staff, direct, and control. Some college and corporate management courses were still teaching these same management functions thirty years later.

Times have changed, however. In today's environment, particularly in knowledge-based professions, workers frequently know how to do their jobs better than their managers. Although the five older management functions are still valid, the leading organizations are delegating them further down in the organization, in some cases to the individual level, in others to self-managed teams. Meanwhile, today's managers are exchanging the old management tasks of directing and controlling for new functions. Using the new management model, today's leaders empower, coach, recognize, and reward.

This is not to say that the employees run the business; far from it. The organization's senior leadership determines the business's mission, defines its values, and creates and communicates a vision. The leadership also sets performance goals. The difference in the new management model is that management empowers the people in the organization to find and implement the most effective and efficient ways to perform the mission and attain the goals while observing the organization's values. As part of the new management process, the leaders also give employees feedback on how well they are accomplishing the mission, meeting goals, and living by the organization's values.

## Recognize and Reward

Besides giving employees feedback on how well they are doing their jobs, leaders also recognize and reward people for their accomplishments. This recognition can be as informal as a pat on the back, a thank-you note, or a commendation at a sales or team meeting. It can also include rewards such as a night on the town, a cash bonus, a merchandise prize, or a trip to a company recognition event. It can be a salary increase or even a promotion. Each of these forms of recognition has value when managers use it appropriately.

Most managers recognize people for an accomplishment such as reaching a goal. In a sales organization, recognition usually comes from closing a large order or achieving a sales quota. Marketing commends people for completing a major project such as a successful advertising campaign, a new product launch, or a market research study. Improvement teams are recognized for solving a chronic problem or improving a key business process. Certainly recognizing people and teams for their accomplishments will continue to be appropriate.

However, when managers recognize people, they accomplish other leadership objectives as well. Recognition is a form of performance feedback. It is also a way to say thank you for doing what the organization thinks is valuable. Even more important, positive recognition is the most effective way to reinforce desired behaviors. People tend to repeat the behaviors that they believe will be rewarded. In addition, when a manager visibly recognizes an individual or team, it sends a clear message to everyone else, telling others what the organization really values. Using recognition as a way to reinforce positive and useful behavior is a much more effective way to influence behavior than reprimanding people for what they are doing wrong.

An example of a behavior that leading companies want to encourage is participation on teams. In the past, companies have recognized people for their individual performance. Now companies are recognizing teamwork and individuals' contributions to the team effort.

The leading companies also want to encourage certain ways people solve problems. Historically, people have been recognized for quick fixes. But as Jo Shute, director of organizational effectiveness at the James River Corporation has observed, "Companies that reward fire fighting, breed arsonists." Now companies want people to use a formal problem-solving process, to ensure that root causes are identified and eliminated, preventing the same problems from happening repeatedly.

Xerox is an example of a company that revised its recognition and rewards program to support its move to reinforcing team behaviors and using processes that bring about lasting fixes. Like most companies, Xerox had been oriented to recognizing the individual performer and had associated rewards primarily with money. Then it extended its program to include groups of individuals and teams. It also broadened its forms of recognition, beginning with a simple thank you. Another change was to make sure that managers recognized people in public, not in the privacy of their offices. Lastly, Xerox identified the specific "role model" behaviors it wanted managers to recognize, behaviors such as using the quality improvement tools and team participation.

It is just as important to recognize role model behaviors in sales as in the improvement process. Traditionally companies recognize salespeople for attainment of sales objectives. However, largely uncontrollable circumstances often contribute to a salesperson's performance, making some salespeople shine and others miss their quota objectives. A good sales territory, a low quota, or a large unexpected order will have a positive effect on the results of even the least effective salesperson. A poorly designed territory, high quota, bankruptcy of a key customer, or poor economic conditions can have a negative effect on the best salesperson's performance. When companies recognize and reward good sales practices, the behaviors that lead to sales results, they create a stronger salesforce that performs better in the long run.

## Stay the Course

Making a commitment is easy. Sticking to it is often another matter, and according to Warren Bennis, one of the most important qualities of effective leaders is their willingness to stay the course (Loeb, 1994). That course is often a long and sometimes rocky one. Yet research indicates that it takes time to get results from the improvement process and, more importantly, to get the culture change needed to sustain that process. The Westinghouse Quality and Productivity Center has helped over 150 clients implement their own quality improvement processes. The center's research indicates that it takes an average of two and a half years to get significant results. The U.S. General Accounting Office study (1991) of the early Baldrige Award finalists and winners came to exactly the same conclusion. A consultant's rule of thumb for estimating how long culture change will take is that it takes one year for every layer of management. (At a recent consultants' meeting, one comedian suggested that the number of years required for real change is the square of the number of layers of management in the organization.) In any case, change takes time and does not come easily.

In the late W. Edwards Deming's famous Fourteen Points for the Transformation of American Industry, the first point is, "Create constancy of purpose for improvement of product and service" (1986, p. 24). Warren Bennis agrees that successful leaders have constancy of purpose, saying, "One of the things you hear about least effective leaders is that they do whatever the last person they spoke to recommended"(Loeb, 1994, p. 241). The companies that are recognized leaders in the improvement process have been doing it for years and apply it in every area of their organizations.

## The Role of Managers: Management

The distinction between leadership and management roles in an improvement process is never a sharp one. For example, the creation of a compelling vision is part of the leadership role, but a vision will remain a dream without a plan to make it happen. Creating a plan to support the vision is usually considered a management function. Nonetheless it is an important part of the improvement process.

### Create an Improvement Plan

The companies that have been most successful in implementing the six best practices began by creating an improvement plan. They based their plans on customer and employee input. These plans established a direction and set improvement goals and target dates. They also assigned and allocated company resources. Although usually separate from the organization's business plan, they aligned with it and supported it.

Many of these companies found that in the beginning, having a separate improvement plan did emphasize the improvement process. However, most learned quickly that keeping the business strategy and improvement plan separate sent the wrong message: it told people that solving problems and improving processes were separate activities from the day-to-day operation of the business. To make continuous improvement part of the organization culture, these companies soon made their improvement plans an integral part of their business plans.

GTE's quality management process has been one of the most successful. Since beginning its quality journey in 1981, the company has improved product and service quality, increased customer satisfaction, and reduced costs. In 1994, GTE's directories division received a Malcolm Baldrige National Award in recognition of its efforts.

However, the company did not get the results it was looking for immediately. Although it had lots of anecdotes about improvements, the results were not reflected in the key business measurements. After three years, GTE leadership took another look at the change effort. They found that quality management had not become part of the way the company wanted to conduct its business. Therefore, in 1985, the company developed a new approach, called Quality, the Competitive Edge. This approach started at the top of the business and was rolled out through every layer of management. The message was clear: quality management is the way top management wants to run the business. It worked. The new approach got the return on investment the company wanted. It succeeded by making the improvement process an integral part of the company's business strategy.

Mutual of New York (MONY) took a different path. The senior executives of that insurance company built quality management into their business strategy for the 1990s, and they did it from the very beginning. MONY's top quality officer, Jan Howard, said, "In 1988, we defined our business strategy for the 1990s. The first step was to determine the markets we were in and the markets we wanted to be in. We matched that up with our distribution system and developed a supporting business structure." Part of that structure included quality management. MONY's senior management selected quality management to provide the "tools and techniques and a methodology from which to approach [the] business."

Howard was responsible for the day-to-day implementation of the plan. In 1990, she began with an education program for MONY's top management. According to Howard, "One of the precepts is that if you don't have senior management commitment, you might as well bag it, because it is not going to work." Howard spent over a year on an education and awareness program for MONY's top management team. In this program, she described the quality process and its origins, why MONY had chosen to get involved, what the competition was doing, how the organization would have to be reshaped, and what the new culture would look like. With an understanding of the quality process, MONY's executives then created a vision for the company.

The next step was to make the rest of the company aware of the new mission and vision and to provide general education on the basic quality concepts. Howard spent more than four hundred hours presenting to people all around the country as she began her "buy-in process." The awareness training was followed by looking for best practices in the field sales organization. Howard pulled together teams of top salespeople from around the country. Their purpose was to share best practices and to look for ways to become even more effective. The teams focused on ways to reduce or delegate nonselling activities and increase the time salespeople could spend with their clients.

Creating and following a plan is important, but the real measure of success is how well it works. In MONY's case, the results received national recognition when one of Howard's teams received *Sales & Marketing Management* magazine's top salesforce award in 1995, and Howard appeared on the magazine cover. MONY's Top Producer Group 2 team was the only salesforce in the competition to receive an A or A+ in all five judging categories in the Gallup survey that identified the winners. The team had boosted sales by 47 percent in a one-year period and did it by providing better customer service (Brewer, 1995a).

MONY's plan is not finished yet. The teams continue to look for ways for salespeople to increase their selling time with their clients. The best practices being developed by the Top Producer Group 2 team and others like it are being spread across MONY's salesforce. High-performing salespeople are brought into the company's sales training to share their best practices, and the company is encouraging salespeople to form more teams across the salesforce.

Making the improvement plan part of the business strategy is not limited to large companies such as GTE and MONY. Many smaller companies have made companywide improvement part of their business strategies as well. However, it is unusual to find it happening in a retail automobile dealership. Most auto dealers operate on a day-to-day basis; few of them have any kind of business strategy at all. Dallas-based Park Place Motorcars is an exception.

Park Place Motorcars executives have a business strategy that focuses continuous improvement toward the company's number one objective: long-term customer satisfaction. The company's strategy is to change the typical auto dealer culture and get everyone working toward a common goal. Business plans in each of the dealership's departments support the companywide strategy. The compensation plan for most of the dealership's employees also takes customer satisfaction into consideration. Like GTE and MONY, Park Place is getting results. Over 90 percent of its customers are "very satisfied" with their experience with Park Place, and the company's Mercedes Benz dealership, one of its three stores, is ranked tenth in the United States in sales and fifth in service.

GTE, MONY, and Park Place Motorcars are just three of the companies that have made a formal improvement process part of their business strategy. Virtually every company that successfully implemented a major improvement process has done so. They all recognize that the real leverage comes from making the improvement process part of the corporate strategy. Failure to do so relegates the process to second-class status at best; something that gets done when there is time to get around to it. In companies where that is the case, the improvement process usually ends up in the dustbin of abandoned management fads.

## Measure

Another key part of management's role is measurement. This includes developing measurement systems, collecting data, and making decisions based on those data. Measurement systems are an integral part of the business strategy, giving management feedback on how well its plans are working. Measurements tell the organization how well it is doing relative to its performance and improvement goals, its competition, and its customers' requirements. Measurements are also a key part of business process management, keeping management informed on how well processes are working and the effect of process improvements. Finally, when managers use measurements properly, they are a powerful motivational tool. According to one internal consultant at General Electric, 65 percent of improvement comes just from putting a measurement on something.

### Measurements and Strategy

For measurements to be effective, management must first align them with the organization's business strategy. If the strategy is to increase customer loyalty and retention but the key sales measurement is the number of new accounts sold, the organization has failed to align its strategy and its sales measurements. If the company's strategy is to grow through new product innovation and a measure of sales performance is to get at least 25 percent of revenue from products developed in the last four years, the company has aligned its business strategy and its measurement.

One example of aligning measurements with the company strategy comes from a small meat-packing firm in Arkansas. In the early 1960s, this company had six salespeople, who were measured, recognized, and rewarded for their gross sales volume. After the company automated its accounting system, it was able to rank customers and salespeople on the basis of profit as well as volume. Much to management's surprise, the first ranking report showed that salespeople who sold the lowest volume generated the highest profits for the company. Their profit rankings were the reverse of their sales volume rankings. The company had been measuring the wrong thing and recognizing and rewarding the wrong people.

### Common Measurements Across Departments

It is also important to align measurements across department lines. Consider this example. A business unit of a large company provides a popular on-line computing service. To access and use the service, customers need custom computer terminals and software leased by the company's sales department and installed by systems support professionals. Although the sales and system people are in separate departments, the business unit expects them to work together on teams.

The salespeople are measured and compensated on the basis of how much they can sell. So far, so good. However, the business unit is measured on a fixed capital budget that limits the amount of hardware that it can purchase for resale to the customers. Also, one of the systems support function measurements is the function's headcount, or staffing level. It is has a limited number of people to install the equipment and train customers to use it. See the conflict between the way the business unit measures sales and the budgets and head count?

The salespeople can easily lease more equipment than the business unit can provide and the systems support people can install and support. And the measurement and compensation systems provide an incentive for sales to do just that. The results: salespeople compete with each other for limited resources. Systems people are challenged to keep all of the salespeople and customers happy. Customers are not satisfied when they cannot get the equipment or support they need after sales has told them how great it will be when they do get it. The teams do not work well because of the mismatch in measurements and the contention that this causes.

A classic example of misaligned measurements frequently can be seen in the measurements for sales departments and sales training. The sales department is usually measured on selling and supporting products and services, and many companies have also added a customer satisfaction measurement. One element of customer satisfaction comes from salespeople with good product knowledge. Sales training is often measured on productivity, calculated on cost per student day. In some companies, the training department is even a profit center, charging back its costs to the sales department. Training is also evaluated on student feedback.

Training's cost-per-student-day measure promotes large classes that apply to as many people as possible. This allows training to amortize the cost of the course developers and trainers across a large number of students. However, it also forces training managers to cancel classes that are below capacity. It discourages training, for example, on products that do not apply to the whole salesforce. Fewer and larger classes taught only on mainstream products may be more productive for the training center but may not support the needs of the salesforce. If salespeople have to wait for classes or cannot get training on a niche product, sales and customer satisfaction suffer. Making training a profit center also conflicts with sales departments that operate under a budget. When expenses are tight, they stop training salespeople at the very time they need to increase their sales skills or product knowledge.

Student evaluations, the other classic sales training measurement, reflect how students liked the class and instructor, but are a poor measure of how well each student learned the information or skill, whether the student used the course material on the job, and whether it resulted in increased sales. Only a few sales training organizations bother to match sales training to sales results.

One such organization is Heublein, Inc., the Hartford, Connecticut–based distributor of wines and liquors. Heublein is one of the very few companies that has measured the effectiveness of sales training where it counts, in sales revenue. Robert J. LaMontagne, Heublein's training director, can say with confidence that the company's sales training does work.

### Align Measurements with Customers

It is just as important to align measurements with customers as to align them across divisions and departments. Many companies overlook this idea as they focus on measuring what is important to them. Their internal measurements often have no relationship to their customers' highest priorities. For example, one food-processing company reported that its measures used to be designed to catch customers doing things wrong, such as placing an order with less than forty-eight hours lead time, arriving late to pick up an order, or buying in less than a minimum order quantity.

When companies align their measurements with their customers, they learn how well they are meeting their customers' most important wants and needs. From a product viewpoint, that may mean fast delivery, customized products, or excellent after-the-sale service. In sales, the greatest customer requirement may be for salespeople who understand the customer's business, quick contract approval, or on-line access to product information. At its highest level, aligning measurements means that the company tries to make its customers successful however those customers measure their success.

### Align Measurements, Compensation, and Priorities

Sales managers send a powerful message when they align their strategy with their measurements and their compensation, recognition, and reward systems. They are telling salespeople what is important and how well they are doing. Then they back that message up with compensation, rewards, and recognition for the people who contribute to the goals of the business. When they do not align their strategy, measurements, and rewards, they send mixed messages and confuse the salespeople. In turn, they lose credibility.

Consider the findings of a Dartnell Corporation salary study (Table 2.1). It revealed that companies often regard certain sales practices as being important yet do not back them up with sales incentives.

Granted, many of the sales organizations that participated in the Dartnell study may have had measurements that were not tied to the compensation system. The study did not address that. From personal experience, however, I find that most salespeople only pay attention to the measurements that are linked to compensation.

### Measurements and Values

It is one of management's leadership roles to ensure that the organization has a strong set of values. These values guide the day-to-day activities and support the vision and strategy. Managers can instill appropriate values in part by aligning measurements, compensation, and recognition and rewards. For example, if a company

**Table 2.1.  Sales Priorities Versus Sales Incentives.**

| Sales Task | Percent of Companies Surveyed that Consider It Important | Percent of Companies Surveyed with an Incentive for Salespeople |
|---|---|---|
| Retaining existing customers | 98.7 | 30.4 |
| Selling to major accounts | 92.3 | 29.5 |
| Finding new accounts | 91.3 | 34.1 |
| Improving profit contribution | 90.6 | 53.1 |
| Reducing selling costs | 62.5 | 16.7 |

*Source:* The Dartnell Corporation, 1996, pp. 150–155.

*Note: n* = 250

values customer retention, it will measure how well the salespeople keep existing customers. As the first line in Table 2.1 shows, 95 percent of the companies surveyed reported that they do value customer retention. However, only 31 percent reinforce that value by measuring and compensating salespeople for how well they live by it. The remaining 64 percent are either unaware that their values and measures are not aligned, or they do not really value customer retention after all.

The first step in aligning values and measurements is to determine what the organization currently values. Simply asking executives and managers what the company values will identify their espoused values. The second step is to find out whether their espoused values are the same as the values that actually guide their behaviors. Employees, customers, suppliers, and other stakeholders can provide that information. What managers actually measure, how they compensate, recognize, and reward people, and how they spend their time also point to their true values. If management's espoused values and practiced values are the same and have roughly the same priorities, the managers are congruent and credible—and their organization is in the minority.

The next step is to determine how well the practiced values support the organization's vision and strategy. Consider a vision of long-term partnerships with key customers. The strategy to accomplish that includes having salespeople with in-depth knowledge of the customers and the product line. Supporting values might include

- Taking time to learn and understand the customer's business
- Selling solutions that are in the customer's long-term best interest
- Taking time to learn the company's products and services
- Achieving high customer satisfaction

In this case, if the company pays its salespeople 100 percent of their earnings through commissions and measures them on monthly sales goals, their compensation and measurements are not aligned with the vision and strategy. Paying salespeople a relatively high percentage of earnings in salary and giving them incentives to gain product knowledge, learn more about customers' long-term requirements, and achieve high customer satisfaction are more in line with their vision and strategy.

What happens when measurements and compensation are not aligned with the organization's strategy and vision? Several examples have appeared in the business and consumer press in the last few years. One of the most visible occurred when Sears Automotive Centers were accused of recommending unnecessary repairs and parts to their customers. It is hard to imagine that the strategy of the giant retailer was to grow through such an unethical business practice. However, the company measured and compensated automotive center personnel on business volume. This did not align with the espoused values of the company and resulted in negative nationwide publicity and legal action in several states.

Some of the country's best-known insurance and brokerage firms have suffered through highly publicized scandals when their salespeople used misleading practices to achieve high earnings and reach ambitious sales targets. But high sales objectives and commission earnings are common in these industries, and many companies are successful while still avoiding the dubious practices that got their competitors in trouble. The latter companies rely on a strong set of values that emphasize ethical behaviors.

Mutual of New York provides an example. Part of MONY's strategy is to set an industry standard for ethical selling. To achieve this, MONY trains every salesperson in ethical sales practices. To emphasize its importance, the training is delivered by agency managers, not the training department. After completing the training and reviewing study materials, the agents take an ethics exam. Fail, and they take it over until they pass. The company clearly supports its strategy with strong ethical values (Brewer, 1995a).

### Measurement Priorities

One theme that is common among many leading companies is the way they prioritize their companywide measurements. Where most companies focus on financial results first, these companies put their customers and employees at the top of their list. They find that by satisfying their customers and taking care of their employees, their sales volumes and profits take care of themselves.

Xerox discovered the value of putting customers first early in its quality journey. When it began its improvement process, it established profit and quality goals, giving each one equal weight. It did not take long for profit to become first among equals. Company mangers realized that they had to change their priorities to get the quality improvements they needed. They established a new set of goals, putting customer satisfaction at the top of their list, followed by employee satisfaction. Market share and profits ranked third and fourth. Other companies have made the same discovery and established customer satisfaction as their top priority. According to Xerox's John Lawrence, "It puts the focus of people's efforts on the most important aspect of the business, the customer. From that, all else follows."

One notable exception to the customer first philosophy is Federal Express. This company puts employees first, customers second, and financial results third. Management's belief is that it takes satisfied employees to keep Federal Express customers happy. In a company where almost half of the company's 94,000 employees are in contact with customers every day, satisfied employees are getting the job done. The company tracks customer satisfaction almost daily and keeps its customer satisfaction index in the high 90 percent range.

All of this is not to diminish the importance of profits. Without profits, the organization would ultimately go out of business and customer satisfaction would drop to zero. However, when companies put profits and other financial measurements at the top of the priority list, managers are tempted to make short-term decisions based on the cost side of the profit equation. This results in reduced investments in things like training, research, and development, and the improvement process. Managing by the financial measurements is like trying to coach a football team while constantly watching the scoreboard. As in football, in sales and marketing the action is on the field.

### Unintended Consequences of Measurements

When developing measurements, consider the law of unintended consequences. According to *Fortune* columnist, Daniel Seligman (1995), this law is generally associated with Columbia sociologist Robert K. Merton, who wrote about the idea sixty years ago. It states that, "Political action often leads to unexpected if not counterproductive results" (p. 175). Seligman provides many examples of legislation gone awry. One of the best is the tax the U.S. Congress put on pleasure boats. Intended to soak the rich, it almost put the boat-building industry out of business instead.

Often, measurements ill conceived by management can have similar results. Take the example of the annual sales quota in the computer industry. It seems logical at first. Managers give their salespeople a sales quota measured in the dollar volume of computers and services customers accept in the calendar year. However, in setting the quota, sales managers take into consideration all the business in the backlog, that is, business sold in previous years but not yet shipped to the customer. The unintended consequence of the annual quota is that salespeople have an incentive to sell *and* install equipment in the same year, whether or not it is in the customer's best interest. After all, if the salesperson takes an order this year for delivery the following year, the sales manager just builds the transaction into the next year's quota. The annual quota flies in the face of the objective most companies have set of developing long-term customer partnerships.

We have already seen other examples of measuring sales results without considering the best interests of the customers. Recall the examples of Sears Automotive Centers and some of the large insurance and brokerage firms. All have been burned by the high focus on short-term sales results and a high percentage of earnings coming from commissions. A marketing manager in an electrical equipment manufacturer said that before management recognized the impact of short-term sales goals, the prevailing attitude was, "Don't worry about next year, and damn the customer."

Some companies have shifted away from measuring and compensating for sales revenue and now focus on the profitability of sales. In many cases, this provides a more effective measurement. However, it too can have an unintended consequence. Consider how measuring and paying on profits can impact new product sales. New products are seldom profitable early in their life, but at the same time, because they are new, they may require a disproportionate amount of sales time. They may not get this time when profitability of sales is an important measure.

The point is not to give up on measurements and compensation tied to performance. Just be aware of the potential for unintended consequences. Examine every measurement to make certain that its effects align with your organization's vision, values, and strategy.

### Simple and Few

Now consider the number of measurements in your organization. Most of the leading companies have between three and seven key companywide measures, and they are in a priority sequence. It is virtually impossible to focus on more. That is not to say that each functional area, such as sales or marketing, does not have other measures. They do. However, each department's measurements should support the companywide measures, and departments too should limit the number of measurements to which they manage.

In the 1970s, IBM found that its sales branch managers had 75 measurements to track. The company decided that 75 was too many and set about to reduce the number. A few years later, IBM reviewed the branch manager's job again and found that the number was approaching 250. Management decided to try to get it back to 75. Obviously, no one can even keep track of 250 measurements, or even 75. In reality, the branch managers focused on about three sales measurements plus customer satisfaction, budget, and headcount.

Finally, nowhere does the KISS principle (Keep it Simple, Stupid) apply any more than in measurement. Whether measurements are for tracking sales performance or determining the effectiveness of process improvements, people are more likely to respond to them when they are simple and easy to understand. It helps if the measurement data are easy to collect and analyze as well.

## Communicate

Communication is also an important part of the improvement process and has both leadership and management dimensions. Leadership is more than just defining the organization's mission, vision and values, developing a strategy, and setting goals. It is also doing whatever it takes to communicate that information to everyone in the organization. Without a complete awareness and understanding of that information, the members cannot align their efforts and support their common objectives.

Executives and managers own the formal processes through which information flows down, up, and across the organization.

They transmit the mission, vision, values, plans, and goals down the organization. They also convey measurements and feedback on how well organization members are executing the plan and meeting objectives. This performance feedback is vital. Without it, people tend to make up their own reality.

One element of the open organization culture, one of the six best practices, is sharing information. Effective communication processes provide ways to do this. For example, if a sales team in one location solves a chronic problem or develops a more effective sales process, the event's value is limited unless the salespeople in every other location learn about it. If one division has established relationships with a key customer, other divisions cannot benefit without a way to access the customer information.

In addition to companywide learning and sharing of information, good communication processes enable organizations to coordinate improvement efforts. Many companies with multiple locations find they have more than one person or team working on the same problem. They need effective communication processes to reduce or eliminate duplication of effort.

## Getting Management Commitment

As described earlier, any major change effort requires the commitment and participation of the organization's leadership. This is true whether the organization is a sales branch office, a marketing division, or a company. It is also true when two or more companies work together, in a partnership with a customer or supplier, in a supply chain, or even in a marketing alliance in which the members have complementary products and services. The leaders of these organizations must all demonstrate their commitment in the ways discussed in this chapter.

What does it take to get commitment to sustained leadership of any organizational change effort? Michael Herrington, vice president, quality, at World Color, Inc., states there are three drivers: impending financial collapse, demanding customers, and a born-again CEO (Herrington, 1991).

Impending financial collapse drove the quality revolution in the late 1970s and early 1980s when Japanese competition forced U.S. companies to focus on product quality. For example, it was in

1979 that then Xerox CEO David Kearns learned that the Japanese could sell higher-quality copiers at a retail price equal to his company's manufacturing cost.

Customer demands are also driving changes and forcing commitment. Consider the example of Wal-Mart and other leading retailers. These companies are changing the way their suppliers sell and support them. Wal-Mart, for instance, wants an EDI connection with its suppliers. When major customers demand change, they often create the potential for financial collapse. Together, these two drivers constitute a real or potential crisis that leads to management commitment.

That leaves Herrington's third driver, the born-again CEO. This leader recognizes that there is a better way to manage and lead an organization. He or she reaches this conclusion without any major outside influence. In my own experience, these leaders amount to about 5 percent of all senior executives. They include people like Ralph Stayer at Johnsonville Sausage, Ray Marlow at Marlow Industries, and Fred Smith at Federal Express. Note that both Marlow Industries and Federal Express are Baldrige Award–winning companies.

Getting commitment at every management level without a crisis or a born-again CEO can be challenging, but many companies are proving that it can be done. They realize that unless they make continuous improvement part of the organization culture, they will ultimately face financial collapse or their customers will demand change. Better to start the journey voluntarily and in a more orderly fashion than an impending crisis allows.

The most powerful way for executives and managers to get commitment is to change the measurement and reward system. G. Howland Blackiston, president of the Juran Institute, reports that neglecting this change is the most common reason that improvement initiatives fail.

Xerox, for example, is a company that got middle-management commitment by changing the way managers were evaluated and promoted. Shortly after Xerox began its quality journey, it conducted an employee opinion survey. One survey question asked whether employees' managers (1) were role models in the quality process, (2) knew how to use the quality tools, or (3) did not support the program. The survey revealed that, in the eyes of their employees, most managers did not support the quality process. To help resolve the problem, CEO David Kearns instituted a new companywide policy. To be eligible for promotion, managers had to be noted as "role models" for the "Leadership Through Quality" attributes. When asked why Xerox did not just promote managers who got outstanding business results, he replied, "We needed outstanding business results that were sustainable, and that required a change in our culture. It is quite a rude awakening to be told that you are not eligible for promotion even though you just experienced some recent successes." Obviously, the approach worked, and Xerox continues to be a leader in continuous improvement long after David Kearns's retirement.

Getting commitment from higher-level managers and executives is obviously more difficult. Before his 1994 retirement, management consultant Joseph Juran often suggested making the case to senior management in the language they understand best: financial results. During one of his last speaking engagements, someone asked Juran how to respond when his financial vice president pointed out another Baldrige winner with poor financial performance. Juran suggested that he look at what would have happened if he had invested $1,000 in each of the Baldrige winners.

*Business Week* picked up the challenge and engaged the help of the Associates for Improving Management, a Peachtree, Georgia, consulting firm, to find the answer. The firm calculated the return on a hypothetical $1,000 investment made in each Baldrige Award winner on the date the award was announced. They calculated the return on the same investment in the S&P 500 and compared the results. The S&P investment would have returned a healthy 33 percent. However, the hypothetical Baldrige fund did much better, returning a whopping 89 percent. It's hard to ignore performance like that (*Business Week*, 1993, pp. 7–8).

Here are more ideas that may persuade higher-level managers to commit to an improvement process:

*Listen to peers.* Although managers may not value input from subordinates, they do listen to their peers in other organizations. Get them to visit companies that are successful and talk to the senior executives there. The Baldrige Award winners are good references. They commit to sharing information as a prerequisite to applying for the award.

*Benchmark performance.*  Compare the organization's performance to that of others. Often management sees increasing sales, profits, and customer satisfaction and is happy with results, but when managers compare their performance to industry leaders, they find they are being left behind.

*Listen to customers.*  The company's customers may not yet be demanding change, but they will often support the need to improve if they are asked. Research has shown that of all the management tools, listening to customers has the highest relationship to company profitability.

*Pilot programs.*  If senior managers will not commit to a major improvement effort, get them to agree to a small pilot test. Implement some of the best practices in a sales office or district and measure the results. Before starting the project, be sure to get agreement on two things: how to measure success, and what management will do if the pilot is a success.

## Conclusion

Change, whether incremental improvement or radical restructuring, does not just happen. It requires leadership and management based on a foundation of a lasting commitment by everyone in the organization. Of all of the best practices, management commitment stands alone at the top of the priority list.

# Chapter Three

# Listen to Customers

Listening to customers is not a new idea. After all, listening is one of the most important skills that salespeople can have. They won't last long without it. In addition, most companies conduct frequent market research studies to identify customers' wants and needs for products, services, support, and administrative processes.

The vast majority of companies also do customer satisfaction research to find out how well they are meeting their customers' requirements. According to a study of dozens of management tools and techniques by Bain & Company and the Strategic Leadership Forum, the use of customer surveys is the second most popular practice. Bain & Company's director Darrell Rigby reported that 85 percent of the companies responding to the study used customer surveys, and 47 percent said they were frequent survey users. What is even more important, the use of customer surveys was identified as one of the practices that provided the most financial benefit.

The U.S. General Accounting Office got similar results in its 1991 study of Baldrige Award winners. "Customer Focus" was at the top of its list of the six practices that set these companies apart from the other applicants. According to the GAO, companies carried out this top practice by using "focus groups, surveys and meetings to better understand their customers' requirements and value expectations" (p. 29).

Unfortunately, listening to customers to identify ways to improve sales and marketing is much less common. Yet, without knowing what customers think about these functions, trying to improve them is no more rewarding than throwing darts in the dark. You cannot tell where the target is or whether the darts are reaching their mark. Strangely enough, many organizations begin their improvement process without ever talking to a single customer.

For the sales and marketing functions, external customers are the people who make or influence buying decisions. The objectives of listening to these customers are to identify

- What information they need
- How and when they want to receive that information
- How well sales and marketing are currently meeting their information requirements
- How sales and marketing can improve
- How well improvements work after they are made

Remember, too, that both sales and marketing have internal customers. These customers also have information requirements, and their input is also important to the improvement process.

There is one more reason to listen, and it may be the most important of all. Customers just want to be heard. According to research conducted by Learning International *(Profiles in Customer Loyalty,* 1989, p. 4), the Stamford, Connecticut training firm, 77 percent of all buyer decisions are based on three things:

- I like the people
- They know my business
- They respond to me

Addressing these three critical decision factors requires effective listening to the customer.

## Information Content (or What to Listen For)

To identify what to listen for, we need to examine some of the elements of a process. In Chapter One, I noted a definition of process as a series of activities that take input, add value, and produce an output that goes to a customer (Harrington, 1991, p. 9). Figure 3.1 shows the basic process model. If this were a manufacturing process, suppliers would provide components as input, the company would add value by assembling the components into a product, and the output, the manufactured item, would be delivered through the distribution system to a customer.

### Figure 3.1  Basic Process Model.

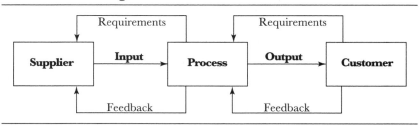

The two arrows that point from the customer back to the process in Figure 3.1 represent the flow of requirements and feedback from the customer to the company. The requirements tell the company what the customer wants and needs. If the product being assembled is a personal computer, the customer's requirements might include processor speed, memory size, disk capacity, and price. They might also include hardware reliability, service levels, training, documentation, and support. The customer feedback tells the company how well the product and supporting services are meeting those requirements.

An example of a process involving sales and marketing in the computer company is calculating and distributing pricing information (see Figure 3.2). Manufacturing provides cost information to the finance department. Finance calculates prices and volume discounts and sends them to the marketing department. Marketing packages the information into sales manuals, brochures, and catalogues and distributes them to sales. Sales delivers the information to the customer decision makers and influencers.

This process is essentially the same in a bank introducing a new personal loan package, an insurance company offering a commercial property policy, or a distribution firm with a new product line. In each case, product information flows to the marketing department to be packaged, then to the salesforce to be delivered to the customer. Just as in the case of the manufactured product, the process includes ways to gather customer requirements. The difference is that the requirements are for the information the customer needs to reach a buying decision.

**Figure 3.2. Computer Pricing Process.**

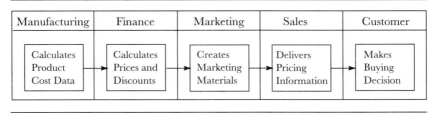

| Manufacturing | Finance | Marketing | Sales | Customer |
|---|---|---|---|---|
| Calculates Product Cost Data | Calculates Prices and Discounts | Creates Marketing Materials | Delivers Pricing Information | Makes Buying Decision |

The process model (Figure 3.1) also includes ways to get feedback on how well that information meets the customers' requirements. The feedback helps the company identify problems and opportunities for improvement in the areas most important to the customer. After the company makes the improvements, the process produces more output, and the feedback loop again provides information on how well the output meets customer requirements.

Gathering customer requirements would be simple if a sales or marketing person could just ask for them. However, customers are not always aware of all their own requirements. Even when they are, they do not always express them. When they do list their requirements, they do not always provide enough detailed information. Understanding this phenomenon is important in gathering, defining, and validating customer requirements. Figure 3.3 organizes customer requirements into four categories.

*Stated requirements.* One of the responsibilities of the sales and marketing staff is to find out specifically what the customer wants and needs. The staff begins by asking the customer directly, and the customer's responses are called *stated requirements.* These requirements are for both the products or services being sold and for the information the customer needs to decide to buy. The arrows below the boxes in Figure 3.3 illustrate that both the salesperson and the customer are aware of these requirements.

*Assumed requirements.* Assumed requirements are more difficult to determine because the customer thinks they are obvious and does not bother to specify them. They are frequently based

**Figure 3.3.  Four Levels of Customer Requirements.**

| Stated | Assumed | Withheld | Unknown |
|---|---|---|---|
| "This is what I want or need." | "I thought you knew I needed that." | "I did not know I could get that." | "I never thought of that." |

Customer ➝

Salesperson ➝

on organization or industry culture and tradition or common business practices. Assumed requirements are often obscured by vague language. How often has a customer asked for a "proposal" without specifying exactly what he or she wanted in it? The salesperson assumes the customer wants a letter with prices and delivery while the customer wants a thirty-page document that includes product information and an implementation plan. The arrows in Figure 3.3 illustrate that the customer is aware of the assumed requirements and the salesperson is probably aware of some but not all of them. It is part of the salesperson's job to be absolutely sure that he or she has identified the customer's assumed requirements. The objective is to turn assumed requirements into stated requirements.

*Withheld requirements.*  Because the customer does not think the salesperson can fulfill certain requirements, he or she does not bother to state them. In one example, a chemical company noticed a customer had stopped buying a product used to purify water at the conclusion of a manufacturing process. When the salesperson called the customer to find out why, he learned that a competitor was now supplying a chemical that was introduced at the beginning of the process to keep the water clean throughout. The chemical company offered similar products, but because the customer was not aware that they offered this solution to his problem, he never asked for it.

Another responsibility of the salesperson is to ensure that the customer is aware of the selling company's capabilities that go beyond products and services. These capabilities might include, for example, electronic data interchange for order entry and billing, unique financing arrangements, or on-site training and support. It is often these additional capabilities that differentiate the successful companies from their competitors.

The customer is aware of withheld requirements. Part of the sales job is to identify and respond to these requirements as well as to the stated and assumed requirements.

*Unknown requirements.* Unknown requirements are completely beyond the customer's awareness; they are the things the customer has never thought about. One of the best examples of a product that filled unknown requirements is the fabulously successful Sony Walkman. The teenagers who were walking around with fifteen-pound boom boxes on their shoulders were not asking for a small cassette tape player that they could put in their pockets and listen to privately with earphones. Had they been asked for their requirements, they would probably have requested a boom box that weighed less.

Identifying unknown requirements is much more difficult than identifying other wants and needs, and yet it is probably the most important capability for satisfying and retaining customers. In business-to-business sales, it calls for the ability to step back and view the customers in relation to their industry, their competition, and the changing business and regulatory environment. In consumer sales, it requires an understanding of changing values, concerns, and lifestyles. It is also critical to look into the future to anticipate changing requirements and the impact of new technology. The organizations that master all four categories of customer requirements will be the survivors.

## Information Sources

The next step in examining the best practice of listening to customers is to identify all potential sources of customer input to the improvement process.

## Current Customers

The leading companies clearly recognize the value of their current customers. They view them as an asset and realize that it costs about five times as much to acquire a new customer as it does to retain an existing one. They know it is easier to sell additional volume and new products to current customers than it is to develop new accounts. With the trend toward reducing the number of suppliers each customer uses, companies and their salespeople are working hard to retain their existing customer base.

For all these reasons, most companies have a process for listening to their current customers. The leading companies use several complementary methods. Recall, for example, how Eastman Chemical uses a combination of customer satisfaction surveys, a complaint-handling process, customer partnerships, and sales reports to gather requirements and track satisfaction.

## Lost Customers

Virtually every business loses some customers or orders. In business-to-business sales, customers go out of business, move away, switch to competitors, or find alternative products or services. In consumer sales, the possibilities are even greater. Customers may switch brands or buy through different channels. Their interests or hobbies may change. They may move away or die. Hardest to detect are the business customers or consumers who simply buy a little less every year from one supplier while shifting business to others.

The common theme among lost customers is that they have all taken action. They have decided to go elsewhere. The company needs to know the reason for the lost customer, order, or business volume. This is vital input to the improvement process, yet most companies do nothing to tap this information source.

One example of a company that does follow up on losses is AccuRate, a Whitewater, Wisconsin, manufacturer of dry material feeders. AccuRate surveys customers who receive proposals for AccuRate products but elect not to place an order. This may result from a competitor's getting the business or from a decision not to order anything at all. Although AccuRate sells products exclusively through manufacturer's representatives, the company surveys these lost customers by direct mail. About 30 percent respond. Information on why AccuRate lost an order is routed to everyone who can benefit from seeing it, including product engineers, managers, pricers, sales representatives, and the manufacturer's representatives.

When the company asked the manufacturer's reps why an order was lost, they almost always responded that it was due to price. However, when AccuRate surveyed the lost customers, it found that price was almost never the reason. The most frequent cause was that the manufacturer's rep did not fully understand the customer's requirements and did not propose the right solution. AccuRate responded by improving training and support for the manufacturer's reps, increasing their close rate.

## Prospective Customers

Prospects are the companies or individuals with whom a company has never done business. They often represent major growth potential but have not been reached through current sales or marketing approaches or simply have not chosen to place an order. Consumer product companies invest heavily in listening to prospects, typically through telephone research, focus groups, and interviews. In the business-to-business sector, fewer companies take advantage of this source of input, although the same listening techniques apply.

## Competitors' Customers

Listening to competitors' customers is another area where there is significant potential to learn about what customers need and want. Customers in this segment have already decided to use a product or service, but they are getting it from a competitor. A major old-line restaurant chain, for example, failed to listen to other chains' customers. It hired market researchers to interview customers as they left the chain's own restaurants to determine how they liked the food, service, and value, and the responses were generally positive. However, there were fewer people coming out of the restaurants than before, and the interviewers were not talking to the people who were eating at such fast-food restaurants as McDonald's, Burger King, KFC, and Pizza Hut. If they had, they would have learned that competitors' customers valued fast service and different kinds of foods.

## Indirect Customers

So far, current, lost, prospective, and competitors' customers have been discussed as if they are direct customers. For some companies, they are. However, many companies sell through a channel that may include one or more levels of distributors, dealers, agents, brokers, or other distribution partners. Frequently these companies do not have direct contact with the end users or consumers of their products or services. In these cases, companies treat the intermediaries as both customers and an integral part of the company. Although it is important to listen to the distribution partners, the company must find ways to listen to the end users or consumers as well. Companies like Motorola, Square D, and AccuRate all sell through distribution channels. They survey the end users of their products, their indirect customers, and share the results with the members of their distribution channels to help them improve their sales, marketing, and service operations.

## Internal Customers

One more potential but frequently ignored source of input to the sales and marketing improvement process is internal customers. In many companies, these internal customers receive the orders that sales closes. They also need the customer requirements and market and competitive information that sales gets directly from customers. Marketing also has a variety of internal customers. However, in most companies these internal customers are almost never asked for their requirements or to provide feedback.

## When to Listen (or Timing Is Everything)

When a company asks for customer feedback, it can do it on a scheduled basis such as sending out an annual customer satisfaction survey. It can also ask for feedback after an important customer interaction such as receiving an order, delivering a product or service, or resolving a problem. Before examining each of the listening methods, we need to understand when to apply them.

## Periodic or Scheduled Surveys

Most companies conduct customer satisfaction surveys on a scheduled or periodic basis. Ideally the company will have enough customers so that it can select a statistically significant sample each month or quarter and survey that sample by mail or telephone. This approach provides a frequent view of customer satisfaction and the ability to track trends over time. If the customer base is too small to provide a statistically valid sample, the company may survey all its customers annually. When that is the case, the company will need other ways to track satisfaction between the annual surveys. In today's market, major shifts in customer satisfaction can occur within a twelve-month period.

Periodic surveys are an excellent way to track overall satisfaction with a company. However, in some situations, they are not sensitive enough to measure the effect of changes that the company makes. For example, if customers receive monthly invoices and the company improves the billing system, every customer will experience the result, and a periodic customer satisfaction survey will quickly reflect customer reaction to the new billing system. However, if the company improves product training for the salespeople, only those customers who have made a purchase recently are likely to notice the improvement. The feedback from a periodic survey to the sales training department will be weak at best.

The periodic customer satisfaction survey can also mask problems if only a few customers have personal interaction with the company during a survey period. Take the case of Brooklyn Union Gas. BUG received good customer satisfaction ratings from its customers in periodic surveys. When it surveyed customers who had just had a personal interaction with the company, however, it found that 40 percent were dissatisfied. It was only by looking at the customers who had called for service, questioned an invoice, or had some other personal contact that BUG was able to identify specific problems (Royal, 1994).

## Transaction-Based Surveys

To overcome problems associated with periodic surveys, some companies supplement them with transaction-based surveys. Pitney Bowes, for example, offers small businesses and home offices a postage meter and scale for processing outbound mail and sells this package through its direct marketing channel. After each sale, the company sends each new customer a package that includes a thank you letter, customer information, and a survey form. The survey asks the customers how satisfied they are with their new postage meter and scale and with the experience they had with the sales and delivery process.

After the sale, the customer's main interaction with Pitney Bowes is a quarterly invoice and an annual meter inspection visit. The company conducts periodic surveys on a sample of existing customers to measure their ongoing satisfaction with the product and after market services. It uses the results of the periodic survey to assess and direct follow-up contact with the customers and for product improvement efforts. And it uses the thank-you letter survey to measure individual or channel sales performance and the effectiveness of the order fulfillment process. Together the periodic and transaction-based surveys provide Pitney Bowes with a complete picture of customer satisfaction.

## Listening Methods

Virtually every successful company uses at least one formal method for listening to its customers, and most employ several complementary approaches. Some of the methods identify customer requirements, others gather feedback and measure customer satisfaction and loyalty, and a few meet both objectives. Many of these methods are used to get customer input to improve products and services. However, my purpose here is to describe how these methods are used for input into the sales and marketing improvement process.

## Written Surveys

The written survey is the most frequently used formal method for listening to customers and is an integral part of virtually every customer satisfaction tracking system. Its strength is in gathering feedback from a large number of customers in a form that can be easily processed for statistical analysis and reporting. The data can be sorted into a number of categories such as department, business unit, division, product or service, sales branch office, geographical region, and customer type. Low scores pinpoint areas where the improvement process can best be applied. High scores identify internal benchmarks and role models.

Survey forms can be mailed or hand delivered to all of a company's customers or a statistically valid sample. Sending surveys to every customer clearly communicates a company's interest in listening to its customers, and despite rising postal rates, mail surveys still enjoy one the lowest costs per response of any form of research. The written form also eliminates the interviewer bias that may be present in other forms of research, and respondents can complete the survey at their convenience and their own pace. In companies selling to other businesses, the low cost of the direct mail survey makes it practical to contact several people within each account.

For all of the benefits of the written survey, there are drawbacks. Unless the response rate is very high, the results may not represent the attitudes of the total customer population. Based on my experience, customers who respond to mail surveys are more frequently either very happy or very dissatisfied. Those in the middle, the neutrals, tend to respond less frequently. Also, the results represent the opinions of customers who like to fill out surveys and omit those who do not.

Because the survey is written, there is also no opportunity to probe for additional, in-depth information. Other methods for listening to the customer such as face-to-face and telephone interviews and focus groups are necessary for that purpose. For this same reason, the written survey is used primarily for feedback and is not a good source for determining customer requirements.

To encourage completion of the written survey and avoid respondent fatigue, the form should be relatively short. The most effective surveys are no more than two pages long. This limits the number of questions that can be devoted to any specific area of the business, such as sales or marketing. To get detailed feedback in these two areas, a dedicated survey must be conducted or other means of listening used. However, even with these limitations, the written survey is the cornerstone of most customer satisfaction systems.

## Telephone Surveys

Although written surveys remain a mainstay in satisfaction research, the use of telephone surveys is increasing. Telephone surveys enjoy a higher response rate than written surveys conducted by mail. Therefore sample sizes can be smaller, and the results more representative of the total population. In addition, the company can be certain of who is actually responding to the survey. Telephone surveys also allow the person conducting the interview to clarify the meaning of questions for the respondent and to probe for more detailed information where appropriate. This capability also makes the telephone survey useful for identifying or validating customer requirements as well as gathering feedback. Finally, telephone surveys can provide customer information more quickly than mail surveys.

The biggest disadvantage of the telephone survey is its cost per response. This cost makes it impractical to survey every customer unless the company has a very small customer set. Another drawback is that the telephone survey is intrusive, and people's resistance to unscheduled telephone research is growing. Even with a willing respondent, the duration of the call limits its effectiveness in asking detailed questions to probe for assumed requirements. Call duration limits also make it difficult to discuss company capabilities at length, information the customer may need to reveal withheld requirements.

Xerox has measured customer satisfaction for years using periodic mail surveys. However, it has recently added transaction-based telephone surveys to its survey architecture. Xerox places over 10,000 calls each month trying to find people who have made buying decisions for document processing products. The respondent may have bought a Xerox copier for the first time, replaced an older Xerox machine, or added printers or copiers. He or she may also have decided on a competitive copier to replace a Xerox machine or another competitor's machine.

In every case where someone has made such a decision, Xerox wants to know what factors were most important: machine features, reliability, cost, service capability, or the relationship with the salesperson. By analyzing survey results, Xerox can identify by customer size and type, geographical location, and competitor what is driving customer decisions. According to Peter Garcia, Xerox director of customer satisfaction, the results tell the company where to invest. Is the need in new products, increased copier reliability, better service, or more training for the salespeople? According to Garcia, Xerox can predict the outcome of a competitive sales situation with up to 85 percent accuracy.

## Face-to-Face Interviews

Interviewing customers and prospects face-to-face is one of the most effective listening methods available. Well-structured and well-conducted interviews provide high-quality feedback on customer satisfaction; they are excellent for identifying and validating the requested, assumed, and withheld categories of customer requirements. Although it is possible to conduct enough face-to-face interviews to get quantitative, statistically valid data, the approach is much more frequently used to gather qualitative information.

The strength of face-to-face interviews comes from the presence of a trained interviewer who has the ability to use all types of questions and to clarify any that are not fully understood by the respondent. The interviewer can deviate from the planned survey guide when necessary to probe for more detailed information. Face-to-face interviews frequently uncover customer issues, concerns, and even opportunities that the company never considered. The interviewer can also present information about the company itself or a specific product or service, use visual aids, or even demonstrate a product as part of the interview.

Face-to-face interviews have a very high response rate, particularly when the company is a major supplier or well-known and respected company. Also, the interview can be conducted at a time and place convenient to the respondent. Because the interview usually amounts to a structured conversation between two people, the responses tend to be more open and honest and free from the influences of other people than the responses of people in focus groups. To be completely bias free, the interview must be conducted by someone skilled in interview techniques and with no vested interest in the outcome. This requirement frequently dictates the use of an outside research firm.

The high-quality information obtained by face-to-face interviews comes at a price. The cost per response is higher than for other forms of listening. The approach is also very time consuming, and scheduling interviews is difficult, particularly when the respondents are spread out geographically.

## Focus Groups

Like the face-to-face interview, the focus group is an excellent source of customer feedback for assumed, requested, and withheld requirements. In the focus group, a small number of people are brought together to discuss a particular topic. It might be the sponsoring company, its product or service, a new product concept, overall customer satisfaction, or a new sales approach or marketing program. The group of eight to twelve people is facilitated by a trained leader who asks questions and conducts a group discussion. Although the focus group is most frequently used for feedback on consumer products, it has application in business-to-business studies as well.

Also like the one-on-one interview, the focus group depends on the skill of the facilitator for its success. The facilitator enters the group meeting with a set of questions or issues that the client company wants addressed. However, he or she also has the ability to ask all forms of questions and to pursue interesting and useful avenues of discussion as long as they fall within the frame established by the client.

Although focus groups can be conducted at a company or customer location, they are generally held at a research firm's facility in rooms designed for the purpose. These rooms have adjoining viewing platforms separated by one-way glass that allows company representatives to watch and listen to the group without influencing or interfering with the process. These research facilities can also make audio and video recordings of the group process, which can be reviewed later by others at the client company. Actually seeing and hearing customers discuss a product or marketing program in person or on videotape has a much greater impact on the client than simply reading a transcript or summary of the focus group outcome.

Using a dedicated focus group facility has a strong advantage, but it has disadvantages as well. It takes time for customers to travel to the facility, in addition to the time they spend participating in the group. Also most respondents expect to receive some compensation for their time. This is particularly true when the client is not identified or when the focus group is dealing with a consumer product or service. Although the cost per interview is lower than the face-to-face interview, it is still relatively expensive on a per-response basis.

The facilitator must be proficient in conducting focus group meetings. He or she is responsible for keeping the group on the subject, making sure the required topics are covered in the time available, and ensuring that everyone contributes and no one dominates or unduly influences the group.

## Blind Surveys

In all the survey types described so far, the company may or may not be identified to the customer. One company that uses the unidentified, or blind, survey is Square D. This company employs a professional research firm to conduct blind, transaction-based telephone surveys of Square D customers who have made a recent purchase. Interviewers begin by stating that the call is being made in behalf of an electrical equipment manufacturer who is interested in measuring its customers' satisfaction. Then they ask the customer to describe his or her last buying experience. At no time during these calls is Square D identified as the client.

There are several benefits to the so-called blind survey. The calls often uncover information about competitors. They are also a way to gather requirements when the company does not want customers to know it is working on a new product or service. Finally, some companies believe that customers are more open when the research is anonymous.

There are also disadvantages to blind surveys. Most companies want their customers to know that they are interested in their customers' opinions. When the company is not identified, the customers have no way of knowing that their supplier is listening and wants to know about their issues and concerns. In addition, it is more difficult to get customers to agree to interviews when the company is not identified. This in turn raises the survey cost.

## Mystery Shoppers

Mystery shopping is the practice of engaging people to visit or call sales or service locations and act as customers. Their objective is to evaluate the sales and service experience directly and report their findings. Mystery shopping surveys are used primarily in such consumer product areas as banking, retail, and fast food. However, they are also used in telecommunications, hospitality, and other industries.

Companies selling business-to-business can also apply the mystery shopper method of testing sales and service delivery processes. One sales vice president in a large manufacturing company regularly telephones his sales branch offices. He determines how long it takes for someone to answer the phone and how his call is handled before he identifies himself. His standard, incidentally, is that a human being must answer the telephone within three rings. Another executive reported that his salespeople send in coupons or call the company's 800-number to ask for information. Then they measure how long it takes the company to respond.

A few years ago, IBM customers gave the company's phone mail system their lowest rating on the company's annual satisfaction survey. They complained that employee announcements were not current and that they were frequently caught in "phone mail jail." IBM responded by creating a staff to call IBM departments around the country to determine whether employees' voice mail announcements were current. Then it reported the findings to the department managers for action. These mystery shoppers have successfully changed the company culture. Today most IBMers update their voice mail announcements daily, and a real person is usually just one transfer away.

Using a mystery-shopping process is a good way to gather customer satisfaction feedback. Done in volume, mystery shopping can generate information for qualitative analysis across a large organization with many locations. However, it can be focused on specific outlets, sales branches, distributors, dealers, or agencies.

For the process to work effectively, the shopper must be unknown to the person being surveyed. This requires a frequent turnover among mystery shoppers. Also they must be carefully selected to represent a typical shopper, not a professional observer. Some companies even recruit real customers to be their mystery shoppers.

## Customer Councils

Customer councils are groups of customers who meet with company representatives to discuss topics of mutual interest. They may be end users, such as council members at NeXT Computer, or distributors, such as council members at OSRAM SYLVANIA. In most cases, the company selects the customers, usually from the company's key accounts. Council meeting topics may include products and services, pricing, administrative processes, and sales and marketing programs.

One example of a company that has a strong dealer network and uses customer councils very effectively is Steelcase, the Grand Rapids, Michigan–based manufacturer of office furniture and systems. According to Ken Dutkiewicz, director of Steelcase dealer market management, "The Steelcase dealer council is made up of members elected by all of the dealers. They meet with us about four times a year to discuss the dealer needs."

One benefit of the customer council is that it helps build a strong partnership between the customers and the company. The exchange of information between council members also helps them become stronger and more effective competitors in their local markets. The feedback on customer satisfaction levels and requirements statements for new products, services, and marketing support are usually well accepted by the company because they come firsthand from trading partners. The council also acts as a sounding board for ideas and improvements proposed by the company.

Although they are very effective, the councils do have limitations. To be an effective size for group discussions, the councils are relatively small. Due to their small size and the fact that members are typically selected from the largest and best customers or distributors, the councils are not representative of the total customer population. For this reason, they are best used to provide an additional dimension to other listening methods, not as the company's sole source of customer input.

## User Groups and Associations

User groups and associations are also potential sources of customer requirements and feedback. Their members share a common interest in a specific product or product category. Most of them meet periodically to share information, experiences, and problems and solutions. Some groups are tightly linked to the supplier of a product; others exist independently.

Besides being a source of input, these organizations help build a sense of partnership between the company and the group members. Because most group activities occur in meetings attended by company representatives, the interaction has the benefit of face-to-face communications, and when customers have positive experiences, the good news travels quickly.

On the downside, large user groups can be costly to support, depending on the level of company involvement. Also some organizations develop a life and direction of their own, and in some cases user groups have even invited competitors to participate. Although the groups are often large, they still may not represent the views of the typical user of the product or service. Therefore the company needs to temper user group input with information from other sources.

## Executive Contacts

The contact between company executives and their customer counterparts is also a source of requirements and feedback. Some of this interaction happens during the normal course of business. During meetings between company and customer executives, customers frequently express their requirements or discuss their satisfaction with the company. Some companies assign their key accounts to senior executives who maintain contact with these accounts on a scheduled basis. In a few cases, the executives even have responsibility for overall customer satisfaction in their assigned accounts.

In Motorola's Executive Customer Advocate Program, it is the executive's job to stay in contact with his or her assigned customer, learn the customer's strategy, and determine where the customer is going and what its communications requirements will be over the next five years. At Eastman Chemical, the senior executives also have key account responsibility and call on their assigned customers several times a year. Executive contact helps establish a relationship at a higher level in the account and keeps the senior executives in touch with customer requirements and the factors that influence their buying decisions ("Follow the Leader," 1994).

Getting customer input at the top levels of the organization has many benefits. The input comes from the highest level in the customer organization, the level that has the best view of the customer's future direction. The information comes face-to-face, the most effective way to gather high-quality information. Having company executives call directly on customers also demonstrates the organization's commitment to listening to the customer. Finally, it gives the executives a better understanding of what is going on outside corporate headquarters.

Like all other listening processes, executive contacts have some drawbacks. Because of the limited number and high cost of executive contacts, the method is not useful for gathering statistically significant data. It is best used in support of other approaches. Like members of customer councils, the customers involved in the executive contact program tend to be the biggest and best. Executives rarely see smaller customers, users of competitive products, or the unfriendly and uncooperative customers.

Another limitation stems from the fact that executives are rarely trained in effective interview techniques nor are they available to spend time in in-depth conversations clarifying assumed requirements or identifying withheld requirements. As a result, executives have been known to get input from one or two calls on a large customer, generalize the results, and make major business decisions on their own small sample.

## Sales and Other Customer Contact People

Everyone in the company who deals directly with customers is a potential source of customer requirements and feedback. In most companies, salespeople lead this list. They are in frequent contact with the people who make and influence decisions to buy products and services. The best salespeople know their customers well; they understand their customers' businesses, future plans, competition, and industry. They are also the first to hear about problems and the first to recognize opportunities. Most sales organizations have a formal process to collect input from salespeople. They use call reports, activity reports, special situation reports, loss reports, product requirements, and employee suggestion systems to gather that input.

Some companies, such as California & Hawaiian Sugar and Globe Metallurgical rely on feedback from their salespeople rather than on formal surveys. As Norm Jennings, quality manager at Baldrige Award–winning Globe reports: "Our salesperson is right there with the customer. Feedback is immediate. Not only our sales and marketing people but also our functional area people, like myself, are in daily contact with our customers. We know their inventories, we know their order patterns, we know their problems, we know what they want in the future, we know their goals and where they are going. We have instantaneous feedback."

As Jennings suggests, one of the biggest benefits of sales input is its immediacy. If problems are significant enough or opportunities large enough, salespeople make the company aware very quickly. If there is a customer satisfaction problem, salespeople have a vested interest in getting it resolved promptly. If the customer needs a new product, feature, upgrade, faster delivery, or volume discount or is inviting in the competition, the salesperson is the first to know and anxious to report.

However, there are disadvantages to using salespeople as the only source of customer information. Sales input can be biased. Salespeople often have a strong personal interest in the outcome of action taken on behalf of their customers. Also, some customer input may not reflect positively on the salesperson or sales process, and many organizations still shoot messengers. In addition, many salespeople have not received training in good interview techniques. They may ask leading questions that bias the answers. And not all salespeople will report at the same level of detail. For all these reasons, input from the salesforce is best used to complement other methods of listening.

## Joint Customer Planning Sessions

The joint customer planning session is one of the least well known and used listening methods. This method is unique to just a few leading companies, and many of them consider it such a competitive advantage that they have been reluctant to discuss it. It is one of the most powerful techniques for listening to customers, and it can provide an effective step in beginning or expanding a customer partnership.

The Calgon Corporation is one leader in the use of joint customer planning sessions. Calgon put a quality management process in place in 1989 and initially focused on internal operations. In April 1992, Calgon's president gave the company's director of quality management, Stan Karmilovich, a charter to determine where the company was and where it should go next. Karmilovich's assessment revealed that the company was doing well internally with its quality management process. However, he recognized that the company had still not asked its customers, "Where can we bring more value to you?" He also saw an opportunity to get the salespeople, the company's service engineers, more involved.

The result was a new program that Calgon called the Quality Commitment Process (QCP). Calgon designed it to get customers and service engineers together to identify projects that would bring added value to the customer. The QCP begins when Calgon invites four to eight key managers from a customer to a Quality Encounter, a meeting with their salesperson and district sales manager. The objective of the meeting is to identify improvement opportunities related to Calgon's products, systems, applications, or services. A Calgon facilitator leads the meeting, and the company's district manager and service engineer sit quietly in the back of the room taking detailed notes.

The facilitator begins the meeting by thanking the customer for his or her business and explaining that this is not a sales presentation. The facilitator then reviews the specific products and services currently being used by the customer and explains the Quality Commitment Process. Then he or she invites the customer to suggest areas for improvement. What follows is a typical brainstorming session that produces from twenty to thirty-five suggestions. The customer team then establishes priorities for the items suggested. Often the Calgon representatives can resolve many of the problems on the spot.

The Calgon service engineer then develops an action plan and leads each improvement project to conclusion. The engineer keeps both the customer and Calgon management apprised of progress regularly. After each project is finished, the engineer and the customer review the original list of opportunities to pick the next issue to address. The Quality Encounter is repeated at least once a year or when the customer feels it is important.

Although the QCP focuses on the wants and needs of individual customers, the collective results are reviewed at Calgon headquarters. This helps identify issues that are common to more than one customer and require headquarters attention to resolve. After having conducted over 150 Quality Encounters, Calgon is extremely pleased with the performance of the program. Customers are also happy with the opportunity to identify value-added activities for the service engineers.

There are several variations on Calgon's theme. As part of AT&T's Shared Expectations process, customer representatives brainstorm what they expect from AT&T and what they think AT&T expects of them. At the same time the customers are meeting, the AT&T account team convenes in a separate room. Their instructions are to identify what they expect of the customer and what they think the customer expects of them. Then the customers and AT&T representatives gather together and compare their results. The salespeople often discover that they do not have the clear understanding of customer expectations that they thought they did.

Other companies as diverse as Century Furniture, GE, and Texas Instruments have used similar approaches, and all have achieved positive results. The common themes are the use of salespeople as a channel to gather information, a commitment to improve the products and processes at the customer level, direct input from the customer, and a willingness to listen to constructive criticism of current practices and offerings.

There is one caveat concerning this technique. The company must approach it with the sincere objective of making real customer-focused improvements. That requires commitment from the salesperson, the sales manager, and the management team. It also requires that the participants all understand the improvement process and can use it effectively. If the customer perceives that the meeting is a thinly veiled sales presentation, it can seriously damage the customer relationship.

Many customers are not waiting for planning sessions, mail surveys, or telephone interviews to tell their suppliers what they think.

They are more willing than ever to complain when their suppliers are not meeting their requirements. Some customers are even sending periodic report cards to their suppliers to give them performance feedback.

## Customer Complaints

Most companies have some kind of process for handling dissatisfied customers and customer complaints. These processes may include return of merchandise procedures, liberal contract cancellation clauses, financial rebates and credits, and letters and visits from executives. It is always in the company's best interest to listen to dissatisfied customers and take action to resolve their complaints where possible.

An effective complaint system does more than just track complaints to make sure they are resolved. It also accumulates statistics on the number and kinds of complaints. By reviewing the patterns, the company can recognize the most frequent or most costly complaints, identify their root causes, and take corrective action to make certain they do not happen again. Of course, the analysis can also determine patterns of complaints by product or service category, sales location, business function, and customer type or demographic characteristic.

A well-designed complaint system shows the company's commitment to customer satisfaction and provides almost immediate feedback on what customers think about company products and services. The complaint statistics can also highlight unmet customer requirements and pinpoint assumed requirements. Without analysis of complaints, the complaint system will produce quick fixes to problems but not the lasting process changes that will eliminate root causes.

There are some cautions about using complaint handling and tracking systems as a source of input. First, it is not always possible to probe for more detailed information about causes of dissatisfaction. Second, complaints do not come from a random sample of the customer base; therefore they do not represent a complete picture of customer attitudes. Finally, the most frequent complaints are not always about the issues that have the greatest impact on customer satisfaction and loyalty.

## Customer Report Cards

Another form of unsolicited customer feedback is the supplier report card. This is a relatively new form of feedback that has come out of the quality movement and is gaining in popularity in business-to-business relationships. John Steel, vice president, marketing and sales, at Baldrige Award–winning Zytec, reports, "Many of our customers give us very formal customer report cards, some monthly, some quarterly, telling us how we are doing in quality and reliability and service and what they expect of us by the end of the next quarter or the end of next year."

Like customer complaints, report cards require the company to have a process to receive them, record the results, and send the information to the appropriate people in the organization for review and appropriate action. Of course these recipients include the salespeople assigned to the account. However, because each customer's report card is unique, the types of information a report card provides will differ from one customer to the next, making comparisons difficult. These differences also make it almost impossible to analyze the data statistically.

These report cards are an important form of customer feedback, providing information that the customer has deemed important for the company to know. Although report cards do not provide the opportunity to ask questions, their measurements are usually straightforward, and input is consistent from one period to the next. Tracking the results from one customer over time can reveal trends in performance for that specific customer.

Also, like the customer complaint system, report cards may not identify the items most important to overall customer satisfaction. If the report card form a customer uses is the same from period to period, it may not reflect specific problems or issues that are outside the scope of the form and are changing quickly. Clearly, information from the customer report card should be included among the sources of customer requirements and feedback but not be relied on as the only source.

## Listening Methods Conclusion

All of these listening methods can suggest improvements for the sales and marketing functions. The leading companies generally select several complementary listening approaches in order to create a complete and accurate picture of customer requirements and get feedback on how well these requirements are being met. Table 3.1 summarizes the listening methods and describes specifically how they apply to sales and marketing.

## What to Do After Listening

After a company has listened to its customers, it must follow through on what it has learned.

### Respond Immediately to Current Problems, Issues, or Concerns

Almost all the listening methods may uncover current problems, issues, or concerns. In many cases, these issues will not even relate to the subject at hand. For example, during a telephone survey to gather information regarding direct mail marketing, the customer might state that the company's sales representative has not been returning telephone calls, that an order is behind schedule, or that there is an unresolved billing error.

Written surveys are no different. Customers often write in unsolicited comments on the survey forms, whether the instructions ask for them or not. For this reason, every form should be reviewed to check for write-in comments, looking particularly for current problems. Unsolicited customer input calls for immediate attention, and the listening process should include a way to direct it to someone who will address it quickly. It should also be recorded in the company's complaint handling system for follow-up and analysis.

Several leading companies also report that they contact every customer who marks an item in either the "very dissatisfied" or "dissatisfied" category. In most cases, salespeople are responsible for following up to resolve such issues. Failure to respond to any problem will discourage future customer feedback and may be ignoring a festering problem or even a business opportunity.

### Give Survey Feedback to the Customers

Several companies report their survey results back to their customers. They include current findings, how the findings compare

**Table 3.1. How Listening Methods Apply to Sales and Marketing.**

| Method | How Well Does It Represent the Total Population? | Relative Cost per Response | Information for Sales and Marketing | Used for Requirements, Feedback, or Both? |
|---|---|---|---|---|
| Written survey | If response rate is high, written surveys can be very representative. If rate is low, there is a bias toward (1) people who like to fill out surveys and (2) people who are very happy or very unhappy. | If response rate is high, cost per response is among the lowest. If response rate is low, cost per response is correspondingly higher. | If survey is scheduled and covers many company aspects, information for sales and marketing is very limited, probably just answers to a few key questions. If survey is transaction based (after a sales or marketing program experience), all the information can relate to sales or marketing. | Primarily feedback. |
| Telephone survey | Good representation of the intended population. | Medium. | Same as for written survey. | Both. |

| Method | Representativeness | Cost | Description | Type |
|---|---|---|---|---|
| Focus group | Good representation of the intended population. | Medium. | Same as for written survey. However, focus groups tend to be used to study specific issues, not general customer satisfaction, and can offer excellent input on ways to improve sales and marketing activities. | Both. |
| Face-to-face interview | Good representation of the intended population. | High—in most cases too high to get statistically valid data. | Excellent source of qualitative input. Used to identify factors most important to customers (which can then be explored in written and telephone surveys). | Both. |
| Mystery shoppers | If mystery shoppers represent typical shoppers, results will be representative. | Medium. | Good source of input on direct sales. Can measure things like how well the company responds to inquiries and requests for information. | Feedback. |

**Table 3.1.  How Listening Methods Apply to Sales and Marketing (cont'd).**

| Method | How Well Does It Represent the Total Population? | Relative Cost per Response | Information for Sales and Marketing | Used for Requirements, Feedback, or Both? |
|---|---|---|---|---|
| Customer councils | Most are small and made up of best customers; rarely representative of the total population. Also do not include prospects or lost and competitive users. | High. | Can supply good input on sales activities and marketing programs. Usually lots of opportunity for interactive discussion with customer representatives. | Requirements and feedback. |
| User groups and associations | Most are made up of frequent or high-volume product users and generally do not include prospects or lost and competitive users. | Medium to high. | Can be good source of input on how frequent, committed users want to learn about new products and services. | Requirements and feedback. |
| Sales and other contact people | Not well. Only active customers and prospects come in contact with sales and other company representatives. | Low. | Information about sales and other contact people may be high. However, because it is collected by the very people it concerns, there is a high potential for bias. | Both. |

| | | | | |
|---|---|---|---|---|
| Executive contact | Not well. Executives deal with the largest and best customers and prospects. | Medium. | Potential is high. | Both. |
| Joint customer planning sessions | Not well. Conducted only with interested customers. | High. | Very high. Excellent on an individual account basis. | Both. |
| Complaint systems | Not well. Represents only customers with problems. Also, complaints may not represent factors most important to customer buying decisions. | Low. | Potential for input on sales activities and marketing programs in direct proportion to how often they do something wrong and customers complain. | Feedback. |
| Report cards | Not well. They tend to come from the largest and most quality conscious customers. | Low. | Sales and marketing activities rarely included in unsolicited report cards. | Feedback. |

to previous survey results, and what action the company plans to take. Sharing the results demonstrates that the company is listening and that it is willing to be open and honest with its customers. This encourages customer feedback on future surveys. Even more important, the public display of the results provides an incentive to the responsible executives and managers to make the improvements necessary to raise customer satisfaction.

The Bausch & Lomb Eyeware Division provides an example. The division conducts periodic surveys of its direct customers: sunglasses distributors and retailers. After an analysis of the responses, the division publishes a quarterly twelve-page brochure that summarizes the results. It includes information on the key drivers of overall satisfaction: order processing and distribution, brand image, product offerings, fit and comfort, and product quality.

## Take Action

The next step in the listening process is to take action based on the customer input. This may sound basic, but not every company understands this key point. Take the example of a well-known electronics company. Several years ago this company had a unique and technically excellent product that it sold through independent retail dealers. To grow sales, the marketing department wanted to sign up new dealers, so it commissioned a study to find out what would influence potential dealers to carry the product.

A research firm conducted face-to-face interviews with a sample of the company's current, prospective, and ex-dealers. The survey findings were not what the company wanted to hear. Both current and ex-dealers revealed that the company frequently did not answer the telephone or return telephone messages. It did not support an older product line with parts and service. The majority of the dealers interviewed did not consider the company a good supplier, even though they acknowledged that the company's product was technically superior to that of the industry leader. To make matters worse, the company's reputation was common knowledge in the dealer network. As a result, potential dealers were simply not interested in carrying the company's product line.

The company did not receive the research findings well. The marketing department just wanted to know what to say to sign up new dealers. It did not want to hear what it was doing wrong or what needed to be fixed in other parts of the business. In the final analysis, the company did not take action on their customers' input. The result? Six years later this well-known company closed its doors forever, leaving hundreds of employees without work and thousands of users with orphan products.

An executive with another company in the same industry shared a similar problem. The senior executives in his company were constantly traveling between meetings with customers and visits to company sites. They were inundated with information. They spent so much time listening, they almost never had time to reflect on what they heard and take appropriate action. While they were listening, the market changed, but their business strategy did not. When the executives finally awakened to the problems, they were so severe that it took a 40 percent staff reduction and a whole new strategy to turn the business around.

Listening is not an end in itself. The objective is to take informed action supported by the results of listening.

## Report Improvements to Customers

After taking action, the next step is to let the customers know about the improvements. As the late Sam Walton said, "It is not an improvement if the customer does not know about it." Some companies, such as Eastman Chemical, communicate their improvements through their direct sales people. According to George Trabue, Jr., past president of Eastman Chemical Company's Worldwide Sales Division, the sales organization has two roles in the listening process: "One is to listen to the voice of the customer and then to give the input to everybody in the company on the improvement opportunities. Then, once we have made changes through our improvement projects, the sales organization communicates those back to the customers."

## Pitfalls in Listening

Listening to customers seems so easy. Just design a survey form and mail it to the customers, make some phone calls, interview a few key decision makers. However, this simplicity masks the potential pitfalls. Here are some of the most common mistakes.

## Listen to the Right People

This may seem obvious, but it is vital to identify and listen to the right people. If the objective is to gather requirements and get feedback for sales and marketing, the customer decision makers and influencers are the target audience. However, many companies have missed this target.

Consider the example of IBM in the early 1980s. The company's marketing division considered its primary customers to be the executives responsible for the function that was then called the data processing department. These were the people who made or strongly influenced decisions to buy large mainframe computers. IBM listened to them carefully through a variety of listening methods. At that time, few IBM managers considered that the real customer might be the end users of computing and that the data processing executive was just the distributor of computing services.

As it turned out, end users' requirements were not being fully satisfied. They wanted new applications developed more quickly, faster response to changes in their requirements, more flexible systems, and more control over priorities. In many companies, the data processing department failed to respond. The end users turned to micro-computers and then to mini-computers and personal computers (PCs). Because IBM had not done an effective job of listening and responding to the needs of the end user community, the company lost a great deal of business to the mini- and micro-computer companies that did.

When conducting surveys, companies often rely on their salespeople for a list of contact names. Although this is a logical approach to identifying the right people to listen to, it may lead to an unintended consequence if salespeople are measured on customer satisfaction. After all, what salesperson in his or her right mind would supply the name of a customer contact who might provide a negative response if that would affect the salesperson's evaluation or income. In this case, the sales manager or other disinterested party should select or at least review the list of contact names.

## Identify the Most Important Issues

After identifying the right people, the next step is to ask them the right questions. Many companies begin their survey design by asking their managers and executives for a list of the questions they want to include in the survey. The problem is that these questions are created from the point of view of the company, not the customers, and these questions may not address the issues customers think are most important. Motorola's MCEI vice president and director of quality and strategic planning Shapour Arami describes what happens: "Usually, when we designed the questions, we pretty much already knew the answers. Too determine what was important to the customer, we did a 'critical need assessment.' Those needs are what we survey now."

Asking managers and executives to create a list of questions may also create another problem: too many questions. As mentioned earlier, the most effective written surveys are no more than two pages long. Longer surveys tend to have much lower response rates. Even when customers do complete and return longer surveys, respondent fatigue may affect the answers. Also, when a large number of questions are created this way, they tend to contain redundancies and overlaps. Often a list of seventy-five or more items can be reduced to two pages of questions with no loss of vital information.

After determining the right questions, effective satisfaction surveys provide a way for the customer to rank the relative importance of each item. It is also important to include a way for the customers to compare the company's performance against that of competitors or to world-class suppliers. Performance and satisfaction are relative.

## Get Adequate Responses

Some companies report a problem with getting enough responses to their written customer satisfaction surveys. However, if the survey is well designed, short, and asks relevant questions, and if the customers perceive that action will be taken, this is not normally a major problem.

John Nelson, vice president of marketing and sales at Baldrige Award–winning Marlow Industries describes how that company gets a high response rate to its survey:

> We did a preliminary survey and asked the customers what questions they wanted on the customer satisfaction survey. We found

out that almost all of them wanted fewer than ten questions. They
wanted them to be quick and cover a broader band, and so we pat-
terned our survey after what our customers said that they wanted.
Two out of the eight questions on our survey deal with marketing
and sales activities. We leave an area at the bottom of the form to
ask for any areas of improvement that they might suggest, and they
usually fill that out. They do not like to spend more than fifteen
minutes on it. And for that we get about 85 percent of our surveys
back. I attribute that to the fact that the surveys are simple and
easy. They are what the customers want.

Don Scoggin, vice president of marketing programs at Unisys,
describes how that company increased its customer survey response
rate:

The response rate used to be less than 50 percent. To improve
that, we provided incentives to the sales representatives to hand
deliver and return the customer surveys. In the last three cycles,
we've gotten over a 90 percent return rate. We want to hear from
all of our customers. We know that it is critical. We also want
immediate feedback on the actual transactions that we have with
a customer, so beginning this year in one region we plan to include
a survey with our proposals. We want to measure how well we are
identifying the customers' business problems. We also want to
know the customers' opinion of how we are applying technology
to those problems and whether the proposals are clear and have
a professional style.

The Wheelabrator Corporation in LaGrange, Georgia, uses an
even more persuasive method of getting customer feedback. The
company pays the salesperson's commission only after the customer completes and returns the survey. Draconian, maybe, but it
works.

## Analyze Results

The ultimate measure of how well a product or service meets the
customers' requirement is whether, given the need and opportunity, customers will buy it again and whether they will recommend
it to others. If there is a high correlation between high customer
satisfaction measured by the methods already described and repeat

purchases and recommendations, then the feedback processes are valid and useful. However, if the correlation is not high, then other factors are at work. The organization must then employ other methods to identify the customers' withheld and unknown requirements. Also, even when a high correlation exists between overall customer satisfaction and repeat business and recommendations, it is still important to learn specifically which requirements most influence overall satisfaction.

Xerox and Pitney Bowes have both found a high degree of correlation between high satisfaction and repeat business. John Lawrence reports that Xerox is focusing on customers who are in the "very satisfied" category. He says, "What we are really interested in is trying to figure out how many of our customers are delighted and what it takes to delight them. We are past just looking at 'are you satisfied or are you not satisfied.' We want to move people to the top end of the scale because we know what the ramifications of that are."

At Pitney Bowes, there is the same view of the "very satisfied" or "delighted customer." While participating in a seminar on improving sales and marketing, Archie Martin, vice president of customer service, shared Pitney Bowes' experience with the customer's degree of satisfaction: "Customers who are very satisfied are 80 percent more likely to do business with us again. Those who are just satisfied are only 20 percent more likely to do so."

Bausch & Lomb is another company that understands the need to focus on the factors that most influence overall customer satisfaction. Elizabeth Gillmeister, director of quality planning, is responsible for customer satisfaction research in the Eyeware Division. She uses the statistical technique of multivariate regression analysis to determine which factors are really important:

> We do a regression analysis on all of our surveys to determine which experiences with our product and service offerings are most important to our customers. When I first introduced this statistical technique to people here, I used a hospital analogy. I ask the people, "What is the patients' biggest complaint in a hospital?" The answer is the food. Based on that information, would you do anything about the food? Actually, you would not, because if you did a regression analysis, you would find that food has absolutely no impact on overall satisfaction. Patients do not expect good

food. More important, food has no impact on your measures of
erosion which are, "Are you willing to come back to this hospital
if you need it?" and, "Would you recommend this hospital to
someone else?"

A quick review of customer satisfaction survey forms from several leading companies reveals that they all contain these two key
questions: "Would you buy from us again?" and, "Would you recommend us to others?" A regression analysis can be applied to the
results of these surveys to determine the relationship between responses to these two indicators of overall customer satisfaction and
each of the other questions on the survey. When hospitals apply a
regression analysis to their customer satisfaction surveys, they find
that the most important factor in customer satisfaction is the care
provided by the nursing staff and physician interaction.

The correlation between high customer satisfaction and repeat
sales and endorsements is not 100 percent. Marianne Crew, vice
president, technical support of TSS (an IBM-Kodak joint venture),
reports that some IBM customers express a high level of satisfaction on surveys but still use some competitive products and services. In contrast, there are other customers who report a lower
satisfaction level but use IBM products and services exclusively.

## Pitfalls Conclusion

These are just some of the problems that can come from using an
unguided approach to customer satisfaction surveys. The customers' responses may not provide valid information on which to
base improvement activities. The results may even be misleading.
For most companies, it is useful to get professional assistance to develop a first survey and evaluate its results. After that, the company
can bring the survey process in-house by hiring a research professional or training a current employee.

## Barriers to Listening

Listening to customers for requirements and feedback seems like
such an obvious thing to do. For various reasons, however, many
companies still have not put formal processes in place to perform

this vital function. Let's look at some of the barriers to effective listening and ways to overcome them.

## Company Culture

Probably the biggest barrier to listening to customers is the culture of the organization itself. Cultural barriers can be based on many existing behaviors and beliefs. The company may simply resist change of any kind. Decisions may have been made based on the intuition or opinion of the company leadership. There may be a belief that the company already knows the answers. Worse, the company may believe that it knows better than the customers what they want or need. It may even be that no one has ever thought of the idea of listening before.

Changing the culture of an organization means changing its basic behaviors and beliefs. This comes only after company leadership recognizes that there is a real need to change. This recognition may come from outside the company through public appraisal, unsolicited customer feedback, or a major business loss. It may come from within the company as the leadership observes a decline in competitive position or business performance and looks around to see what more successful companies are doing. It may also come from an enlightened leader who recognizes the value of listening to customers and champions the cause of change. However change happens, it almost certainly starts at the top of the organization.

An example of how a public appraisal got one company started listening to customers comes from GTE. The November 29, 1982 issue of *Business Week* reported that a GTE subsidiary, General Telephone of California, was "widely perceived to be the worst telephone company in the U.S." Nancy Burzon, director of quality education at GTE, describes the situation: "We didn't believe it. We denied it. We went back to our measures and said, that couldn't be true. And then we started some benchmarking." The results verified the problem, and GTE was thrust into a companywide improvement initiative, complete with a variety of requirements and feedback processes. Today, GTE has improved its customer satisfaction across the board and currently leads the competition in several key markets. In 1994, GTE Directories was a recipient of the Malcolm Baldrige National Quality Award.

Any public source of information may get the attention of the company's management. Organizations such as Consumer Reports evaluate many consumer products and services, rate and rank them, and publish the results. Publications on a wide variety of subjects from investments to golf, from automobiles to home maintenance, evaluate and publish product and service ratings. Industry associations often survey customers and publish the results for their members. Any of these independent and highly visible sources of information may provide the evidence needed to get management's attention and get a formal listening process started.

If the company has customers who provide report cards, make sure that input reaches the company leadership. Provide company leaders with statistics and examples from the complaint system. Couple these with information on major competitive losses and declining market share. These all add up to demonstrate the need for a better understanding of customers' requirements and for additional feedback on their satisfaction. The fear of financial loss is an excellent motivator.

Sometimes a public rating or unsolicited customer feedback is not available, and there is no enlightened leader in the organization to show the way. In this case, providing executives with stories of companies who have listened to customers and the results they have attained may be useful. The successful companies may be direct competitors or other organizations that serve the same customer base. Another approach is to arrange for the executives to make face-to-face calls on customers who have effective listening processes in place. These customers have a vested interest in having high-quality suppliers who listen to their requirements and act on their feedback.

## Listening Takes Too Long, Costs Too Much

Two of the most common objections to listening to customers are "it takes too long" and "it costs too much." In some cases, these objections are raised to obscure underlying cultural issues. In others, the objection does not consider the costs of not listening.

Consider the idea that listening to customers takes too long. The culture in many organizations rewards quick fixes to problems. When a problem occurs, recognition goes to the people who rush in and "put out the fire." The message from the organization is,

"We don't have time to listen to customers. We have to solve today's problem today." Of course it is important to fix the immediate problem. However, in this kind of culture, there is little or no reward for the person who identifies the root cause of a problem and implements a lasting solution that will prevent the problem from ever happening again.

In today's business environment of tight budgets, executives often raise the cost of listening as an objection. Clearly there are costs involved in implementing a listening process. Using a consultant to structure and conduct a formal customer survey may be a substantial investment. Even conducting joint customer planning sessions entails some costs. Executives also raise the concern that if they find out something needs to be changed, that too will require an investment of time and money.

These may all be valid concerns. However, what are the costs of not listening? How much money is the company spending on marketing programs that are not meeting the information needs of the decision makers? How much money is sales spending for training on new sales techniques when the customer wants salespeople with technical product information or problem-solving skills? How much money is administration spending to improve a traditional order entry process when the customers want to use electronic data interchange? How many sales is the company losing to competitors who are listening to the customers, showing interest, and taking action?

## Listening Creates More Work

Another concern is that listening to customers may create additional work. Calgon, for example, recognizes that its Quality Encounters do identify projects that take the time of Calgon salespeople. Here is how quality management director Stan Karmilovich addresses that issue.

> Sometimes the service engineers are concerned about how much work I am generating for them. We manage that by saying to the customer at the conclusion of the Quality Encounter, "You have told us what is important and where we really need to spend our time. Now, we already spend a lot of time at your facility. Are there things we are doing around here that you look upon as less

valuable than some of the things you have asked us to do? Can we trade some of the things we are currently doing for some of the things you have listed, spending our efforts where it brings you the most return? Are there things that we are doing that may be redundant with what some of your own people are doing?" I counsel our service engineers to try to make some trade-offs where we need to and not to look on this as just more work.

Sometimes it takes a demonstration to show managers that there may be significant differences between their own beliefs about customer attitudes and requirements and those of the customers themselves. To demonstrate the discrepancy, survey a sample of customers regarding their requirements, priorities, and satisfaction levels. Then ask the managers to answer the same survey questions in the way that they think the customers responded. Summarize the results from both groups and present them back to the managers. Recall that this approach is an integral part of the AT&T Shared Expectations process.

This technique frequently demonstrates a gap between internal beliefs and reality. It is particularly effective in sales offices and marketing departments. Be prepared to defend the listening process. Some people will deny the results and even question the validity of survey techniques. However, most people will accept the outcome and recognize the value of listening to the customers. Although not everyone will become a supporter, this approach will convince many people of the value of listening.

## Conclusion

Sales and marketing need input from their current and past customers, prospects, and competitive users on which to base their continuous improvement activities. To be most effective, they need to use several complementary listening methods tailored to their specific customer set. Although listening to customers appears to be easy to do, there are pitfalls and barriers along the way. However, the input from listening will provide the requirements and feedback that they need to implement the other best practices. Without that information, they are just guessing.

# Chapter Four

# | **Focus on Process**

Successful sales and marketing organizations all listen to their external and internal customers, but they do not stop there. They apply what they learn to identify and improve their key business processes. It is through these processes that they deliver information to their customers. Their objective is to ensure that the process output meets their customers' requirements and that they operate in an efficient manner. To accomplish this, they are using formal improvement techniques such as business process improvement, reengineering, and benchmarking.

Chapter One defined a process as any activity or group of activities that takes input, adds value to it, and produces an output that goes to a customer. Chapter Three introduced the basic process model (Figure 3.1) that shows the relationship among process elements. This model serves as a foundation for all improvement techniques.

Figure 4.1, a functional flowchart, shows a simplified view of an order fulfillment process in a manufacturing company. The order begins with the customer, flows through the sales branch office, order entry department, manufacturing, and shipping and returns to the customer in the form of a product. In addition, invoicing information for the product flows from manufacturing to the billing department and on to the customer. The boxes in Figure 4.1 represent activities in the process. Each activity has a supplier, adds value, and has a customer. Each activity also needs requirements and feedback from its customers. To improve any process, it must be viewed from beginning to end.

**Figure 4.1.  Order Fulfillment Process.**

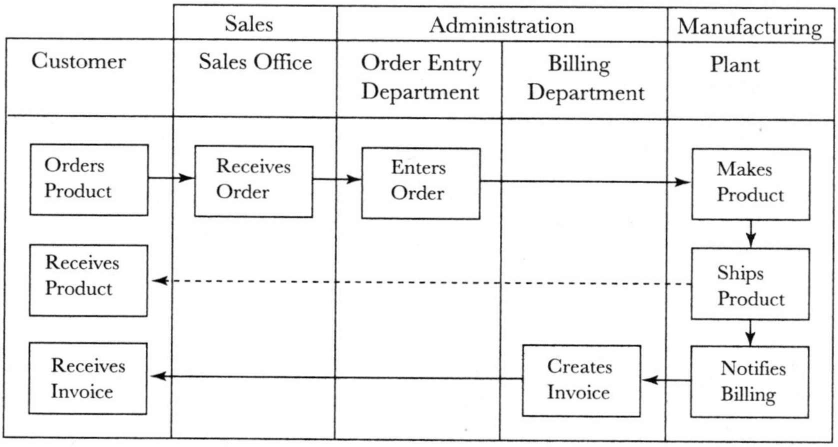

| | Sales | Administration | | Manufacturing |
|---|---|---|---|---|
| Customer | Sales Office | Order Entry Department | Billing Department | Plant |
| Orders Product → | Receives Order → | Enters Order | | Makes Product ↓ |
| Receives Product ◄ - - - - - - - - - - - - - - - - - - - - - - - | | | | Ships Product ↓ |
| Receives Invoice ◄ | | | Creates Invoice ◄ | Notifies Billing |

## Sales and Marketing Processes

Sales and marketing people do not often think in terms of processes. That makes it is difficult for them to recognize the processes that do exist in their areas. Here are just a few examples of processes that the leading companies have identified and improved in the sales and marketing functions:

- Lead qualification
- Proposal preparation
- Contract preparation and approval
- Order entry
- Sales forecasting
- Recruiting and hiring
- Training
- Performance evaluation
- Literature request fulfillment
- Trade show lead follow-up and tracking
- Advertising campaigns
- Advertising lead follow-up and tracking
- Product launch

- Direct mail
- Marketing support material development
- Sales cycle from customer interest to product delivery
- Product development cycle from customer interest to delivery

## Sales and Marketing Process Improvement Results

By improving their business processes, leading companies are achieving breakthroughs in sales and marketing productivity and customer satisfaction. Here are examples of the results some of these companies are achieving.

One of the most common customer complaints is the length of time it takes to get sales literature. Texas Instruments was taking an average of 4.8 days to respond to each of the 250,000 inquiries it received each month. The company analyzed the processes used to fulfill these requests and decided to start all over with a clean sheet of paper. The result was a new process that treated every inquiry as if it were an order. This reduced to ten hours the time required to fulfill an information request, and cut processing costs in the bargain.

The proposal preparation process was the subject of improvement at Unisys and Medicus Systems. Unisys is the well-known computer hardware and professional services provider. Its customers responded with increased satisfaction when improved proposals were submitted. Medicus Systems is a software development firm with products serving the needs of health care industry. It reduced the variation in routine proposals by using a standard set of documents, numerically ordered. Further, it streamlined internal communications between sales and administrative support personnel who helped create proposals. Proposal quality improved, and cycle time was reduced significantly.

During the 1980s, Amica Mutual Insurance Company reduced the time required to make policy changes from an average of two weeks to less than two days. Amica continue to work on the process and is approaching twenty-four-hour turnaround. According to John J. Connors, Jr., Amica's vice president, "It is very likely that when a policy holder calls with a change, it is in the mail the very next morning."

When Texas Instruments redesigned its order entry process for products, the objective was to reduce cycle time and improve on-time delivery. TI was able to reduce order entry time from fourteen days to three. An unexpected benefit was an improvement in order quality as well. TI reports a 60 percent reduction in the number of inquiries handled in sales offices on lost shipments and missed deliveries. The TI salespeople now use the benefits of the improved processes and electronic data interchange as a way to differentiate their company from the competition.

## What to Call Process Improvement

Many labels have been applied to the techniques used to improve business processes. Some of the common terms are *business process management, business process improvement, business process reengineering, continuous process improvement, sociotechnical redesign,* and *systems analysis.*

As with many of the other improvement techniques, there are virtually no standard definitions for these terms. To add to the confusion, different companies have applied different labels to what are essentially the same techniques.

## Common Characteristics of Process Improvement

Although each of the techniques listed here has its own nuances, they all share several important characteristics.

*They are cross-functional.* The most important of the common characteristics is cross-functional focus. These process improvement techniques are all based on the idea that business processes flow through many departments or functional areas of the business. The order fulfillment process in Figure 4.1 demonstrates this idea. It is this cross-functional view that makes major improvements in process effectiveness and efficiency possible.

*They are customer oriented.* Processes have customers, and whether the customers are internal or external, they are the reason the process exists. The process customers decide the quality of the process output, that is, how well it meets their requirements.

*They involve the people who work within the process.* No one knows business processes better than the people who are part of them, who work with them every day. Improvement techniques all recognize the value of getting these people involved in process improvement. Most of the techniques use teams to define, analyze, and improve the processes, including people from the processes on these teams. These techniques also employ a process owner, an executive or manager from within the process, who is responsible for improving and managing the process

*They include all process elements.* It is easy to think of processes as just the procedures that people follow. However, there are other elements in any process, including the people and equipment in the process and the information that passes through it.

*They are process model based.* The techniques all use a basic process model. Although the models may vary, most include the elements shown in Figure 4.2. Chapter Three discussed the right side of the model (Figure 3.1). In the case of sales and marketing, this side illustrates delivery of information to the customer. To do that effectively, sales and marketing need to understand their customers' requirements and get feedback on how well they are doing. Note that sales and marketing provide requirements to their own suppliers. Just as sales and marketing need to understand their customers' requirements, the suppliers need to know the requirements of sales and marketing. The suppliers also need feedback on how well they are meeting those requirements.

**Figure 4.2.  Basic Process Model.**

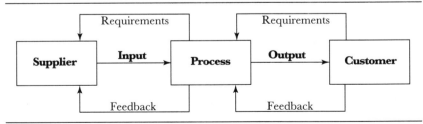

## Improvement Itself Is a Process

Each of the improvement methods is itself a formal process. Each includes a series of steps that takes input, adds value, and produces an output. The input is information about the process to be improved. The value added comes from defining the process, gathering customer requirements, measuring the process, analyzing the process, and recommending and making specific changes. The output may be an improved process or whole new process.

The improvement techniques also share a common set of objectives: to make business processes more effective and efficient. The following sections look more closely at three of them: business process improvement, business process management, and process reengineering. Later, this chapter also discusses two other popular techniques, process benchmarking and ISO-9000, to see how they apply to sales and marketing.

## Business Process Improvement

Business process improvement, or BPI, is the most commonly used technique and provides a model to which we can relate the others. Figure 4.3 illustrates the steps in BPI. The approach presented here is based on a study of methods used by over a dozen leading companies and consulting firms. Although the exact number of steps varies slightly from company to company, and each company organizes and labels the steps a little differently, the underlying sequence and content of the steps is very similar.

### Step 0: Commit

Chapter Two discussed the need for management commitment to the improvement process. This commitment is necessary at the top of the company and at the senior level of every part of the business that takes part in business process improvement including sales and marketing. Because commitment must take place before BPI begins, I have called it Step 0. This step includes four management tasks: establishing company guideposts, understanding BPI and management's own role in it, making the commitment, and creating a supporting organization.

### Figure 4.3. Business Process Improvement.

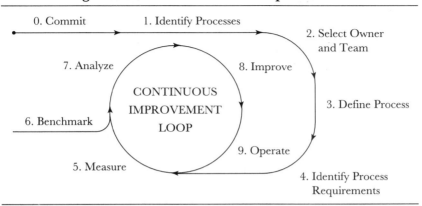

### *Establish Guideposts*

To be effective, BPI must support the company's mission, vision, and strategic direction and be based on the company's core values. It should also support the mission and strategy of sales and marketing and the organization's other functional areas. If company leadership has not yet established or identified these key business guideposts, now is the time to do it.

### *Understand BPI and Management's Role*

The senior executives themselves must have an understanding of the process improvement techniques and their roles and responsibilities in them. They also need to know what results to expect and how long it will take to achieve them. Finally they need to know that major changes in the organization structure may be necessary and resources may have to be shifted. They do not need any surprises in these areas after they have made a major commitment.

### *Make the Commitment*

After the members of management understand BPI and their role in it, they are in a position to make an informed decision to proceed. This decision includes several factors. The first is the scope of the effort. Is it a pilot project to check out BPI, or is it a full-blown companywide effort? Does the scope include one critical process or all of the company's key business processes? The scope of the process will help determine how much time the senior managers will have to invest in the process and an estimate of the staffing and resources required.

### Create the Supporting Organization

Most companies already have an executive team in place that can manage the improvement process. This team includes the CEO and the executives who report to him or her, including representatives from sales and marketing. When the process improvement initiative is conducted within a business unit, division, or major department, the supporting executive team may be at the senior management level of that unit. We can refer to the group that manages the overall improvement effort as the *executive improvement team,* or EIT. The EIT sets up separate teams to work on each process or major subprocess that the organization plans to improve. We can refer to them as *process improvement teams,* or PITs (PITs are discussed in Step 2).

## Step 1: Identify and Select Processes

After establishing a firm management commitment, the organization is ready to begin business process improvement. The first step is to pick one or several key processes on which to focus. A key business process is one whose failure would do significant harm or cause the business to fail. For most companies, this definition will certainly cover some of the sales and marketing processes. When a key process does break or is longer competitive, the company may be in crisis. In this situation, the process on which to focus is a given, and BPI begins at Step 2 (selecting an owner and a process improvement team). Fortunately, most organizations do not begin BPI in crisis. They have time to identify all of the company's key processes and select one or several on which to focus.

### Identify Key Processes

The EIT may identify the organization's key business processes or it may delegate the task to a management or employee team representing the major departments. The simplest way to identify key processes is for the team to brainstorm a list. Another approach is to list the company's key outputs and then identify the processes that create them. When identifying sales and marketing processes, remember to consider output that goes to internal as well as external customers.

### Establish the Process Selection Criteria

One of the most important criteria for selecting processes is what the customers think of the process output. In their view, how important is it, how does it compare to the competition, and does it need improvement? Here are some additional questions that the organization will want to consider in selecting processes:

- Does this process support the company's mission, vision, and strategic direction?
- Is this process part of the company's core competencies?
- What will happen if the company does not improve this process?
- How much of the company's financial and human resources does the process consume?
- Is there an executive sponsor for this process?

## Step 2: Select Process Owner and Team

This step includes four tasks: choosing a process owner, selecting a process improvement team, defining owner and team responsibilities, training the owner and team.

### Choose the Process Owner

The process owner is an executive or manager within the business process who has authority and responsibility for the overall results of the process. (This role is in contrast to the traditional organization role in which an executive or a manager is responsible for a functional area.) The job of process owner is not an additional position on the organization chart. The executive improvement team assigns ownership to someone who already has responsibility for some part of the process. For a major processes, the owner will be at a high level in the organization and may even be a member of the EIT or management committee.

There are several criteria that the EIT can use to select a process owner. The process owner may be the executive or manager who

- Has the most resources in the process
- Does the most work in the process
- Suffers the most pain when things go wrong
- Has the most to gain when things go right
- Is in the best position to make changes to the process
- Is accepted by executives or managers who own other activities in the process
- Wants the job

Although the specific responsibilities of the process owner will vary by company, they fall into two general categories, operations and management. In the operations category, the owner is responsible for making sure the process meets its mission-specific objectives. For the sales processes, mission-specific objectives include revenue and profit growth and customer satisfaction.

The process owner is also responsible for managing the improvement process and attaining improvement goals. This includes taking the process through the remaining six BPI steps. It also includes resolving issues between various functional areas within the process and reporting process status and results to the company's senior executives. Process improvement goals might include reducing response time to customer inquiries, eliminating errors on orders entered, or reducing salesforce turnover.

### Select the Process Improvement Team

The members of the process improvement team represent the major activities within the process and are responsible for carrying out the remaining steps in BPI. To do this, they need to be very knowledgeable in how their activity works. They also need to work well in a team environment and be willing to support the team's mission, which is to improve the process. They are not there to promote the interests of the functional department they represent. Except in a small organization or process, the process owner will not be the PIT leader or even an active day-to-day participant. A team member will fill the leadership role. Having salespeople on major improvement projects will be necessary in many cases, and this presents some unique challenges (discussed in Chapter Five).

Many of the companies that contributed to this book emphasized the importance of having an information systems (IS) representative on every process improvement team. The IS team member brings knowledge and understanding of systems analysis and design, of the potential of technology in general, and of the organization's existing and planned IS capability.

### Define Responsibilities: The PIT Charter

After forming the process improvement team, the next task is to provide its members with a clear understanding of their charter. The charter includes the team's mission, level of authority, available resources, and how the team will be measured. In the ideal organization, the process owner is the link between the EIT and the team and communicates the charter. Although defining responsibilities sounds like a basic management principle, it is surprising how often teams start out without this critical information.

The team will also receive specific process goals. These are the objectives the company or EIT has set for the improved process. For example, Carl H. Arendt, recently retired from the Westinghouse Quality and Productivity Center, reports that the center's goals for initial process improvement are always set for at least a 65 percent reduction in process cycle time. Other goals for the improved process include error elimination, cost reduction, and customer value enhancement, and these are usually set by the team itself with management concurrence.

### Train the Process Owner and Team

The process owner and team members need a complete understanding of BPI. Team members also need to know interview techniques and have team skills. All these should be included in the team's formal training.

## Step 3: Define the Process

Defining the process includes creating a mission statement, establishing boundaries, documenting the flow, and identifying the critical success factors. Unless the process is relatively simple, the process improvement team members will have to be relatively skilled interviewers to gather or validate information from other people involved in the process. These interviews will also be a good source of ideas on how to improve the process.

### Create a Process Mission

The first task for the team is to create a mission statement that describes the purpose of the process. For example, the mission of IBM's customer fulfillment order process is, "To manage the order from the customer's point of view and to ensure that the customer's order will be accepted defect free and delivered as ordered." To have the order accepted defect free means entering an order for a computer configuration that the software will support and manufacturing can build.

### Establish Process Boundaries

The next task for the PIT is to establish boundaries around the process. This is necessary to keep the project manageable. In most companies, almost all the business processes touch one another at some point. Without clearly defining process boundaries, knowing where one ends and others begin, it is difficult for the team members to control the size of their project. Think of the possible result as "mission creep."

The process improvement team establishes process boundaries by answering the following questions:

- Where does the process begin?
- Where does the process end?
- Which activities are included?
- Which activities are excluded?
- Who are the customers of the process?
- Who are the suppliers to the process?

### Document Process Flow

The next task is to describe the process within the boundaries. The PIT does this by creating a high-level functional flowchart like the one in Figure 4.1. Flowcharting the process is the first step in determining exactly how the process works now, and it provides the basis for a more detailed examination of the process later.

Although it may seem a complex and technical task, flow-charting a business process is relatively easy. The team members simply identify all of the activities in the process. Then they create a diagram showing the sequence in which activities occur and the information that flows between those activities. The result is the functional flowchart, or process map. The flowchart represents the whole process. The boxes represent the activities or steps within the process. Usually each activity is performed within a single department. Steps that occur within the activities are called tasks.

### Conduct a Process Walk-Through

Think of the functional flowchart as a map of the process. However, as noted semanticist Alfred Korzybski said, "A map is not the territory" (1958, pp. 58–60). During the process walk-through, the PIT explores the territory. The objective is to validate the functional flowchart and to gather more information about each activity within the process.

The process walk-through is required for large complex processes. Even though PIT members understand the process, it is virtually impossible for them to know everything that happens. If the process is small, the team members may be aware of every activity and task. However, they still need to gather and document additional information about the process. They do this in the process walk-through. Conducting a process walk-through is a relatively easy task. Just as the name implies, members of the team walk through, or follow, the process from beginning to end. They examine each activity, observing and interviewing the people who perform the tasks that make up each activity. They record the information gathered in each interview and move on to the next activity.

### Reevaluate the Process Definition

The PIT's next task is to review the process definition in light of what team members learned in the interviews and data gathering. This will almost certainly produce a number of surprises. They will have uncovered cases where written procedures are out of date or there are no formal procedures at all. Where such procedures do exist, PIT members may have found that people circumvent them because the procedures are too bureaucratic or slow and are not responsive to customer needs. In some cases, people will have already taken the initiative and improved the process without recording their changes or even telling anyone.

Some of the findings will affect the process boundaries. The process map will have to be redrawn to reflect the way the process really works. This is why using Post-Its, a chalk board, or computer software to record the process flow is useful. It makes changing the process map much easier.

One of the most frequent findings in the process walk-through is that defective input from other processes causes many of the errors in the process output. Take, for example, the product launch process at Pitney Bowes. When the process improvement team began to study that process, team members found that the root cause of many of the problems lay in actions taken, or not taken, during the concept phase of product development. In order to improve the product launch process, they had to change the process boundaries to include activities during the concept phase.

## Step 4: Identify Process Requirements

Process requirements are the wants, needs, and even demands that the process and its output must satisfy. Most requirements come from the process customers. For sales and marketing, once again, the external customers are those people who make and influence buying decisions, while the internal customers receive the output of some sales and marketing processes and thus have requirements as well. In addition, every activity within the process has a specific customer, and those customers also have requirements.

It is the job of the PIT to identify all of the customers during the process definition step. In this step, the PIT gathers as much information as possible about each customer's wants and needs. During the interviews, PIT members record the customers' stated requirements and ask probing questions to uncover their assumed and withheld requirements. They may even brainstorm with the customers to discover their unknown requirements.

If the interview stopped at this point, the PIT would probably have a wish list rather than a requirements statement. Therefore, the PIT needs to qualify the importance of each requirement and assign a weighting factor to it. The interviewers also need to know how the customer will use the process output. Understanding the customer's intent often helps to identify alternative ways to meet the same requirement.

After gathering customer requirements, the team's next task is to document them and validate them with the customers. When this task is complete, the requirements will meet these four criteria:

*They will be specific.*  The wording of each process requirement must be precise. It is not enough to say, "Responses to telephone inquiries from media advertising must be made in a timely manner." A specific requirement would state, "Sales literature mailed in response to telephone inquiries from media advertising must be delivered to the post office within twenty-four hours of the receipt of the customer call."

*They will be measurable.*  There must be a way to measure whether the requirement is being met. In the previous example, it is relatively simple to log customer calls and the time the response was sent.

*They will be documented.*  The process requirements statements will be in writing. In this form, they will provide the basis for process measurement, analysis, and improvement (the next three BPI steps).

*They will be agreed-to.*  The PIT reviews the requirements with the customers to ensure that they agree with the team's wording. This criterion ensures that the requirements clearly represent the customers' wants and needs.

Meeting customer requirements is the reason for the process. Those requirements are paramount. However, there are other important sources of process requirements. They include

- The people in the process
- The process owner
- The business owners
- The community
- Federal, state, and local governments

## Step 5: Measure the Process

To paraphrase an old management axiom, "If you do not measure a process, you cannot manage or improve it." Without a measurement system that collects reliable process measurement data, it is not possible to know how well the process is performing over time or in comparison to other processes. Neither is it possible to know whether improvements have had their desired effect.

### Types of Process Measurements

Generally speaking, process measurements measure two things: effectiveness and efficiency. Effectiveness is a measure of how well the process is meeting its requirements; efficiency is a measure of process or output cost. Measurements of effectiveness have the highest priority. If a process is not meeting its requirements, particularly its customer requirements, it does not really matter how little it costs to operate.

For most companies, the primary measure of sales and marketing process effectiveness is the business volume that a process produces. However, there are other possibilities. Because part of the mission of sales and marketing is to provide information, effectiveness measurements can also show how well these functions are getting information to their external and internal customers. Sales and marketing process measurements answer questions such as these:

- Is the information what the customer wanted and needed?
- Is it in the form and at the level of detail the customer wanted?
- Is it delivered when the customer wants it?
- Is it error free?

Productivity measurements also fall into this category. In sales, these include calls per day, proposals submitted per month, or time spent with customers. In marketing, these include response rates to direct mail campaigns or the number of qualified leads generated through telemarketing.

The second type of measurement addresses efficiency. These are financial or cost measurements. They reveal things like the cost of an average sales call, a direct mail piece, a qualified lead, or even an order. Because many companies still place a greater focus on financial results than customer satisfaction, these are probably the most common process measurements.

### Add Measures If Needed

The PIT gathers information on how the process is currently measured in Step 3. In Step 4, the team identifies process requirements. These become some of the standards against which later process measurement data will be compared. In Step 5, the PIT decides whether the existing process measurements are adequate to determine how well the improved process meets the team's requirements. If they are not, the PIT may add measurement systems to the current process and collect data about the revised process's performance. The team may also conduct special one-time surveys to gather information.

After adequate process measurement data have been collected, they are recorded as a baseline of process performance. At the completion of the BPI, the team will measure the process again and compare the results to this baseline to gauge the degree of improvement.

## Step 6: Benchmark the Process

Process benchmarking is a formal procedure used to identify and compare similar business processes. These processes may be either in other parts of the same company or in other companies. Normally, companies look for the very best processes, those that achieve world-class results. They then compare their baseline data to the baseline data for these other processes.

If the company decides to do such benchmarking, this is the point at which the input enters the improvement cycle. The team may have been collecting information about what other companies are doing in parallel with BPI Steps 3 through 5. However, it is only now that they really know enough about their own process to make visits to other companies worthwhile. (Benchmarking is described in more detail later in this chapter.)

## Step 7: Analyze the Process

The next step is to analyze all of the information that the PIT has gathered and to select an improvement method to use in Step 8. There is no one best way to do this. Analysis is just applying good common sense. The specific approach depends on several factors, such as the size of the project, the skills of the PIT members, and the resources available. Here are some ideas:

### Assemble All Process Information

The first task is to assemble all of the information that the PIT has collected. It includes

- Process definition
- Statement of mission
- Process boundaries
- High-level flowchart
- Process requirements
- Baseline data from process measurements
- Benchmark data
- Known chronic problems
- Customer and employee suggestions
- Customer satisfaction data

### Review Process Requirements

The process requirements drive improvement. The next task is to determine how well the process currently meets its requirements. If the PIT members have not done this already (Step 5), they now rank the process requirements in order of importance. Using the measurement data, they rate how well the process currently meets the requirements. They also determine how well the benchmark and competitors' processes meet the same requirements.

There will be conflicts between some requirements. For example, the customer wants fast turnaround, the employees do not want to work extra hours or a second shift, and a manager wants to review the work before it goes out. How can the customer requirement be met? What are the trade-offs? Are the best-in-class benchmarks or the competitors able to meet the requirement and how do they do it?

The requirements review will identify the areas in the process that need the most attention. There may be a greater question, however: Should there be a process at all? Processes, and departments for that matter, often develop lives of their own. They may have grown out of a real business need in the past but have outlived their usefulness. As Alexander Woollcott reportedly said, "The worst sin of all is to do well that which shouldn't be done at all." General Electric's highly successful Work-Out program identified many activities and processes that had outlived their usefulness at that company.

### Review Process Activities and Flow

Next the PIT traces the process flow and examines each activity in the process, looking for improvement opportunities. When the PIT first developed and validated the process flowchart in Step 3, the team members probably recognized many activities that were done at more than one point in the process. They may also have noticed that some necessary activities were not being done at all. However, now they have the benefit of well-defined process requirements, measurement data, and possibly benchmark information to guide their process review.

As the PIT members examine each activity, they also determine its added value. In his book *Business Process Improvement* (1991, pp. 138–140), H. James Harrington suggests that activities fall into three categories:

*Real value added.* These are activities that must be performed to meet external customer requirements. In sales, a real-value-added activity is providing the information the customer requires to reach a buying decision. In many companies it also includes writing up and entering orders.

*Business value added.* These activities do not contribute directly to meeting customer requirements. They are necessary, however, for running the business. For example, activities that collect sales data for reporting and commission payment are not needed to meet the requirements of the external customer, but they are still a necessary part of running the business.

*No value added.* These activities do not contribute value to the process. In some cases they may be duplicate or redundant steps that have been inadvertently built into the process over its life. When these steps are discovered, they can be dropped. Steps built into the process to fix errors also do not add value. However, automatically eliminating them might allow errors to reach customers. The process has to be improved so that errors are not made in the first place.

Another form of no-value-added activity is what Harrington calls bureaucracy. These are the management sign-offs and approvals that often take so much time and frequently add no value. For example, when TransCanada Gas Services, Ltd., examined their contract approval process, they found that a vice president had to review and approve every contract even though 80 percent were standard terms and pricing. The executives of another company were asked why they wanted to approve every major proposal, an activity that added to the time it took to respond to the customer.

The answer: the executives just wanted to know what was going on. The company found a better way to keep them informed, a way that did not slow down the proposal process. Bureaucratic activities often add to the process cycle time and cost without contributing to process requirements.

As they review the process, the PIT members can also look for ways to apply technology, another of the best practices for continuous improvement in sales and marketing. By doing it at this stage, team members can avoid a mistake made by many companies: using technology to automate their existing processes rather than to improve them. Automating processes that are ineffective or prone to defects just allows the organization to make errors more quickly and in greater volume. The better approach is to apply technology after the process has been analyzed, to improve it or to do things that are not possible without it. See Chapter Seven for more information on the application of technology.

### Develop a Recommended Approach

At this point, the PIT is ready to decide exactly what to recommend in Step 8, the improvement step. Through analysis of the process activities, the team members probably have already identified better ways to meet process requirements, cut cycle times, improve customer satisfaction, reduce defects, and cut costs. The team can now compare the improved process to the benchmarks and a potentially reengineered approach. Of course for processes that do not support the company's core competencies, another alternative is to outsource them. After selecting an approach, the PIT is ready to take its recommendation to the process owner and executive improvement team for review and approval.

## Step 8: Improve the Process

In this step, the organization makes the improvements or converts to the new process developed by the PIT. The effort involved in this step is in proportion to the magnitude of the changes. It can range from making small adjustments in the procedures to starting over with a whole new process. Because there is such a wide variety of possible approaches, this chapter can only list some of the elements that might be necessary.

## Tasks in the Improvement Step

- Create a detailed design of the improved or new process.
- Build in measurements for each activity and the overall process.
- Validate the design with the process customers (and all other sources of requirements).
- Document the new procedures.
- Design a conversion from the old process to the new or improved process.
- Acquire any new computer, network, and communications capability needed.
- Write or update computer software.
- Train the people in the process.
- Pilot test new procedures.
- Measure results.
- Convert to the new process.

### Build in Process Measurements

One of the items on the list deserves special attention: measurements. It is critical to build measurements of effectiveness and efficiency into the process at key points along the way. Well-placed process measurements can identify problems early in the process, before they are detected by the customer who receives the process output. They also provide an ongoing indication of how well the process is working and supply information for future continuous improvement activities.

Although measurements are specific to the process they measure, here are some guidelines that may help when putting measurements in place. First, get the customers and the people in the process involved in creating the measurements. They know what is important and how to measure it. Then tie measurements to the process requirements. Next build the measurements into the process rather than adding them later. Often they can be taken automatically, as part of information systems processing. Keep them simple and easy to understand and collect. In most processes, each major activity should have some measurement. That allows errors to be caught when they occur and not at the end of the process when they are costly to correct.

The intent is not to add unnecessary work. In some cases, fewer measurements may even be appropriate, as long as they are the right measurements.

### Who Is Involved in the Improvement Step

The PIT has done most of the work up to this point, and there may be a temptation to create a new implementation team and let the PIT members go back to their regular jobs. Donna McNamara was a key player in Pitney Bowes' BPI efforts, and she cautions against this idea. McNamara reports that "it is important to have the same people who do the analysis also do the implementation." The PIT members have an investment in the success of their recommendations, and they know more about the way the process currently works than anyone else in the organization. In addition, they have already worked together and become a cohesive and effective team.

In addition to the PIT members, many other people will take part. Depending on the magnitude of the change, some people in the process will have to learn new ways to do their jobs. Others may have to learn whole new assignments. The people in the process will play a major role in converting from the old way of doing things to the new.

The process customers can also make a significant contribution. Getting them involved in the design helps ensure that the process meets their most important requirements. By helping design the process, they get an appreciation for the trade-offs that may have to be made if some of their requirements are in conflict. They also get a sense of ownership in the process and commitment to its success if they take part.

Suppliers can also contribute in this step. If they are external suppliers, they have the benefit of seeing how their other customers have approached the same process. Taking part in the design also helps them understand exactly what they are expected to supply and when.

### Improvement at Every Step

Although Step 8 is labeled as the improvement step, improvement can occur at almost every step along the way in BPI. Just the act of identifying processes in Step 1 may reveal some that are redundant and others that produce an output that no longer fills a need.

Defining the process in Step 3 may reveal activities that provide little or no added value. Potential improvements may be uncovered during any of the following steps as well.

In many cases, it will make sense to make improvements as soon as the opportunity is discovered. When this happens, be sure to measure the effect of the change when it is made. Most executives want to know the return on their investment in process improvement. Measuring and getting agreement on the effect of changes helps solidify the continued use of BPI, and it is easy to forget the results of a change made early in the effort when the project is completed six months later.

## Step 9: Operate the Process

In Step 9, the new or improved process is in operation and accomplishing its stated mission or purpose. It may seem strange to include operation as a part of process improvement. After all, the changes have been made, the people trained, and the conversion completed. However, it is only by operating the process and measuring its effectiveness and efficiency that the organization can determine how well it works and how much better it is than the one it replaced.

Not measuring the results of the BPI is one of the biggest failures in process improvement efforts. Many organizations have an aversion to measurement. They prefer to operate on anecdotal evidence that the improvements have been made, and they have no way to know for sure whether the new process works any better than the old one. Improving a business process is just like designing a new advertising campaign or developing a new sales compensation plan, however. The only way to find out how well it works is to put it in place, measure the results, and compare them to previous experience.

## Business Process Management

Business process management, or BPM, looks just like BPI, except that the company repeats the improvement cycle continuously. Refer again to Figure 4.3. After a process has been improved, operates, and is measured in operation, the process improvement team analyzes the measurement data, makes further improvements, and the cycle continues. The process owner is responsible for the ongoing performance of the process. The PIT meets periodically to review the ongoing process measurements, analyze the results, and continue to improve the process.

Although many companies claim to be doing business process management, very few actually are. After going through the improvement cycle one time, most companies seem to lose interest and move on to other things. This is true even when they have gotten excellent results from their initial BPI efforts.

## Process Reengineering

Reengineering is the hottest management fad of the decade. It is the Total Quality Management of the 1990s. Almost every major company claims to be doing it, and where it has been done properly, the results have been nothing short of phenomenal. Companies have turned themselves around using the approach. Processes have been streamlined, customers better satisfied, cycle times reduced, and costs cut. Unfortunately many companies have misused the term, applying it to massive staff reductions with no real change in their processes. The result in these cases has been more work for the remaining staff, higher error rates, longer cycle times, and lower customer satisfaction. So what is reengineering and how does it relate to sales and marketing?

In their book *Reengineering the Corporation* (1993), Michael Hammer and James Champy define reengineering as "the fundamental rethinking and radical redesign of business processes to achieve dramatic improvements in critical, contemporary measures of performance, such as cost, quality, service and speed" (pp. 31–32). Their book title suggests the idea of *corporate reengineering;* their definition speaks of *process reengineering.* The examples they include in their book suggest that both exist, and both are important.

In some cases, corporations have literally reinvented themselves. They have started with a clean sheet of paper and redesigned the way they look. They have stopped doing some things, outsourced others, focused on their core competencies, and created whole new processes where none existed before. Hammer and Champy include several examples of this approach in their book. I call this corporate reengineering.

In process reengineering, the term Hammer and Champy use in their definition, the focus is on the process, not the whole company. It means starting all over with a blank sheet of paper and designing a whole new process. Hammer and Champy also include examples of this type of reengineering in their book. Our interest here is process reengineering, and from here on I will refer to it simply as reengineering.

To put reengineering into perspective, look at the change continuum shown in Figure 4.4. It runs from no change at all on the left to complete change or reengineering on the right. Between the two points are various degrees of improvement to the existing process. These might involve minor improvements to various process activities, major revisions, or even reengineering some activities within the process.

Think of reengineering as part of BPI or BPM, not a stand-alone tool. Without having gone through the first seven steps of the process improvement cycle shown in Figure 4.3, a company cannot reengineer. It is these steps that define where the process is today and where the company and the customers think the process should be in the future. It is during the analysis in Step 7 that the process owner and improvement team select the appropriate method for improvement. Their analysis of the current process design, measurements, and requirements will indicate how far along the change continuum the company needs to go. Starting out with the idea of reengineering is beginning with a solution in mind without having first understood the problem to be solved.

There are several things that reengineering is not. First, it is absolutely not solely staff reductions. Although many companies have been able to do more work with fewer people by improving and reengineering processes, the improvements came first. When

**Figure 4.4.  The Change Continuum.**

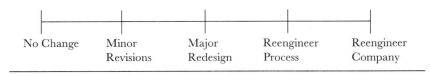

| No Change | Minor Revisions | Major Redesign | Reengineer Process | Reengineer Company |

companies reduce staff before improving processes, there are not enough people left to get the job done as it is currently designed, let alone to make the process improvements necessary for increased effectiveness and efficiency.

Reengineering is also not new. Contrary to Hammer and Champy's assertions, companies have been redesigning processes from scratch for years. My own business career began in 1961, and redesigning processes was not new even then. However, what is new is the *need* for radical redesign. Companies have grown, competition has increased, and costs have skyrocketed. It is the need for reengineering that is new.

It is also helpful to understand that most of the time, the term reengineering is a misnomer. It implies that the processes were engineered in the first place. Most were not; they just grew. Due to their functional organization structure, few companies looked at their processes from beginning to end. Each function just did its thing. As companies subdivided their business functions for the sake of efficiency, their business processes became more complex. As the processes became more complex, companies added more and more controls to ensure accuracy. All of this added up to the long and complex business processes that exist today. BPI, BPM, and process reengineering address this typical process history. Furthermore all have been applied successfully in sales and marketing functions.

One of the most dramatic examples comes from the major retail chains such as Wal-Mart, Kmart, and Target. They are completely reengineering the way they do business with their suppliers. Using the capabilities of point-of-sale scanners, satellite communications, and computers, they have designed processes that record sales data at the store check-out stand and communicate that sales information directly back to the manufacturer. In some cases, the chain actually authorizes the manufacturer to use the sales data to replenish store inventory. The suppliers literally place the orders with themselves.

The ability to get sales data almost instantly makes it easy for manufacturers to test market new products and try out marketing programs. They select a few stores in target markets, introduce the new products in those stores, and provide various kinds of marketing support. Then they measure sales. The cost and risk are minimal, and customer feedback is almost immediate. Although they have not developed these systems under the banner of process reengineering, the result clearly fits the definition.

Another example comes from the Wheelabrator Corporation in LaGrange, Georgia. The company had about fifty people in the sales and engineering departments. The salespeople worked with distributors and customers to identify requirements for the company's custom-built machines. The engineers then used the requirements to design the equipment. The first process improvement step the company took was to combine the engineering and sales departments. This move eliminated the hand-off of information from sales to engineering; customers' requirements went directly to the people who used them to design the products. Then the company redesigned the process. This reduced the number of people required to handle the work by 80 percent. Business volumes remained at the same level, costs went down, and customer satisfaction went up. The leadership at Wheelabrator started with a clean sheet of paper when they designed their sales process.

## Benchmarking

A benchmark can be defined as a standard measurement. Benchmarking, then, is simply the process of comparing something against a standard. In organizations, benchmarking is the comparison of people, products, services, or processes with standards of excellence. In his book *Benchmarking* (1989), Xerox's Robert C. Camp defines the process somewhat more narrowly as "the search for industry best practices that lead to superior performance" (p. 12).

Xerox brought the practice of benchmarking to prominence in the 1980s. Today that company has raised it almost to an art form. Benchmarking was and remains today a key part of Xerox's quality improvement process, a process that has itself become a benchmark for many other organizations.

### Types of Benchmarking

Like reengineering, the practice of benchmarking is not really new. It has existed for many years and in many forms. All of them have been applied successfully in sales and marketing. Here are the various types.

### Personal

Almost everyone has personal role models in his or her field of interest. For a golfer, it may be the best player in his or her regular Saturday morning foursome, the club pro, a regional amateur champion, or this year's top PGA money winner. For a salesperson, it might be the top revenue producer in the branch office, this year's companywide sales leader, or someone in an unrelated business who has received national recognition for outstanding sales performance. In any case, the role model represents a personal benchmark and is someone to be emulated.

### Product

The idea of product comparisons has been around as long as there have been competing products and the people who sell them. In my own 1960s experience in computer sales, one of the favored techniques in competitive situations was to run a standard job on our machine and the same job on the competitor's equipment. Today, dozens of magazines publish the results of comparison tests on virtually every kind of product from automobiles to computer hardware and software, from insurance policies to dishwashers, from tennis racquets to lawn mowers. All these products are compared to a standard, one that is usually set by the best of the products.

### Organization Performance

Manufacturing and service companies, health care providers, colleges and universities, and even government agencies compare themselves with other organizations on the basis of their performance. These are usually numeric comparisons, based on such measures as customer satisfaction scores, business volumes, profits, growth, costs, and financial ratios. No one would make a personal investment decision to buy an organization's stock without looking at its performance relative to other investment opportunities. Sales organizations compare their results as well. But comparing results only reveals how well organizations perform, not how they achieve that performance level.

### Process

In process benchmarking, organizations compare their processes with similar processes in other organizations. This approach reveals the processes and best practices that enabled leading organizations to achieve outstanding results. The standard may be another department within the same company, another company in the same industry or an organization doing the same thing but in an unrelated industry. It is by going beyond the bounds of the company and even the industry that true world-class processes can be identified. For example, Xerox's benchmark for warehousing operations was L.L. Bean (Camp, 1989). Cigna Corporation's search for world-class salesforces identified six benchmark companies: Anheuser-Busch, Caterpillar, Hewlett Packard, J. P. Morgan Bank, Procter & Gamble, and Wachovia Bank. Not one of these was in the company's own insurance industry ("Cigna Places a Premium on Being the Best," 1993).

## Process Benchmarking as Part of Process Improvement

Process benchmarking can be an important part of process improvement. However, like reengineering, it does not stand alone. It must be performed as part of a formal improvement process such as BPI. Without having done the first five steps of the BPI, it is virtually impossible to conduct an effective process benchmark. Input from benchmarking (Step 6) then becomes part of what is analyzed in Step 7 of the improvement process.

There are two reasons that benchmarking comes where it does in BPI. First, without completing the first five steps, the organization has no baseline against which to compare the benchmark results. The company does not know what to look for or what questions to ask. Without understanding their own process, PIT members are not really benchmarking, they are just taking an industrial tour. Even if they gain access to another company, they will be treated as tourists, not as people seriously committed to process improvement.

The second reason is that many leading companies will no longer agree to being benchmark subjects unless they get something in return. Today, most leading companies are only willing to be benchmark partners when they believe they can learn from the other party as well. There is an exception to this, however. Most companies are willing to be benchmark subjects for their own customers and suppliers. Obviously it is in their best interest to do this.

Although Figure 4.3 shows benchmarking as part of the improvement cycle, it is not required and may not even be useful when a company is just getting started in process improvement. If it is done at that time, seeking world-class benchmarking partners may not be the best approach. A first-year downhill skier trying to master a wedge turn would not learn much from watching a videotape of the Winter Olympics slalom competition. In the same vein, a company trying to improve its consumer products marketing processes for the first time would probably not appreciate many of the refinements of the marketing process at Procter & Gamble.

This conclusion is supported by the International Quality Study (1992) conducted by the American Quality Foundation and Ernst & Young. This study of hundreds of companies in four industries and four countries revealed that benchmarking was most effective among the high-performing companies. According to Ernst & Young's H. James Harrington, benchmarking is of little value and in some cases can be almost disastrous in lower-performing companies.

## The Steps in Benchmarking

Many companies view process benchmarking as simply visiting other companies to ask them what they do and how they do it. However, there is much more to it than that. Like BPI, process benchmarking is itself a formal process. It includes selecting the processes to benchmark, collecting data, analyzing those data, and using the results to improve the processes.

### Identify Processes to Benchmark

When picking processes to benchmark, most organizations will pick the same key business processes that they selected for improvement in Step 1 of BPI. If they want to begin by benchmarking fewer processes, they will to pick those that are most important to the success of the business. Processes that create new products or develop marketing programs fall into this category, and they are the highest priority candidates for benchmarking.

### Gather Public Information

Benchmarking visits to other organizations are not appropriate until the process improvement team completes the first five steps of BPI. However, the company can start gathering benchmarking data by other means as soon as it has selected the key processes. There are many legitimate ways to collect information about how other companies' processes work and the results they get. One of the easiest ways is to pick a couple of sales or marketing trainees or part-time graduate students to conduct preliminary research. They can search the publicly available information and begin to develop information files on each of the key processes. Potential information sources include general business, industry, and professional magazines, newspapers, and newsletters. They also include association meetings and conferences and their printed proceedings. Researchers can also contact or visit association libraries. For example, the American Marketing Association has a major library of books, papers, and periodicals in its Chicago headquarters.

In addition to the literature, there are many other legitimate sources of benchmark information about the processes in leading companies. Customers and suppliers are often willing to provide information about other companies with which they do business. Consultants are often aware of the processes in leading companies and may be able to share some information. Some consulting and research firms provide benchmark information as a service. Obviously, when using these secondary courses, it is important to limit requests to information that is not confidential or proprietary.

All of this preliminary research can be conducted while the organization defines its own business processes, establishes process requirements, and collects measurement data. When these BPI activities are complete, the company understands its own processes and has information on potential benchmark candidates. At this point, several options are available. If the company has collected sufficient information about comparable processes in other companies, it can proceed with analysis of the information and the improvement of its own process.

### Survey Potential Benchmark Partners
However, if the company needs or wants additional information, it can

- Conduct a written or telephone survey of organizations with similar processes

- Commission or participate in a blind survey of companies with similar processes
- Form benchmark partnerships and conduct site visits
- Participate in benchmark groups

Each of these approaches can be used alone or in combination with others. For many companies, the next step in benchmarking is to take the first option and conduct a written or telephone survey of other organizations with similar processes. These surveys are excellent sources of information about business processes and their results. They are also a way to narrow the company's search for benchmark partners and site visits. Some companies develop and administer their own surveys. Others may choose to have them done by a consultant or research firm. In either case, the company's preliminary research will help identify potential survey prospects.

The written survey has several benefits. Because it can be completed over a long period of time, it gives the recipient the opportunity to gather information that may not be immediately available during a telephone call or even site visit. It also helps ensure that every area of interest is covered, and has the benefit of being self-documenting.

Telephone surveys have a higher response rate than written surveys. However, they are more limited in the amount of data that can be collected in a single call. Also, the information is limited to that which is available to the interviewee at the time of the call. The telephone survey is probably better suited to identifying prospects for site visits

Both the written and telephone surveys can be used to identify companies that are willing to participate in future information exchanges and have something to offer. They also can identify the potential partners' areas of interest to ensure that there is value to their participation.

There has to be a quid pro quo for companies to respond to surveys. For most companies, the benefit is being able to share in the results of the research. Most of the research on which this book is based comes from face-to-face interviews with leading companies. For most of them, the benefit was to see a presentation on the research results.

One of the disadvantages companies face in doing their own surveys is that their direct competitors are not likely to take part. Even if they do, their responses are highly suspect. However, if the survey is done by an independent consulting firm and confidentiality of the results is assured, competitors are often willing to take part.

When the survey is done blind, the results are reported back to the participants so that individual companies cannot be identified. Results may be listed by a code such as "Company A," "Company B," and so on. By knowing their own company code, companies can see how they compare to other companies. However, they cannot identify specifically which companies are performing better and worse. They can identify best practices but will not know exactly who is doing them.

One benchmarking study was conducted in twenty-four aerospace and defense contractors by Price Waterhouse (O'Guin, 1995). The study included a written survey followed up by face-to-face interviews by Price Waterhouse consultants. The objective was to identify the industry's key business processes and their importance to company profitability. The project also studied the relationship between profitability and continuous process improvement. The results were no surprise to professionals in either marketing or quality improvement. First, the study confirmed that the most profitable companies were also the most successful at continuous process improvement. Second, the study identified five business processes at which the most profitable companies excelled. Business acquisition (or what commercial enterprises commonly call sales and marketing) topped that list. The companies with the most effective business acquisition processes were not just a little better than their competitors, either. The average close rate in competitive situations for the twenty-four companies was 18 percent. How did the top performers do? They averaged a close rate of more than 60 percent.

Individual company's numbers are highly confidential in the aerospace and defense industries. It was only through this blind benchmark study that the participants were able to learn how they related to their competition. Of course there was more to the survey results than just these performance measurements. The face-to-face interviews conducted by the consultants provided the participants with more details.

### Visit Benchmark Partners

Some companies will be satisfied with the information they have gathered at this point. They are ready to return to BPI and begin process analysis and improvement. Others will want more detailed information that is only available through direct contact with benchmark partners. This requires on-site visits.

The organization can arrange benchmark visits in several ways. If the potential benchmark candidates are customers or suppliers, there is already an established business relationship. If not, peer-to-peer contact is an effective approach. Consultants can also be used to set up visits. In any case, make sure there is something in the relationship for both parties. This might include a willingness to share benchmarking results or an ongoing information exchange.

Just as in any other kind of research, preparation for benchmarking visits is critical for success. It is important to prepare an interview guide or meeting outline to ensure that the key points are covered. Sending a list of questions or areas of interest to the benchmark partner will help the partner gather information and have the right people available for the meeting. Picking the right people to make the visit is also important. At least one person on the team should be familiar with the benchmarking process and be skilled in interviewing and facilitation. The benchmarking team should also include people who are knowledgeable in the key business process being studied.

The objective of the site visit is to gather information. The benchmark team accomplishes this by asking questions and listening to the answers. The team members should avoid the temptation to compare the partner's processes and business practices with company's current or proposed approaches during the visit. This is generally not productive. There will be an opportunity to do that later. During the visit, the focus is on what the benchmark company does, how they do it, and the results they get.

During the visit, it is usually appropriate to take extensive notes. It is also a good idea to gather as much material as possible. In the sales and marketing area, there are usually flyers, brochures, catalogs, and other materials. The team may also be able to get or borrow manuals and training videos that provide information on the processes being benchmarked.

Remember that processes are made up of more than just the procedures. They include people, information, equipment, and the environment in which they operate. The benchmark team should be aware of all of these factors, asking questions about them and observing facilities and information flow. Team members should also find out exactly how the benchmark partner measures the process they are benchmarking. According to Northrop Grumman Norden Systems' operations specialist Peter G. Callahan, "You have to be sure your metrics are exactly the same. We found that the slightest variation in the interpretation of a metric can make the comparisons meaningless."

The last step in the benchmark site visit is to consolidate all of the observations and notes of the team members. This is best done as soon after the visit as possible, while the information is fresh in everyone's mind. The objective at this stage is to pull together all of the information and get it documented, not to analyze, compare, or criticize.

### Input Benchmark Results to Step 7

Once all the information from all the benchmark visits is on paper, it is input into the BPI process at Step 7. It is during this analysis step that the results of all the data collection and site visits can be compared to the organization's current processes and practices. This analysis will identify gaps in performance between the company and the best-in-class organizations. The process improvement team can then determine the best ways to close the performance gap. Again, the improvement team may improve an existing process or design a new one. In either case, the team can include the best ideas from the benchmark companies.

One criticism of benchmarking is that if a company copies the best, this sets an upper limit. They cannot be better. However, the objective of benchmarking is not just to copy the best. It is to see what is possible and how it is attained. Remember the example of the aerospace and defense contractors. If one of these companies knew that the average close rate for the industry was 18 percent and that it was closing 21 percent, management could feel pretty good. However, if management knew that the best companies were closing over 60 percent, they would also know that they had a lot of work to do. Benchmarking demonstrates possibility; it does not set upper limits.

Benchmarking is a powerful technique for business process improvement. Without benchmarking the best, an organization can never be sure how good its practices and processes really are. The NIH, or "not invented here," syndrome has been the downfall of many organizations. One of the popular slogans of the quality improvement movement has been "Steal Shamelessly." Borrow from the best. And remember, even the also-rans have something to offer. They demonstrate what does not work and what not to do.

## ISO-9000

ISO-9000 is an international series of standards for managing and assuring quality. Although it is a relatively new addition to the quality improvement field, it is having a major influence on the way many organizations do business today. Like it or not, many companies that manufacture and sell to other businesses are being encouraged, and in some cases forced, by their customers to adopt ISO-9000 or similar standards. This is particularly true for companies selling in the European market. Although ISO-9000 is most commonly associated with manufacturing operations, a few companies are adopting the standards for key parts of their sales processes as well.

The standards are developed and promoted by the International Standards Organization, or ISO. Located in Geneva, Switzerland. ISO is made up of about one hundred member countries. The United States is represented by the American National Standards Institute (ANSI). Hundreds of worldwide technical committees and working groups work together to develop and update the ISO standards. The objective of ISO-9000 is to establish standards for the elements of quality management. These elements include a quality plan, a quality manual, and process documentation. The idea is that customers can be relatively certain that the products and services of an ISO-9000 company will be of consistent quality.

The current standards address various parts of the manufacturing process, including the following:

ISO-9001. Quality systems: model for quality assurance in design/
development, production, installation, and servicing

ISO-9002. Quality systems: model for quality assurance in production, installation, and servicing

ISO-9003. Quality systems: model for quality assurance in final
inspection and test

ISO-9000 standards can be applied to a plant site, a product,
or a process. Although the process element includes manufacturing processes, it can also include many kinds of nonmanufacturing processes, such as design, pricing, and purchasing. A document
called the "Scope of Registration," defines exactly what is included
in each ISO registration.

Putting an ISO-9000 quality management system in place is
much like implementing business process management. It begins
with top management commitment and includes identifying the
sites, products, or processes to be certified and registered, putting
a staff in place, and learning the ISO-9000 standards. It also included defining, documenting, and implementing the quality management procedures that will ensure the consistency of the product
or service being produced. When these steps are complete, the
company is ready to be registered.

To achieve ISO-9000 registration, the company engages a third-
party auditor. The auditor examines the company's documentation, reviews the process, and interviews the people involved. The
test of the process documentation is this: if all those involved in
the process were replaced by new people, would the documentation allow new employees to continue to operate the process exactly as before? When the company passes the audit, it is awarded
a certificate of registration. However, to maintain the ISO-9000 registration, it must submit to periodic audits to ensure that the standards continue to be observed.

ISO-9000's many advocates point to a number of benefits. Customers who purchase ISO-9000 certified products have assurance
that they are of consistent quality. The customers have the option
of eliminating incoming inspection, and they do not have to conduct supplier audits themselves; the third-party auditor does that

twice a year. This results in reduced costs for the customer. These benefits are particularly important in international trade, where the one hundred member countries recognize the standard.

The company benefits as well. If the company uses the standards in the spirit in which they are intended, they will improve the company's processes as the standards are applied. If all of the company's customers accept ISO-9000 certification, the company will be audited only twice a year. If the company is not registered, it may face the costs and disruption of frequent audits and on-site inspection by many of its customers.

ISO registration also produces sales benefits. The company can advertise its ISO registration, and it will be listed in a directory of registered suppliers. Even companies that do not audit their suppliers may be influenced by a company's willingness to become registered. In some industries, ISO-9000 certification is becoming a requirement to do business with a few U.S. customers, and it is even more important in the European market.

ISO-9000 is not without detractors however. The standards are designed to assure customers that the company follows procedures. This should reduce variation in the product. However, just because the product is consistent does not mean that it meets customer requirements. Also, registration is a relatively expensive proposition. External consultants and trainers are frequently involved. There are also the expenses of developing the quality plan, documenting the plan and the process, and training the people involved. The company also pays for the registration and periodic audits.

Several leading companies have carefully considered both sides of the issue and have chosen to ISO-9000 certify some of the steps in their sales process. These are companies that make and sell complex and sophisticated products, ranging from power systems and electrical products to computers, communication equipment, and chemicals. These companies recognize that their salespeople provide customers with technical product information and often help develop complex equipment configurations. After the customer decides to buy, the salespeople hand off the order to engineers or production people. This sales process must work flawlessly to ensure that the customers get what they order and that what they order meets their unique requirements. As quality manager Norm Jennings at Globe Metallurgical says, "Quality starts with sales."

The Square D Company used ISO-9000 to begin a quality improvement process in sales and marketing. While certifying their manufacturing processes, the company also certified the order fulfillment process. The overall objective was to increase order quality. Bruce Kappel, Square D's quality projects manager, describes the company's order quality measurement as "the accuracy of translating the customers' expectations into an order." The order fulfillment process includes several preorder activities such as pricing products, establishing terms and conditions, generating bids, and creating proposals. Kappel reports that Square D set the following five objectives for the ISO-9000 certification of order fulfillment.

*Establish a basic discipline.* ISO-9000 requires detailed documentation for each key process to be certified. This documentation includes detailed procedures to ensure that the order fulfillment process is consistently applied across the company's 150-plus sales offices.

*Institutionalize gains.* The company continues to improve the order fulfillment process. When they make process improvements, they want to be sure that every location implements the changes and that those changes became a permanent part of the procedures.

*Reduce variation.* When each person in a process has his or her own way of accomplishing a task, there is a wide variation in the process output. Providing documented procedures and a pricing manual to everyone in the process helps reduce that variation.

*Measure marketing differently.* ISO-9000 has brought an additional dimension to measurement. The company is now able to determine how well the order fulfillment process is working. They can also measure the effectiveness of corrective actions or changes to the process.

*Use terms consistently.* The Square D Company has over 150 sales offices and thirty-two plant sites in the United States. In addition, the current company is the product of several mergers and acquisitions. By adopting the ISO-9000 documentation standard, the company has been able to establish a common vocabulary of terms. This has resulted in improved communications across every part of the organization.

The Energy Services Division at Westinghouse has ISO-9000 certified elements of its marketing process. The division began by identifying all of the business's key processes and by defining and documenting their current procedures. This activity identified some holes in the processes. The division corrected these problems, documented the revised procedures, created a requirements manual, and defined the limits of authority and approvals required. All of these activities provided the division with a better understanding of internal and external customers and their requirements. This information was fed back to the people in the process through a comprehensive training program.

One of the division's objectives was to ensure a smooth transfer of the customer order from marketing to the operations function. The objective was to make certain that marketing handed off 100 percent of the orders through formal transfer meetings. These meetings ensure that operations has a complete and accurate understanding of the customer's requirements. This is critical in the complex environment of major power systems. As a result of implementing the ISO-9000 standards and achieving the subsequent process improvement, documentation, and training, the people in the process are much more comfortable with their responsibilities. The process has been in place for more than five years and has proved to be more efficient as well.

Several other leading companies have certified key parts of their sales processes. Among them are the Ethyl Corporation's Industrial Chemical Division; Hewlett Packard, in computers; and The Paradyne Corporation (now part of Lucent Technologies), in communication equipment. The companies who have chosen to use the ISO-9000 standards in parts of their sales processes share certain characteristics. They are all business-to-business marketers. They have also certified their manufacturing processes. They provide complex products or systems, and in some cases they also provide installation and maintenance services. Their products are often custom designed and created for each application. And their customers need very specific and accurate product information on which to base informed buying decisions. Due to these characteristics, the results of an error in the sales and order fulfillment processes can be very expensive to the company and its customer.

All the companies that have ISO-9000 certified parts of their sales processes have benefited from doing it. However, as we have seen, they are all business-to-business marketers in complex and technical industries. Other companies that fall into this category may want to consider ISO-9000. However, ISO-9000 does not have the broad applicability of the other tools discussed in this chapter.

## Conclusion

Leading companies have applied all five of these process improvement techniques to sales and marketing processes. As we have seen, when process improvement techniques are focused on the most important processes and used properly, they can make dramatic improvements in an organization's effectiveness and efficiency.

*Chapter Five*

# | **Use Teams**

Teams have become the organizational building block of the 1990s. The Center for Effective Organizations conducted three surveys of the Fortune 1,000 companies over a six-year period and the most recent survey revealed that more than 91 percent of the respondents were using some form of employee participation groups. The surveys also showed continued growth in the use of such groups over the six-year period (Lawler, 1995, p. 27). According to the American Quality Foundation and Ernst & Young's International Quality Study (1992), companies in both manufacturing and service sectors plan to increase their application of teams.

The sales and marketing functions have accepted teams more slowly. While more than 91 percent of the companies surveyed use teams somewhere in their organization, the number reporting teams in sales is less than 40 percent (Lawler, 1995, p. 97). This is the group that is least likely to be covered by either Total Quality Management or Employee Involvement. However, the number is growing, and the leading companies use teams much more frequently in their sales and marketing functions than they used to. In my own best practices survey, 95 percent of the companies interviewed use teams somewhere in their sales or marketing functions.

Virtually every organization can benefit by increasing their use of teams, and a number of factors are encouraging companies to do just that. The last chapter showed how process improvement techniques depend on cross-functional teams. Teams in marketing develop and launch products faster and more effectively than the traditional approach. Sales teams add value to products and services and increase sales and customer satisfaction. Salespeople also participate in joint customer and supplier teams to solve problems, improve processes, address opportunities, and strengthen partnerships.

Finally, when companies downsize they eliminate layers of management, and self-managed teams assume many of the management tasks.

This chapter considers the structure of teams, how they work and how companies are applying them successfully in sales and marketing. It also identifies the critical success factors for teams. Because teams are not for everyone and are not appropriate in every situation, this chapter provides guidelines for when and when not to use them. The discussion begins with definitions: what constitutes a team and how a team differs from other small groups.

## Definition of a Team

A *team* is defined as a group of two or more people who work together to achieve a common objective. This definition, however, could also apply to other small groups, such as some departments, committees, and task forces. There is more to a team than just people working together toward a common objective.

The best way to illustrate this is to use a sports team analogy. All the team members have a common mission (the sport they play) and a common goal (to win games). They function as a unit. They receive training and are coached to work together. They are empowered to some degree to make their own decisions during the game. They get the credit if they win and take responsibility if they lose.

Like the sports team, the business team comes together for a common purpose, described in its mission statement. The team members are interdependent. No one person can do everything. The team members receive training in the tools and techniques that they will use. A coach or facilitator helps them work together as a team and use the tools and techniques they need to achieve their mission. They make many of their decisions as a team, and they are collectively responsible for the outcome of their efforts.

Contrast that with the typical committee or task force. Rarely, if ever, are the members trained in group dynamics, meeting skills, or a problem-solving process. Although they may work together, they frequently owe their allegiance to the department or function that they represent. They often work toward compromise rather than consensus.

Some managers use the team label for groups that do not meet team criteria. These managers want to be perceived as using teams without making the cultural, organizational, and management changes necessary. Usually, their "teams" are just conventional departments, and the "team leaders" are the department managers. It takes more than a change in titles for a group to become a team, however.

## Benefits of Teams

When teams are used in the right circumstances, they have several benefits over people working independently or in traditionally managed work groups. Here are some of the major advantages.

### Productivity

Several leading companies reported that their use of teams resulted in increased productivity and more efficient use of resources. Steelcase uses teams in the corporate marketing function to develop marketing support for the company's five business units. When a business unit comes forward with a new product, corporate marketing selects a team leader. The team leader then works directly with the business unit on its project.

The team leader forms a team by selecting members from the various groups in corporate marketing. For example, a team might include a merchandising manager, a production manager, a writer, and maybe even an outside vendor. The team has overall responsibility for developing the marketing support for the new product launch. Depending on the size of the project, team members may go back to their own departments and form subteams to deal with specific parts of the launch.

By using this approach, Steelcase gets maximum use of the corporate marketing resources. People can work on multiple teams and support several projects at the same time. Everyone understands and contributes to the whole project through the team meetings. Contrast this approach with a traditional organization in which each department has a fixed headcount and carries out specific assignments. Communication with other departments working on the same project takes extra time and resources. Also there is a tendency for work levels to ebb and flow, with some people overworked and others with idle time.

## Improved Performance

Teams are frequently able to produce better results than individuals working independently. This ability is the result of a phenomenon called synergy. The *American Heritage Dictionary* defines synergy as, "The interaction of two or more agents or forces so that their combined effect is greater than the sum of their individual effects."

A simple training exercise demonstrates how synergy works. A box of about twenty-five items is shown to groups of six to eight people for about fifteen seconds each. Each individual is then asked to write down all of the items that he or she can remember. Next the group works together to create a combined list. To the surprise of no one, the individuals can recall less than half the items they have seen. However, working together, group members can list two-thirds or more of the items. The learning point of the exercise is understanding why the group list is larger than any individual's list. It is due to group members' differences—their backgrounds, experiences, ages, and genders. It is the diversity in group members that enables teams to be more effective than the same individuals working separately, and research shows that the greater the diversity in a group, the more effective it is in reaching its objectives (Rice, 1994).

That's right. The greater the diversity, the more effective the group! Certainly, the more homogeneous groups do tend to get off to a faster start. However, in the final analysis, the more diverse groups come up with more comprehensive and creative results.

All other things being equal, teams will complete projects as fast as, or faster than, managers and employees using a traditional approach. It may not seem so in the early stages of a project, when teams spend time getting organized, establishing roles and group norms, discussing, and reaching consensus. However, when project plans are adopted by the team, implementation goes much more quickly. There are two reasons for this: buy-in and communication.

## Buy-In

Team members buy into and support their group's decisions because they participate in making them. The decisions are the product of a consensus approach in which everyone on the team contributes ideas and opinions. The team develops alternatives and selects the most desirable one that everyone can support. The alternative selected may not be everyone's first choice, but it is one everyone can live with. Team members may take time to reach a consensus. However, once they do, they can implement their decision much more smoothly and quickly than they could using a traditional approach.

In the traditional approach, a manager makes a decision and announces it to everyone who is affected. Support for this decision tends to be lower. There is often disagreement between the parties involved, and they spend time negotiating to work out differences. Because many of those affected had no opportunity to provide input, problems are often uncovered as they implement the decision. Solving these problems also takes time.

## Communication

The second reason that teams can implement decisions more quickly is better communication. When the team makes a decision, the members know about it immediately. The team meeting is the communication medium. If the team is cross-functional, the members represent various departments. They can quickly communicate team decisions to their respective departments keeping everyone informed. When members leave team meetings, they know what they are responsible for doing and how that ties into everyone else's assignments. This is in contrast to the traditional approach, where a manager makes the decisions and communicates them to the other people or departments involved. This communication process takes longer, and people are not always aware of what others are doing and how it relates to them.

## Employee Morale

Opinion surveys at two companies revealed that employees who participate in teams have higher morale and greater job satisfaction than those who do not. One of the companies reported that managers of team members received higher ratings than managers of other employees on how well they did their jobs. The team members also rated their managers' business, technical, and people management skills more favorably. The most revealing question on the survey identified how well team members thought their jobs used their skills and abilities. Sixty-one percent of the team members responded favorably to that question while only 38 percent of the people who were not participating in teams thought the company was using their skills and abilities effectively.

## Personal Development

Another benefit of using teams is personal development. Team members learn and develop skills in solving problems, listening, resolving conflicts, and giving and receiving feedback. Teams also provide people with an opportunity to develop and demonstrate management and leadership skills. Steelcase corporate marketing uses team leader assignments to prepare people for higher levels of responsibility. The company designates product launches as level A, B, or C based on the size and complexity the project. New team leaders begin with level C product launches. As they learn and demonstrate leadership skills and gain confidence, they move up to the more challenging B and A launches. This approach gives people the opportunity to find out whether they like the role and responsibilities of leadership. The company can see how well people perform in a leadership position without actually placing them in a management job. Promotions into management can then be based on a candidate's interest, demonstrated ability, and experience. For the people who lack either the interest in being a manager or the necessary leadership skills, the company provides recognition, rewards, and career opportunities in their professional area.

For all of the reasons seen here, a team is an effective way to organize and carry out a mission. However, not everything within a team's mission should be done by the team working as a group. Many specific tasks will still be performed by individual team members. In corporate marketing at Steelcase, a team designs and manages the overall project and coordinates the activities of the many project contributors. However, it is still the writers who produce advertising copy, the artists who create illustrations, and the designers who lay out brochures.

## Team Dimensions

Teams are not all alike. They are distinguished by five attributes: scope, size, mission, authority, and duration.

## Scope

The scope of a team refers to the span of its membership. A team's scope is narrow if its members come from a single department or natural work group. If a team draws members from across a business unit or a whole company, its scope is wider, and it is referred to as a cross-functional team. Intercompany teams include members from both customer and supplier organizations and have the widest scope of all.

## Size

The optimum team size is from six to eight members. Although a team of two to five people can often accomplish more than the same number of people working separately, teams of six or more seem to be most effective. The practical upper limit for a team is about twelve members. When teams go beyond that number, it is very difficult for them to reach a consensus when making decisions. It is also harder to get everyone to contribute, and members report lower morale when they work on larger teams. When a mission requires more than twelve people, it is usually more effective to break the project down and create subteams.

## Mission

A team's mission describes its purpose, or what it is put in place to do. There are three broad categories of teams defined by their missions.

- *Work teams.* These are teams that perform the work of the organization.

- *Improvement teams.* These are teams chartered to improve the organization and how it functions. Process improvement teams, or PITs (described in Chapter Four) fall in this category. (Of course, work teams can also improve processes and solve problems within their functional areas.)
- *Special purpose teams.* These are teams formed to plan the annual picnic, give away a company scholarship, or handle the charitable contribution campaign. Although they do real work, it is not directly related to the purpose of business.

## Authority

The authority of a team describes what it is empowered to do without approval. At the lowest level of authority, an improvement team can study a problem and recommend a solution. With a higher level of authority, it can take action to solve the problem on its own. A work team with limited authority may be able to discuss issues and recommend action to management. With a high level of authority, it is empowered to make decisions, spend money, and even hire and separate team members. Teams with the highest levels of authority are referred to as self-directed or self-managed teams.

## Duration

Duration refers to the life span of a team. A team may be temporary and exist until a specific process is improved, problem is solved, or opportunity is addressed. A team may also be ongoing and a permanent part of the organization.

## Teams in Sales and Marketing

The next few pages use the attributes just outlined to describe the more common forms of teams, categorized by scope, and show how leading companies apply them in sales and marketing.

## Departmental Teams

Teams with the narrowest scope operate at the departmental or natural work group level. Departmental teams are made up of employees who report to the same supervisor or manager. These teams may carry out either of the general team missions: improvement or the day-to-day work of the department.

The Alexander Group recently surveyed members of the American Compensation Association to find out just how their members use teams in sales. According to Jerry Colletti, president and CEO of the Scottsdale, Arizona, based consulting firm, the survey revealed that 15 percent of the companies that responded use pure sales teams. These teams are made up exclusively of sales people, and their mission is to sell to and support customers, the day-to-day work of their department. In most companies, the primary application of sales teams is to cover large accounts.

Companies also use departmental teams to solve problems and improve processes within the sales function. If they are addressing a problem, they gather data about it, identify its root causes, and develop solutions. A team may recommend the solution to management, or team members may implement the solution themselves, depending on how much authority they have. Process improvement teams use the techniques already described in Chapter Four.

Park Place Motorcars in Dallas exemplifies an improvement team in a sales department. Park Place has three dealerships in the Dallas area, selling Mercedes Benz, Porsche/Audi, and Lexus automobiles. Salespeople in each of the dealerships participate in teams to address sales-related problems. Recently, for example, the Mercedes Benz team addressed a problem that was costing them sales.

The Park Place Mercedes Benz dealership is located in near downtown Dallas. One of the problems it faces is finding space close to the showroom to store the new automobile inventory. These cars cannot be left outside because hail storms are fairly common in Dallas. To solve the problem, Park Place rented space in the basement garages of nearby high-rise buildings, but this created another problem for the Park Place salespeople.

When a prospective customer asks to see a certain model and color automobile, the salesperson checks the inventory log, locates a car in one of the nearby buildings, and sends someone to bring it back for a demonstration drive. However, because the car has been stored in a basement, it may not be ready to show. The packing material may not have been removed. It may not be clean and may even have bird droppings on it.

The salespeople estimated they were losing three to four sales a month because cars were not ready to show. Then, the director of quality at Park Place reports, "The team came up with a unique solution to getting the cars ready to show. It will increase our volume of sales by almost $200,000 and save us money as well." The solution was simple. The company changed the priority for cars going through the company's on-site car wash, giving top priority to vehicles being taken to show customers. Now it only takes about ten to fifteen minutes to get a car ready to show.

Bill Blankemeier, former regional manager for ITT Fluid Technology Corporation in Oak Brook, Illinois, recognized the value of departmental teams and business process improvement. He used them in his region to increase new account sales. Blankemeier started the project by forming a team of four salespeople from contiguous geographic territories. They picked a meeting location in a centrally located city and went to work. Their first step was to pick a sales process on which to focus. Says Blankemeier, "We do a good job working with our existing customers but don't do as well getting new customers. In 1991, less than 5 percent of our business came from new accounts. We decided that this was the area that we wanted to focus on." Using business process improvement (BPI), Blankemeier's team defined the new business process and identified two areas to improve: capital construction and new accounts. Capital construction refers to companies that are expanding and have potential for major incremental business.

The salespeople had been getting new construction leads from an external supplier, and the team discovered that these leads were not very good. The team's first improvement was to switch to a supplier that could provide better capital construction leads. The team then focused on finding more potential accounts in the industries the company serves, such as chemicals, power generation, pharmaceuticals, and pulp and paper. They located another vendor that could provide them with information on all the companies located in their territories. The list includes data on the size of each company, number of employees, SIC code, and product lines.

The team members developed a new process to load the prospect information into their personal computers, analyze it, and delete companies that are already customers. The result is a list of new account prospects organized by location and size. The improved process also includes ways to qualify the potential of a lead before a salesperson begins to pursue it.

Although this was a pilot project and involved just the four salespeople on the team, the results were excellent. Blankemeier reports that "as a direct result, we have already sold over 250,000 dollars in new business, and we have over four million dollars of potential in the pipeline. This is significant business to us." There were other benefits as well. According to Blankemeier, "We learned how to work as a team and to solve problems in a systematic way. We used the process improvement model, flowcharted the process, collected and analyzed data, and identified root causes of the problems we encountered. We found that it is fairly easy to do all of this." The salespeople on the ITT team are also positive about the improvement process and the results they achieved.

Many companies are giving work teams the authority and responsibility for managing their own day-to-day activities. A few companies are testing self-directed teams in sales. Typically, these teams are made up of several salespeople assigned to a single large or key account. They work toward a common sales quota objective, manage their time, and provide mutual support and backup. If these self-directed sales teams are successful, expect to see more of them as the span of control of the typical sales manager increases.

## Cross-Functional Teams

Cross-functional teams have a wider scope than departmental teams. They include members from more than one department or function, and their mission can be either improvement or performing the work of the organization. When their mission is improvement, they can apply the same tools that the Park Place Motorcars and ITT Fluid Technologies teams used. However, they would normally focus these tools on solving organization-wide problems or improving cross-functional business processes. (Chapter Four includes many examples of how sales and marketing people participate in cross-functional process improvement teams.)

### Cross-Functional Work Teams in Sales

The use of cross-functional work teams in sales is growing in almost every industry. Companies are creating teams with members from different functional areas, such as sales, support, service, and administration. Many companies have more than one division or product line, each with its own salesforce but all calling on the same customers. These companies are including representatives from their different divisions on the same teams. The common element among the team members is that they all serve the same customer or sales territory. To recognize that not all of the team members are salespeople, some companies call these groups account teams or customer teams. The study conducted by the Alexander Group revealed that 25 percent of the companies surveyed were using these cross-functional teams.

Several factors are driving the movement to customer teams, not the least of which are the customers. They want fewer salespeople calling on them, and companies with multiple product lines are responding by consolidating lines in their customer teams. Many customers are trying to reduce the number of their suppliers and are placing all of their business with the few that remain. Companies are trying to survive the cuts and become the preferred suppliers. One way they are doing this is by adding value to their products and services through their customer teams.

Companies as well as customers benefit from these teams. When every function or division that works with a customer is represented on a team and that team has common objectives, the customer, not the objectives of several different internal organizations, becomes the focus. This common focus encourages team members to coordinate their own and the company's resources toward their common customer goals. Teams can also present a more consistent face to the customer than can the multiple functional departments they represent.

To make these cross-functional sales teams work, companies are training team members in group dynamics and problem-solving skills. They assign common objectives such as sales quotas, budgets, and customer satisfaction and loyalty measurements. Companies are also revising their management systems to measure, recognize, and compensate team performance without ignoring individual contribution.

One such company is Marlow Industries, a 1991 Malcolm Baldrige National Quality Award–winner in the small company category. Marlow is a Dallas–based high-technology producer of thermoelectric coolers. The company has segmented its markets according to the end-use of its products and has created what Marlow calls a market segment team for each segment. Each cross-functional team has a market segment manager who is responsible for sales and marketing. In addition, the teams include engineers and customer service representatives. The plant is also organized by market segment, with mini-factory manufacturing areas assigned to build the products for each segment.

An applications engineer supports all four market segment teams. He provides the customers with detailed product information and assists them in determining whether they can buy a standard product out of the catalogue or will require a special product. Using a computer, he analyzes the customer's requirements and even designs a product while he is on the phone with the customer. This preliminary computer design is very close to the final hardware design. As soon as the applications engineer determines which segment the customer is in, he gets the segment team involved.

The next step is for the customer to order the product. Then the market segment team works very closely with the customer to create the exact design. Team members develop the documentation for the product and then bring in manufacturing to make sure it can be produced. The team then goes back to the customer, who buys off on the final design. Once that is done, engineering usually builds prototypes. They are approved by marketing, engineering, and manufacturing.

Marlow's cross-functional team involves sales, marketing, application and manufacturing engineering, customer service, and manufacturing all working together. The market segment team takes the customer through the complete sales, product design, and manufacturing process. Marlow's vice president of marketing and sales John Nelson is enthusiastic about the results of the team approach. "Our cost of quality has decreased. Our profitability has increased. Our returns have gone down. We ship almost everything on time." The team approach has also helped develop customer partnerships and increase customer satisfaction.

Marlow is just one of many leading companies to use this team structure for sales and customer support. Other companies such as AT&T, Westinghouse, and Zytec vary the approach. They also use cross-functional work group teams made up of people with a variety of skills. However, they form teams as needed to focus on specific major sales situations. After the opportunity has been addressed, their teams disband, and the members return to regular assignments or move on to other teams.

Whether they are temporary or permanent, cross-functional teams are proving their value in bringing needed skills and resources to sales situations. Customers like the approach, too. They are more certain that their requirements will be met when everyone is involved during the sales process. The cross-functional approach also helps break down the barriers that frequently exist between the salesforce and other departments. When these barriers are removed, people are more likely to work together to solve problems rather than pointing fingers and blaming each other.

### Cross-Functional Work Group Teams in Marketing

Many leading companies are also using teams to achieve similar results in their marketing functions. Recall how Steelcase uses teams in corporate marketing to support product launches for their five business units. GTE provides another example.

In an effort to improve their telephone operations, the company conducted a major study, called Winning Connections. As a result of that study, GTE established customer segment teams. The mission of these teams is to understand the requirements of each customer segment, define a strategy, determine what products and services are needed, identify the necessary support resources, and get commitment to meet all of these needs. The teams are made up of eight to eleven directors and high-level managers representing GTE's key departments. Although some of the members have limited responsibilities in their respective areas, their membership on the customer segment team is the biggest part of their jobs. Their assignments on the team are permanent, and their responsibilities and loyalties are to the team.

GTE also has product teams that focus on bringing a product family to the market. The product teams support the segment teams. The result of their interaction is an integrated marketing plan. This plan is input for GTE's five-year strategic plan and annual operating plans and budgets.

### Cross-Functional Work Group Teams Across the Business

Some companies are using work group teams that represent all of the major business functions. At the Wheelabrator Corporation in LaGrange, Georgia, the mission of the cross-functional teams began as continuous improvement. Their long-term goal, however, is to become self-managed teams with complete responsibility for running each product line. Sales and marketing are fully involved in the process.

The division began as a traditional organization, including functional departments such as sales and marketing, engineering, and manufacturing. In response to flat product demand and strong competitive pressures, division executives decided to take the blank-sheet-of-paper approach to design the organization and management processes. The first step was to combine the sales and engineering departments. This took down the walls between the two groups and allowed a major reduction in staff while maintaining sales volumes and customer satisfaction.

The next step was to set up five cross-functional teams, one for each of the division's major product lines. Tom Warren, director of equipment sales and engineering, is the team sponsor of the new equipment team. As Warren explains, "Everybody who is involved in the new equipment group is on the cross-functional team. That includes assembly, manufacturing, accounting, sales, engineering, the whole group." The new equipment team has been trained on everything there is to know about the product line. Wheelabrator invited distributors to come in to explain how they sell, how they are organized, and what problems they run into. Suppliers and customers were also brought in. Even a salesman from a direct competitor was invited to explain how he sells against Wheelabrator's product line.

The team used a structured continuous improvement process much like the BPI model described in Chapter Four. Team members examined how everything in the operation fit together from the customer order through shipped product. They identified the specific information they needed from the customer to ensure that the product was right, examined the sales documents, and reviewed manufacturing, assembly, and shipping. Then they identified the major problems. The team fixed these problems immediately if they were relatively easy. In some cases, the team decided to eliminate whole activities. If a project was relatively difficult, like revising the order entry document, the team created a subteam to address it.

One of the challenges was to operate the business and the continuous improvement process without a traditional management structure. The division leadership has eliminated most of the functional middle-management positions and all of the floor supervisor jobs. Those responsibilities are being assumed by the cross-functional teams as they become more self-directed.

Clearly the Wheelabrator Corporation is on the leading edge of change, and the sales and marketing functions are an integral part of the effort. As a result of the reorganization and use of cross-functional teams, customer and employee satisfaction is up, and the division has become one of the most profitable within WMX, Wheelabrator's parent company.

## Cross-Company Teams

The scope of teams is expanding beyond company boundaries. Many of the leading companies are participating in teams with their customers, and their salespeople are frequently team members. These companies are becoming active participants in their customers' improvement and work group teams. In some cases, they bring problem-solving and process improvement skills. In others, they provide product or service knowledge. In either case, they are supporting the movement toward more partnerships between customers and suppliers.

Globe Metallurgical encourages their salespeople to participate in customer teams. During the early stages of development at GM's Saturn division, the Globe salesman was an active member of the power train team. According to Globe quality manager Norm Jennings, "The team not only developed the process of using our product, it also created the delivery system, the inventory system, and infrastructure."

At Foseco, the Cleveland-based manufacturer of products for steel mills, foundries, and the aluminum industry, the salespeople have also begun to participate in teams with their customers. Fred Corpuz, Foseco vice president, describes how one of their salesmen has been working with a West Coast aluminum customer. "He and some of the customer people meet with our people on a partnership basis. We go out to the West Coast with some of our hourly employees, and they come back to our Pennsylvania plant." The mission of the joint team is to work together to resolve whatever issues the customer raises.

One of the companies most highly regarded for its ability to make dramatic organization and process change is General Electric. Recently, GE launched a pilot program to share its change tools with customers. The program is called Change Acceleration Process, or CAP. GE shares the change tools by working together with customers to apply them to an issue or opportunity that is of mutual interest.

The CAP begins when GE and a customer identify a possible issue or opportunity on which to cooperate. A large, multifunction team is assembled, and GE trains the team members on the change tools. This team orientation is about making change happen faster and finding the most efficient way to work together as one. Gary Hessenauer, GE's past corporate area manager, provides an example. "A thirty-seven person team is working on the new 737 project. GE and Boeing will work together in an integrated fashion on the propulsion system. This will be the first time Boeing will sell an airplane without offering the buyer a choice of engines. . . . The plane comes complete with GE engines. The buyer will no longer have the option of Rolls Royce or Pratt & Whitney."

## Team Tools and Processes

To understand the tools and processes that teams use, we first need to understand three concepts: content, task, and relationship. These are the three dimensions of team activities. *Content* is the subject matter on which the team works. *Task* refers to the processes teams use to work on the content. *Relationship* describes the processes they use to address the individual and collective needs of the team members. All three are important.

Content is the information with which business teams work to achieve their mission objectives. For an improvement team, it is the problem that they are solving. For a marketing team, it is the product, customer, and market information the team uses to create a successful product launch. For a sales team, it is the customer requirements data that the team analyzes to create a winning proposal. The content is unique to each team and situation.

Our primary focus here is on the remaining two concepts: task and relationship. These can be referred to as the *process dimensions.* Content is what the team works on; process is how the team works on the content. The process dimensions include the methods teams use to execute their mission. Task refers to the methods they use to solve problems, improve business processes, launch products, or create sales proposals. Relationship refers to how team members interact with each other and how individuals meet their personal needs within the context of the group. It is important for the team members to agree on the task and relationship methods they will use before they address their mission and its content.

Teams have a wide variety of tools and techniques available for the task dimension of their activities, and the mission will usually dictate which tools they need. However, there are two that almost every team requires, a decision-making process and a basic problem-solving process.

One of the first tasks for every new team is to agree on how the team will make decisions. Some companies prescribe or suggest a specific decision-making process for all teams in the organization. Other companies allow teams to pick their own. Teams may use a consensus approach, vote, or just yield to the loudest member. The most effective method for teams is the consensus approach. This method ensures that although everyone on the team may not agree totally with a decision, they can all live with and support it.

The second process basic to almost all teams is a structured problem-solving process. Most companies select one and include it in the training for all their teams. This provides a predefined set of steps and a common problem-solving language across the company. Although there are many problem-solving processes in use, most boil down to the following steps:

- Define the problem
- Identify the root causes
- Create a solution
- Implement the solution
- Measure the results

Data gathering is also an important part of the problem-solving process. It is used to support the steps of defining the problem, identifying the solution, and measuring the results.

Teams also need mission-specific task skills. Improvement team members may need an understanding of tools in areas such as

- Market research
- Customer satisfaction surveys
- Statistical analysis
- Business process improvement
- Business process management
- Process reengineering
- Benchmarking
- ISO-9000
- Information technology

Work team members need task skills in their professional areas. For example, a sales team needs to know the steps to create a proposal or enter a complex order. A marketing team may need to know how to conduct a market research study, develop a product announcement plan, run a business show, or create an advertising campaign. If a team is self-managed, the members also need skills in the management functions assumed by the team. These include employee hiring, evaluation, training, compensation, and even separation.

The relationship skills can also be thought of as social or interpersonal abilities. Some of the most important include conducting effective meetings, listening to others, speaking out when appropriate, taking risks, giving and receiving constructive nonthreatening feedback, and resolving conflicts. When teams use these skills well, it encourages all of the team members to contribute fully. These skills are necessary to make sure that the members work together and that they meet their own personal needs.

As important as attention to relationships is, it is often the least observed. This problem is rooted in a business culture that focuses on the task and content aspects of team activities. Without a focus on relationships as well, however, teams are often dominated by a few members, and other members limit their contributions. Members spend time in conflict and make decisions based on emotion rather than facts. As a result, the team does not live up to its full potential, and the members leave feeling unfulfilled and unwilling to participate in future team activities.

Figure 5.1 shows the relationship between the relationship and task dimensions. Team members need to keep these two dimensions in balance. Teams that focus too much on tasks will not get the most out of all team members, and the results may not be optimum. Teams that focus too much on relationships will have good morale but will not perform at a high level. Groups that just focus on content will not accomplish as much, will not enjoy their work, and do not qualify to be called teams. Team members need to keep both process dimensions in balance as they address the content issues and work toward their mission objectives.

## Team Structure

There are several roles to be played by team members and other people in supporting positions.

### Team Members

The most important role is that of team member. Collectively team members develop action plans, gather information, make decisions,

**Figure 5.1. Process Dimensions of Teams.**

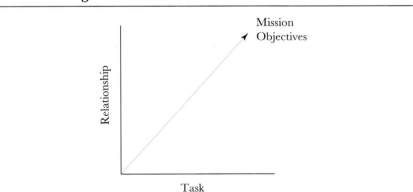

and carry out the work of the team. Here are some of the guidelines to consider in selecting team members.

The most important factor is a commitment to the team and its mission. This is measured by team members' showing up for meetings, carrying out assignments, and observing the task and relationship processes that they all agree to follow. When team members lack commitment, the team will not have a sense of urgency, other tasks will take priority over team activities, and the team will miss milestones and completion dates. It will not be effective in accomplishing its mission.

Some people do not want to be part of any team. If a person does not want to participate as a full member, it is often better to ask or allow him or her to drop out. If the team absolutely needs that person's business knowledge and experience, he or she can participate as a specialist or "subject matter expert" only when the team needs the input.

Having something to contribute to the team is also important. For most members, their contribution is their content or subject matter knowledge. If the team mission is to improve a business process, team members usually understand at least their own part of the process. If the mission is to sell and service a large account, they need to understand the industry and their specific account. They also need to understand their company's products and how to apply them.

There are other things that team members can provide besides content knowledge. They also have to contribute time to carry out team assignments such as conducting interviews, gathering information, analyzing data, and preparing reports. In some situations, it may even be helpful to have some team members without content knowledge. These members bring a novice's view to the team. They can visualize how things might be because they are not encumbered with the knowledge of how things are. These members do not know why they cannot do something, and so proceed to do it.

Task and relationship skills, as described earlier, are also important. However, team members can acquire these skills through training when the team is formed. They are not a prerequisite to team membership.

## Team Leader

In most teams, one of the team members becomes the *team leader.* The leader may be appointed by management or may be selected by the team members. The job can be a permanent assignment or may rotate periodically among the members. Although specific responsibilities vary from team to team, the leader usually conducts the team meetings and represents the group as the contact point for management and other teams in the organization. To carry out these responsibilities, the leader needs training in team leadership skills.

The team leader may be a manager, supervisor, or nonmanager. However, if the team leader is a manager and the team members normally report to him or her, it is very difficult to keep the team from falling back into the traditional manager and employee relationship. For teams to be effective, members must be comfortable in expressing their ideas and concerns. In addition, the role of the team leader is to facilitate the team processes, not to tell people what to do. When managers try to lead teams made up of their own employees, most find it very difficult to give the team the latitude it needs to carry out its mission. It is too easy to revert to form and intervene, just telling the team members what to do, how to do it, and by when.

## Other Team Member Roles

In addition to the team leader, there are other roles or positions the team may choose to fill. The one common to almost every team is *scribe.* The scribe is a team member, usually selected by the team, to record ideas and suggestions, keep minutes of meetings, and publish the team's output. Because these are clerical activities, the scribe role is usually rotated among the members. However, the fact that the scribe's functions are not exciting and interesting does not mean the role is not important. Team meeting minutes help ensure continuity from one meeting to the next. Good documenting of meeting results helps eliminate the need for the team to go back over the same ground again and again. Communicating team progress and results keeps coworkers and management informed.

Some teams identify requirements for other positions such as *timekeeper* or *parliamentarian.* There are no rules for how teams divide responsibilities. The only objective is that each team's organization contribute to its mission and objectives.

## Specialists

Team members do not always have all the skills, experience, information, or support they need. When this happens, they may ask people outside the team to contribute. These people are referred to as *specialists.* They may be other employees of the company or they may be suppliers, customers, or consultants. They meet with the team when needed and provide information or support, but they generally do not participate in the team decision processes.

## Sponsor

Some companies have identified a need for *team sponsors.* Also known as *champions,* team sponsors are typically managers or executives. Their role varies, but usually includes advocating the team's mission and recommendations, obtaining resources, and helping overcome internal barriers to getting things done. The sponsor is a team resource but not a member and certainly not the manager or leader of the team.

## Facilitator

There is one more role that is necessary for optimum team performance: the *facilitator.* This role differs from the others in several ways. Where the other roles focus primarily on the content dimension of team performance, the facilitator focuses exclusively the two process dimensions, relationship and task. The facilitator's job is to help the team deal with relationship issues and to choose and use effectively the task processes. The facilitator role also differs in that can be filled by someone outside the team, by the team leader, or by the team members themselves.

The role of facilitator is important to team success for several reasons. First, teams go through predictable stages of development as they form and begin to work toward their mission objectives.

During these early stages, teams are not fully functional and at times may even be dysfunctional. Qualified facilitators are trained to recognize these stages and to intervene to help guide the group through them.

Mature teams also experience problems. Project deadlines approach; old members leave and new members join; assignments change; events beyond the team's control affect its performance. Sometimes teams just get stuck on a problem or issue. In these cases, they can benefit from the intervention of a trained facilitator.

Facilitators can also help overcome a cultural problem. Most organizations still reward people for fast action and quick fixes. They frequently fail to take time to determine the root cause of problems, preferring to take some kind of rapid action. This is frequently expressed in the old saw "Ready, Fire, Aim." This approach usually results in fixing symptoms, not solving real problems. Under the pressure of the moment, team members focus on problem content and ignore the important relationship and task dimensions that will lead to a better solution. The facilitator can help the team stay on track, resolve the relationship or people issues, and use effective tools and techniques properly. This approach can result in fixing the root causes of problems so that they never happen again.

The greatest challenge that most facilitators face is staying focused on the relationship and task dimensions and staying out of the content dimension. Some facilitators believe that having no knowledge of the team's subject matter helps them resolve this problem. Another challenge is staying neutral in team discussions. The facilitator's job is to be a completely impartial observer of the team processes, intervening only when needed to help the team reach its own decisions and mission objectives.

The most common role for facilitators of teams is *facilitator as coach*. In this situation, the team leader conducts the meetings, and the facilitator is present to provide assistance and support. If the facilitator observes relationship issues, he or she may intervene, providing guidance and direction. The facilitator may also recognize when the team does not have a tool or technique needed to solve a particular problem. At that point, he or she may demonstrate the technique or provide the necessary training. The facilitator may also help the leader prepare for meetings and provide feedback on the team's and the leader's performance.

As team members work together over time and the team passes through the normal group development stages, it becomes effective and productive. The team leader becomes skilled at facilitation, and team's need for an external facilitator diminishes. At some point, the team becomes self-facilitating as the members learn to recognize and address the relationship and task issues. At some point, the facilitator can withdraw, contributing only when the team reaches an impasse and needs external assistance.

In organizations where teams are formed to solve problems or address short-term opportunities and the people are experienced team members, having a facilitator assigned to a team may not be necessary. However, it is still useful to have one available when needed. Even experienced team members need help from time to time, and the chemistry of every team is different.

In some cases, a facilitator may be called on to lead a team. This *facilitator-as-leader* situation may be appropriate when the team has a short duration assignment to address a problem or opportunity quickly and then disband. This approach has the benefit of moving the team quickly. Its disadvantage is that the team members do not have the opportunity to develop and demonstrate their own leadership skills. Their ownership in the outcome may also be lower.

## Critical Success Factors for Teams

Successful teams don't just happen. Several critical success factors, or CSFs, are required in order for teams to achieve their mission objectives. Some of these CSFs are owned by management, others by the team members.

## CSFs Owned by Management

At least eight critical success factors are owned by management. This is more than twice as many as team members own. That may seem strange at first glance. However, it is simply a reflection of the importance of management's role.

### Mission
Teams need a specific statement of their mission to provide direction and focus for their activities. The team's mission should be

congruent with the organization's overall business strategy, goals, and objectives. For this reason, the mission originates with or is approved by management. It can be general, allowing teams flexibility in choosing specific projects or sales opportunities, or it may be specific, allowing no latitude. In either case, the statement of the mission does not need to be longer than a few sentences.

Although the need for a mission statement sounds obvious, many companies have formed teams, trained the members, and then given them little direction. Without it, teams sometimes pick projects to complete or problems to solve that have little or no positive effect on the business. Many of the early quality circles busied themselves with "quality-of-life" issues or spent hours deciding, for example, where to move the watercooler. When they did, skeptical managers pointed to the team process and said, "See, it doesn't work here." Teams need a mission, and the mission should support business objectives.

### Staffing

The second critical success factor for teams is having the right people on the team and giving them enough time to accomplish their mission. Criteria for team members were discussed earlier in this chapter. The time team members need varies with the team's mission. An improvement team in a sales branch office might meet for an hour a week to identify and solve problems. A process improvement team assignment can require 25 percent or more of each member's time, or it can be a full-time job until the team completes the improvement project. Membership on a sales team will probably be a full-time assignment. A member of a corporate marketing department might work full time on teams but participate in several teams at once. The objective is to ensure that the team members have enough time to address the team's mission.

If team activities are in addition to the members' normal job activities, management is responsible for providing enough time to perform both assignments. When a team is cross-functional and members represent several departments, the managers in all of the functions have to buy into the team's mission. Without this buy-in, the managers will often pull team members away from team activities and back to their normal work assignments.

One way to resolve the conflict between team membership and another current job is to assign people to the team full time. This also makes it possible to accomplish the team's mission more quickly. The disadvantage is that the team members' normal duties have to be assigned to others. In addition, team members are often concerned that an extended assignment on an improvement or special purpose team will take them away from their career path. The leading companies resolve this last issue by recognizing team members for their contribution and making sure that being on a team enhances their careers.

Taking part in improvement teams is a challenge for salespeople, particularly if their commissions represent a high portion of their earnings. Several of the leading companies have come up with creative solutions to that problem. One company reported that its salespeople were on straight commission, so to encourage participation in improvement teams, the company paid salespeople for the time they spent in team meetings. To qualify for payment, the salespeople also had to attain their monthly customer satisfaction objectives.

AccuRate, the dry material feeder company, came up with a different solution. It put together a team of salespeople to improve the company's response time to customer inquiries. To avoid taking selling time, the team met on three Saturday mornings. At the first meeting, team members defined the problem and identified the information they needed. Then they collected data for three months. They met on a second Saturday morning to study the data and redesign their process and set new goals. They then collected data for another three months, to determine how well the new process worked. They met on one more Saturday morning to review the status of the project and put an ongoing measurement in place to make sure they were maintaining their new standard.

Jim Kocher, AccuRate's former president and CEO reports that, "The salespeople are happy with the approach. It did not bite into their selling time. They understand that we want fast response to telephone requests. Their benchmark is IBM. Their goal is for us to respond in one-fourth of the time it takes IBM, and we have been consistently doing that."

Another staffing issue is whether being on a team is voluntary or required. As Eastman Chemical has shown, voluntary teams are very effective when management provides the right mission, training, support, and recognition. However, it is sometimes necessary to require people to take part in a team. This is often the case when specific people have the knowledge, experience, and skills that a team needs. In most cases, these people recognize the need for their participation and will contribute, even when they are being required to do so. As mentioned earlier, in those instances where people do not want to be team members, they can be designated as specialists and provide input to the team when it is needed.

### Resources

Providing adequate resources for a work team is usually not a problem, but it is often overlooked for improvement teams. At a minimum, organizations have to provide an appropriate location for teams to meet and supplies for them to use. For teams with a broader scope and larger mission, resources include a budget for salaries, travel expenses, telephones, personal computers, and fax machines. Funding for external resources such as consultants to design and conduct surveys, assist in benchmarking, or facilitate team meetings may also be necessary.

### Boundaries

Teams need a clear understanding of what they can and cannot do. They need boundaries. Boundaries are like the rules of the game. The mission statement, staffing, and resources form some of the boundaries. Another boundary is also one of the team attributes: its authority. If the mission of the team is to solve a problem, are the members empowered the do whatever it takes to solve it, or are they limited to identifying the causes and recommending solutions to management? Whom can they interview? Department members? People outside their department? External suppliers? Customers? Are there any sacred cows? Are any solutions off limits? What are the financial limits? How much time do they have?

This is one of the most frequently overlooked of the critical success factors, but without clearly specified boundaries teams will create their own. Sometimes this results in timid solutions when bold steps are needed. Other times, massive solutions are designed when time and resources are not available to implement them. However, in today's environment it is probably better to be too bold than too timid. As the old saying goes, "It is always easier to ask forgiveness than permission."

## Training

Although most companies do an adequate job of training in the task skills, many fail to include relationship skills. With good interpersonal and relationship skills, team members move more quickly through the stages of team development and became productive in less time. The members are better able to react when conflicts arise, missions change, new members join, and the team encounters challenges. This training does not require a major time investment; one to three days is adequate.

However, training alone will not ensure that team members will retain or use the relationship or task skills. Managers must measure, recognize, and reward the new skills and behaviors if they are to be applied on the job. The team leader, facilitator, and other team members must also support their use. Without continued reinforcement, the skills will be lost.

People will also lose their skills if they do not apply them. For this reason, it is a good idea to provide team members with the relationship skills and just the minimum of problem-solving skills during initial training. Then provide training in additional tools and techniques as the team members need it. This just-in-time approach to training ensures that team members will learn each technique at the same time that they need and can apply it. Adults learn best by doing. They pay attention best when what they are learning has immediate application. The old advice "Use it or lose it" applies here.

Never assume that training by itself will cause change. According to Jack Caffey, now Hewlett Packard's quality manager in the Professional Services Organization, there was a time at Hewlett Packard when people believed that "if we simply train everyone on the tools, their productivity would improve." In the early days of the quality improvement process at IBM, the same idea prevailed. Business units measured their success by the percentage of people who received training. Never mind that after they were trained, they went back to their regular jobs and did the same things the same way they had always done them. IBM and Hewlett Packard were certainly not unique in the belief that training produces change. However important as training is, it is only one of the critical success factors, and it must be provided at the right time and reinforced by management and peers.

*Facilitation*

Facilitation is the process of helping teams achieve their mission objectives through a focus on their relationship and task processes. This is a requirement for teams at every level in the organization regardless of their scope, size, mission, authority, or duration. Facilitation is particularly important to new teams made up of first-time team members.

With good facilitation, teams become productive more quickly and produce better results. Team members have higher morale and practice interpersonal skills that they can apply in other areas of their work. Managers have to recognize the importance of good facilitation and support it. They do this by encouraging teams to focus on relationship and task processes as well as the content of the team mission. Managers also provide the funding and head-count for team facilitators.

*Support*

In addition to providing the necessary staffing, resources, training, and facilitation, it is up to management to help teams when they run into organizational barriers. These barriers exist in every company. Teams encounter them among the silos of the old functional organization, with its conflicting measurements, goals, and objectives. Sometimes the barriers are managers who have retired in place and want to avoid change at any cost. Sometimes they are executives' pet projects, processes, products, or departments, the organization's sacred cows. These barriers prevent improvement teams from solving problems or making processes more effective and efficient. They stifle innovation and creativity in sales and marketing. In most cases, only management can overcome these barriers. If the team mission is not important enough for management to do that, the existence of the team is probably questionable anyway.

*Measurements*

Boundaries define the field of play; measurements tell the team how the game will be scored. It is up to management to establish or approve measurements of success before the game begins and to ensure that the measures tie into the team's performance and mission. There are two kinds of measurements important here:

performance and mission. Performance measurements show the team how well it is meeting team operating objectives such as schedules or budgets. Mission measurements relate to the team's project. A problem-solving team in a sales office could measure the reduction of customer complaints or of errors in proposals submitted or orders entered. A process improvement team could measure the reduction in cycle time. A sales team could measure revenue growth, profitability, and customer satisfaction. A marketing team could measure internal client satisfaction with the marketing materials it produces. Whatever the case, the team needs to know what is going to be measured and what the targets are.

Management is also responsible for making sure that every team member's performance is measured and evaluated and that the results are communicated to the team member. Consider the challenge of the managers in corporate marketing communications at Steelcase. The marketing professionals who report to them may work on several teams at once, most of which are sponsored by other managers. How do managers get input on employees' individual performances? There are several ways; the most important is customer feedback. The customers in this case are the product owners in the business units—they receive the output from the corporate communications teams. These internal customers are the final judges of how well the team's output meets their requirements, and they are in the best position to provide feedback on the performance of the teams and their members. They give their evaluations to the team members' managers, who consolidate the feedback information and present it to each employee during his or her formal appraisal.

Peer group evaluation is another way to give performance feedback to team members. Using this approach, team members evaluate their peers' contribution. They may provide the input to their peer's managers, who consolidate the information and give feedback to the employees in the appraisal session. They may also give the feedback directly to their teammates. Regardless of how the information is gathered and delivered, one of the key measurements of individual performance is how well each member works in the team environment.

## CSFs Owned by Team Members

Not all of the critical success factors for teams are management's responsibility. Here are three that the team owns.

### Mission

Although management establishes the team's mission, the team must understand it, believe it is important, and accept it. One of the team's first steps is to review its assigned mission. Team members may want to restate the mission in their own words. If they do, they will need to review the restatement with management. If management has given them a broad mission, team members may want to create a more narrow statement, to define the way they plan to go about accomplishing the mission or the specific area on which they plan to focus.

When the team reviews its mission with management, team members can also confirm their understanding of their resources, boundaries, and measurements. Having a clear understanding and agreement up front will help prevent the team from going astray and will avoid disappointments and wasted time and effort later.

### Team Process

The second critical success factor owned by teams is maintaining a balance between the content of their mission and the relationship and task processes. One way that teams do this is by creating a list of operating guidelines. In some organizations, these guidelines are referred to as a code of conduct or aspired-to norms. They represent the behaviors that team members agree will make them an effective team. A typical list of operating guidelines has from six to twelve items. It might include agreements to

- Show respect for others
- Speak when no one else is talking
- Meet commitments to team assignments
- Focus on problems, not people
- Follow accepted group problem-solving and decision processes

Teams post their guidelines during meetings as a constant reminder of how the members have agreed to work together. The posted list also helps facilitators, who can refer to the list as an intervention to dysfunctional team behaviors. Over time, these aspired-to norms become part of the team culture.

### *Flexibility*

Flexibility is a critical success factor that applies to the methods the team uses and the solutions the members create. Flexibility begins with a willingness to ask penetrating questions, to challenge the way the organization has always done things, and to challenge the beliefs and assumptions upon which the organization makes decisions. Flexibility includes thinking creatively to develop new approaches and taking the risks that may be necessary to try these approaches. It also applies to the team's internal processes. If one approach to solving a problem, improving a process, or turning around a competitive situation does not work, the flexible team will try another one. Successful teams are willing to "think outside of the box."

## Issues in Sales and Marketing Teams

Teams that include salespeople present some special issues that go beyond the critical success factors common to all teams. These include goal alignment, recognition, compensation, and geography.

## Goal Alignment

*Goal alignment* refers to the idea that within an organization there are common goals shared by everyone and there may also be individual or departmental goals. Where there are individual or departmental goals, they do not conflict with the goals of other individuals or departments, and they support, or align with, the common organization goals. When a team has goal alignment, the team members share a common goal: attaining the team mission. They may also have personal goals, but these goals are not in conflict with the goals of the team or of other team members.

The issue of goal alignment sometimes arises on cross-functional teams, where members come from different departments. Pitney Bowes recognized the problem when teams were created in the company's sales branch offices. Jaci Allen, Pitney Bowes' director of marketing quality at the time, says: "We had different measurements for administration, service, and salespeople in the branches. For example, the customer service manager was measured on service contracts, the salesperson on new equipment. If a service contract on an old piece of equipment was canceled when a new piece of equipment was sold, the service manager lost ground while the salesperson was rewarded. If a service agreement was sold on an old piece of equipment instead of selling a new piece of equipment, the service manager gained and the salesperson lost." Pitney Bowes resolved the issue by creating a team objective, using customer satisfaction measurements to align branch functions. This objective is a significant factor in sales, service, and administration management compensation.

Improvement team goals of solving problems and improving processes may also appear to conflict with short-term sales goals. At one company, salespeople were included in a headquarters cross-functional improvement team. Everything went well until sales dipped. The sales objectives then took precedence over the team's mission. The salespeople dropped out of the team to devote full time to their sales territories. The improvement team lost valuable members, and the action sent an unwanted message to everyone: short-term sales goals are more important than long-term improvement in the company's operations. This is not to say that short-term sales goals are not important. However, given the long sell cycle for this particular company's products, having the salespeople spend a little more time in the territory had little effect on short-term sales.

## Recognition and Rewards

Salespeople seem to be the center of attention in many companies. When they close a big order, they receive congratulations from their managers and peers. Whey they reach their annual sales objectives, they are recognized again and often receive awards, bonuses, and travel to a recognition event. For most salespeople, recognition is one of the things they like most about their job.

In the traditional sales office, the people who support the sales effort often do not receive similar recognition. They are forgotten, or remembered just in passing, while the salespeople bask in the spotlight of success. Yet no one questions their contribution. A secretary works over a weekend to get a major proposal typed. An administrative person gets a commitment for expedited delivery. A financial person comes up with a creative pricing scheme and special financing. The list of people who contribute to a major sales effort, or even the day-to-day activities in a sales office, goes on. A sale really is a team effort.

The leading companies are finding creative ways to recognize these team efforts. This is especially important when the company designates everyone involved as an account or customer team, and the members work together toward a common set of mission objectives. Certainly teams have most valuable players, but the MVP on a football team is not always the quarterback. On a sales team, the MVP in every competitive win is not always the salesperson. For cross-functional sales teams to be effective, everyone has to be recognized in proportion to his or her contribution. In many sales organizations, sales contests are a favorite motivational tool and form of recognition. Yet because they pit salespeople against each other, they discourage cooperation and teamwork. There is already plenty of competition outside the organization. In addition, internal contests usually recognize the individual salesperson, not the supporting team members.

Ken Norland, president of DSSI, a software value-added remarketer, describes his reaction to a contest run by a major software supplier. "I was furious when they announced the contest. I know of no better way to be divisive in a company than have a contest that pits salespeople against each other, particularly in a complex business like this where there are no single person sales. This type of product always requires a team sell." By the way, that isn't sour grapes. A DSSI salesperson won the contest. (DSSI has since been acquired by Ernst & Young.)

## Compensation

Most companies continue to use some form of commissions and bonuses as incentives for their salespeople. Many of these organizations are now forming account teams to cover their key customers, geographical territories, or specific industry accounts. These teams include people who have never been on an incentive plan before. This creates a dilemma. How should the team members be compensated? There is no one right answer to that question. It depends on the specific company, the industry, and the team's mission and objectives. Whatever the compensation package looks like, however, it has to support the team's common objectives, avoid creating contention and disunity, and be fair to all team members.

If a team's mission is simply to generate sales and everyone on the team works to attain that objective, then some form of commission or bonus plan may appropriate for everyone. This does not mean that everyone has to be paid the same amount of money or have the same percentage of total earnings come from commissions. However, everyone should be compensated when the team sells something.

Compensation becomes more complex when the team includes people who have very different responsibilities and provide different services to the customer. Consider a sales office in a typical office equipment company. There are several distinct functions including sales, installation and service, technical support and training, and administration. Each function has its own set of objectives. When people from all four functions are put on an account team, these objectives don't necessarily go away. The team is now responsible for the objectives in sales, service, technical support, and administration.

To design a compensation package for a team with this mix of functions, first look at the objectives for putting the team together. Then design a plan that supports those objectives. The objectives might be to increase customer satisfaction, support a customer partnership, or gain a higher share of a customer's business. Assume, for example, that the objective of forming account teams at our hypothetical office equipment company is to support long-term mutually profitable relationships. The team could be measured and compensated on customer satisfaction and loyalty and on profitability. In other words, the team members make more money if the customer is happy and likely to continue to buy and the company is making money.

Having a common set of objectives for team members does not rule out an individual component to earnings. It also does not exclude individual measurements as long as they are not in conflict with the team's overall mission and objective. For example, the service representative on the office equipment company team may be measured on how long it takes to install or repair a piece of equipment. An individual bonus may be tied to maintaining a certain standard. This measurement does not conflict with overall customer satisfaction and profitability. It supports those goals.

Account team compensation is still an open issue, and companies are experimenting with various approaches. Some are actually moving away from commissions to straight salary for team members. Others are paying team members a salary and adding periodic bonuses for attaining team objectives. Still others pay bonuses that combine individual and team performance in some way. The individual performance may be on a hard measurement such as a personal sales quota or it may be on soft measurement such as peer group evaluation of a person's contribution. Several companies have implemented division- or companywide profit sharing plans to add a third level to individual and team compensation.

## Remote Salespeople

We have already discussed the benefits of having salespeople participate in improvement teams, but when these salespeople are in remote locations, the benefits come at the expense of time out of the sales territory and travel and living costs. Most of the leading companies believe that the benefits are worth the investment.

Getting remote salespeople trained in team, problem-solving, and process improvement skills is no small feat. One approach comes from Globe Metallurgical. Their larger customers such as GM, Ford, Chrysler, and Dow Corning all have their own in-house training groups and make courses available to their suppliers. Globe's salespeople take advantage of their customers' training offers. This approach has the added benefit that Globe salespeople learn customers' terminology and techniques. This gives them the skills they need to take part in customer teams.

A manufacturer of packaging materials with a twenty-two-person remote salesforce included two days of quality training as part of its annual sales meeting. Other companies take advantage of training offered at industry shows and conferences or provide training videos, self-guided study courses, or computer-assisted training to their salespeople. However, once again, salespeople need to use the skills they learn. Without reinforcement, they will soon lose them.

Companies have found several ways to involve remote salespeople in cross-functional improvement teams. Obviously the most expensive is to bring the salespeople into headquarters for periodic team meetings. In this case, organizing the team around fewer and longer meetings helps reduce the number of trips and makes for a more efficient team. Another approach is to bring salespeople in for full-time temporary duty assignments. This is usually the most cost efficient and accomplishes the team mission quickly. However, it does leave the salesperson's territory uncovered for the duration of the assignment.

One communication tool frequently ignored but very effective is teleconferencing. All salespeople need to take part in team meetings is a telephone. Teleconferencing in conjunction with a few well-planned face-to-face meetings is also a relatively cost-effective approach. (Chapter Seven discusses other forms of technology for including remote salespeople on cross-functional teams.)

## When to Use a Team (and When Not To)

Throughout this chapter, we have seen how leading companies are using teams successfully in sales and marketing. These teams are solving problems, improving processes, addressing opportunities, and even managing projects. However, this does not mean that teams should be used in every situation. Following are some guidelines to help you decide where teams fit in your sales and marketing organizations.

First, review the critical success factors for teams. These are virtually universal and most are owned by management. They must be addressed if teams are to succeed anywhere in the organization. Then ask these questions:

- Is management really committed to the use of teams?
- Will management address the critical success factors?
- Is management willing to delegate the necessary authority that the teams need to carry out their missions?

If the answer to any of these questions is no, then attempting to use teams will just frustrate the team members and will not achieve team objectives. If the answer to all of these questions is yes, the next step is to consider the benefits of using teams and decide how important these benefits are to the organization. To review, using teams results in

- Creative new ways to address opportunities, solve problems, and improve business processes
- Cooperation, coordination, and communication, particularly among people from different departments or functions
- Commitment to a course of action
- Greater productivity
- Better use of people's skills and abilities
- Personal development of team members
- Higher morale among team members

Now let's look at the situations where teams work well. First, teams are very effective for solving problems. They have become a cornerstone of the quality improvement efforts in most companies. When considering whether to use a team to address a problem, it is easier to first decide when not to use a team. Here are the circumstances that preclude team use.

- *When there is no time for discussion.* When there is a fire, people don't form teams to determine the cause, they get out of the burning building.
- *When the problem is not important.* No one gets enthusiastic about solving a problem that is not important, not even as a practice exercise in team training.
- *When the solution is already known.* Teams have been formed to get buy-in to predetermined solutions. This is a waste of time and does not work.
- *When the subject is someone's job assignment.* Giving a problem to a team after it has already been assigned to someone to solve is no different than assigning the same task to two different people. It is a poor management practice.
- *When one individual has greater expertise.* When one person is an expert and has the ability to solve a problem and when other team members do not bring anything to the table, the team is redundant.

As we have seen, teams are also the organization of choice in business process improvement. By creating a team with representatives from every major activity in the process as well as suppliers and customers, all major interests are represented. The team members have the knowledge needed to document how the process currently works, establish customer requirements, measure the process output, identify problems, analyze the steps, and make or recommend improvements. Even when people from outside a process are used to improve that process, they need input from those who actually do the work, and the people outside the process will still function best as a team.

Sales teams work well in covering large key customers. These large-account sales teams work toward common customerwide goals and sales objectives. Although everyone on the team is a salesperson, each one may bring a different set of skills or expertise to the customer. The large-account sales team also provides backup when individual members are ill, on vacation, or away for business reasons. Senior team members help train, develop, and mentor younger members. As senior members leave, the newer members are then ready to move up to greater levels of responsibility. These teams also offer continuity to their customers even though individual team members may leave and new members may join the teams.

Many companies are using customer teams that include salespeople and representatives from other functions such as the technical, financial, administrative, and service areas. These cross-functional teams work well in sales territories with accounts in a specific industry or geographical location as well as with large accounts. They encourage goal alignment and focus on their customers' needs rather than the often disparate objectives of several internal company departments.

Putting sales teams in place has to make sense, particularly to the salespeople who are on them. Just assigning all the salespeople in a sales office to a team and giving them a common sales objective does not meet this criterion. Salespeople usually refer to this as socialism, or worse. The best salespeople carry the team, the poor performers hide, and productivity and morale go down.

In the marketing department, many of the activities are project oriented. They require people from various disciplines working closely together toward a common objective. A new product announcement might require expertise in organizing and conducting business shows, writing press releases, designing and publishing brochures and catalogues, and identifying prospective customers. At Steelcase, the product launch team includes people from the marketing communications group and possibly outside suppliers. Marketing may also have participants in cross-functional product development teams, such as Ford's Team Taurus or Chrysler's platform teams.

Not every activity in marketing is a team effort. Consider creative functions such as the artwork for a brochure, the design of a catalogue, or the copy for an advertisement. All of these efforts are probably best left to the individual creative people. They may be team members when it comes to coordinating the project and ensuring a common theme, but they are artists when it comes to their professions.

## Conclusion

Teams are not appropriate for everyone or in every situation, but virtually every organization can benefit from expanding its use of teams. This is especially true of sales and marketing departments. They can apply teams in almost every combination of scope, size, mission, authority, and duration. These teams build on the synergy of the team members, improve communication and buy-in, increase productivity, raise employee morale, and provide a forum for personal development. To achieve these benefits from sales and marketing teams, organizations must be prepared to address both the critical success factors and the issues unique to teams in sales and marketing. When they do, they have taken another major step toward an open organization culture, the subject of the next chapter.

# Chapter Six

# Practice an Open Organization Culture

"If you always do what you always did, you will always get what you always got." This old Irish proverb held true in business for many years, and company cultures evolved that worked in relatively stable environments. These cultures came about during a time when external market forces and technology were changing slowly, if at all. Competition was not as great and certainly not global. In manufacturing, production runs were long, models were few, changes predictable, and customers easy to satisfy. Companies could decide what they wanted to make and sell without paying too much attention to their customers' wants and needs. Employees were not as well educated, and many were just happy to have a job. The culture promoted the status quo and resisted major and rapid change.

That's all changed. Organizations are realizing that "if you always do what you always did, you will always get what you always got, *until the situation changes.*" In today's business environment, that is almost daily. For survival, organizations need a culture that supports continuous change and improvement. Some are fortunate enough to have had such a culture from their inception. Others have recognized that some elements of their current culture are no longer serving them well, and they are transforming these elements. They are managing for change, listening to their customers, focusing on processes, and using teams. These practices and the others described in this chapter make up the *open organization culture.*

The term open organization culture comes from the U.S. General Accounting Office study (1991) of the early Baldrige Award finalists, where it was used to describe the leading companies' *flexibility, innovation, elimination of internal barriers,* and *high morale.* All of these are important, but an open organization culture includes more than just these four things. This book uses the term to refer to a series of elements that when practiced together, promote continuous growth and improvement.

## Elements of the Open Organization Culture

Members of an open organization culture practice a high degree of awareness about what is going on within the organization itself, their industry as a whole, their customers, and the world around them. Although they focus on their individual, team, and department missions, they also take a global view of the organization and how it fits together with its suppliers, customers, consumers, and the community.

The members of an open organization listen to their customers, suppliers, and employees and take action on what they learn. The culture fosters an open sharing of information. It encourages creativity and innovation in the organization's products and services and in its processes and methods. People measure the results of their actions, celebrate successes, and reflect on and learn from their failures. All these behavior patterns are based on mutual trust throughout the organization.

Contrast these behaviors with what happens in companies with a closed culture. There, people appear to lack awareness beyond their own area of responsibility. They take a personal or departmental view and are either not conscious of or not concerned about the ways their actions relate to internal and external customers and suppliers. They function in a state of organizational numbness. In the closed organization culture, people withhold information, based on the mistaken belief that information kept to oneself is power. The culture discourages risk, innovation, and even change itself. Measurements are usually limited to financial performance. People in closed organization cultures rarely listen to their customers, and when they do they resist taking meaningful action on the basis of what they learn. The prevailing attitude in most closed cultures is one of distrust.

Table 6.1 contrasts additional characteristics of open and closed cultures in a sales organization. These are cultural extremes

**Table 6.1. Open and Closed Cultures in Sales Organizations.**

| Open Culture | Closed Culture |
|---|---|
| Sales management recognizes a trend toward customer partnerships and changes the way it measures and compensates salespeople to encourage long-term relationship sales. | Sales management ignores a trend toward customer partnerships and maintains a 60–year-old full-commission sales plan that encourages small, short-term sales. |
| Salespeople accept changes in the way they sell and support products and services. | Salespeople resist using new sales tactics. |
| The sales department is flexible and responsive in dealing with customers. | The sales department is rigid and bureaucratic in dealing with customers. |
| Sales management encourages salespeople to try new approaches to selling and supporting their customers. | Sales management insists on selling the way it has always been done. |
| Management encourages cooperation and teamwork among salespeople. | Management encourages competition among salespeople. |
| The sales department works closely with others in the organization to serve the customer. | Departments are organizational silos, often competing with each other. |
| Salespeople share information with each other and with other departments. | Salespeople withhold information. |
| Everyone questions everything, looking for ways to improve; there are no sacred cows. | People generally accept the status quo; "This is the way it has always been." |
| People and teams are empowered; front-line salespeople can make decisions. | Management makes all major decisions |
| The sales organization learns and improves continuously. | The sales organization frequently repeats the same mistakes. |
| Relationships between the company, the sales function, distribution partners, and customers are based on openness and trust. | Relationships between the company, the sales function, distribution partners, and customers are based on secrecy and fear. |

of course. In reality, no organization culture is completely open or closed. The degree of openness varies within the organization by individual, department, and division. Even so, the point remains that cultures in the leading companies tend to be more open than those in other companies.

The remainder of this chapter examines these seven characteristics of an open culture: practicing awareness, taking a global view, questioning everything, sharing information, taking informed action, empowering people and teams, and learning and improving continuously.

## Practice Awareness

A cornerstone of the open organization culture is *awareness*. To practice awareness means to be conscious of what is going on beyond one's immediate job, activity, or project. This is not always easy when people are confronted with managing today's problem or project or attaining this month's sales quota. Without awareness, however, the organization does not have the benefit of knowing what is going on in the world around it.

The leading companies encourage their people to practice awareness, and they are receptive to the timely information and knowledge that awareness brings. With heightened awareness comes faster recognition of social, political, and industry trends; changes in customer requirements; emerging markets; new technologies; and competitive activities. Companies use this information to design new products and services, develop new ways to add value and serve customers, improve business processes, and create new marketing and sales approaches.

Awareness can be passive or active, and members of the leading companies practice both types. People who are passively aware are paying some attention to things going on around them, including things beyond the sphere of their normal work responsibilities, but they are not necessarily looking for a new product or service idea, a way to solve a problem, or a way to improve a process. However, by being cognizant of their environment, they are constantly getting new ideas and insights that they can apply when needed. Recall how Sony recognized the need for a portable tape cassette player and developed the Walkman. That product came from the CEO's observation of how young people carried and used the boom boxes available at the time.

People who are actively aware are paying attention beyond the bounds of their everyday work environment in seeking new information and ideas. Obviously active awareness involves listening to customers and benchmarking world-class organizations. It also includes reading books and periodicals, taking part in outside organizations, attending seminars and conferences, and networking with professionals in other companies. Although all of these sound obvious, it is amazing how many companies do not encourage their people to take advantage of the learning opportunities that exist. Some cultures even discourage the input that awareness can bring.

In their book *Flight of the Buffalo* (1993), James A. Belasco and Ralph C. Stayer describe an active awareness program in one company. The company borrowed the approach from author John Naisbitt and from the CIA, and they call it "clip, scan and review." Everyone in the company *scans* ten periodicals that he or she does not already normally read each month. Each person *clips* all the articles he or she thinks are interesting regarding future trends and puts them into a file folder. People clip advertisements, articles, opinion letters, anything they think will have any potential impact on the business in the future, no matter how far-fetched it may seem at the time. The entire company is divided into seven-member interdepartmental "review cells," and people circulate their file folders of clipped articles to the other members of their review cell monthly, so that everyone reviews the clippings in all seven file folders.

Quarterly the seven members of each review cell meet and discuss the important trends they noticed in the clipped material they reviewed. The discussion is built around three questions:

- What is the future event that will have the greatest impact on our business?
- What will happen when that event happens?
- What can we do now to prepare for that event?

Every six months, the trends are reviewed, and the results are shared around the company. Belasco and Stayer report: "We get lots of ideas. Imagine having seven hundred people all scanning, clipping and reviewing! We don't get blindsided anymore. We hear the footsteps. Our customers come to us to find out what's coming. We get lots of discussion about appropriate actions. And we get lots of commitment to a future course of action once the discussions are done" (pp. 129–135).

Although this program may be a bit formal for most organizations, it does exemplify what it means to truly practice awareness.

Most managers are not conscious of the idea of awareness. However, managers in the leading companies invite it through their own behaviors and the policies and business practices of their organizations. They are role models of the behaviors they value, practicing passive and active awareness themselves. They expose themselves to new information and ideas through books and magazines, audiocassette programs, conferences, seminars, and classes. Frequently they are active members of professional associations.

The leading companies encourage awareness in their employees. They recognize them for their insights and new ideas with everything from a pat on the back to formal recognition and rewards. They promote employee learning by paying some or all of the costs of professional association memberships, seminar and conference fees, subscriptions, and books. They also reinforce their desire for the input that awareness brings by being receptive to the new information and new ideas that come with it.

## Take a Global View

In today's high-stress sales and marketing environments, it is easy to get caught up in the crisis of the moment. There are competitive activities, new product launches, customer demands, and a host of other day-to-day issues. These situations all require a highly focused, localized view. This narrowing is compounded in closed organization cultures, which tend to take the parochial view even in the best of circumstances. However, companies with open organization cultures encourage their people at every level to step back from the pressures of their individual and departmental responsibilities and take a global view.

Taking a global view means looking beyond the boundaries of an individual job or department. The global view can be taken from two perspectives. The *organizational perspective* shows how people are grouped together, or organized, and how the groups appear and relate to each other. The *systems perspective* shows how work really gets done through processes and how these processes combine to form systems. The organizational perspective is much more common. People tend to think in terms of their company, division, department, and team rather than in terms of the processes and systems in which they participate. However, both perspectives are valuable in improving sales and marketing.

## Organizational Perspective

When a global view is taken from an organizational perspective, the first step back provides a companywide look, showing how the various departments and divisions are arranged within the company. Another step back brings customers and suppliers into the picture. A third step back provides a view of all the elements in the supply chain and the environment in which that chain operates. The view at each level brings a progressively greater degree of awareness of how all the parts fit together. Knowing how they fit together and how they relate to each other is important to the improvement process.

### Companywide View

Taking a companywide view confirms some of the benefits of the functional organization. For many tasks and activities, it is more efficient. Putting people of similar skills together in one department may mean that the company needs fewer people to do the same amount of work. A purchasing department may make it possible to consolidate orders, reduce the number of suppliers, and get volume discounts. A consolidated marketing function makes for more efficiency and makes it easier to coordinate programs, integrate marketing communications, and project a single image to customers. A consolidated salesforce means one point of contact for the customer. When people are grouped by their function or profession, the management tasks of training, evaluation, compensation, and career development are also easier.

However, a global view of the company also shows the disadvantages of a functional organization. Departments and divisions tend to develop a silo mentality, becoming ingrown and forgetting that their objective is to serve their customers. They create processes designed to make life easier for themselves rather than to serve the best interests of their customers and the company as a whole. Because the company measures the performance of each department and division, they compete with each other, often to the detriment of the company and its customers.

As companies grow, they frequently create whole divisions for each new product line. These divisions are often self-contained and include all the functions they need to develop, market, deliver, and support their products and services, including a dedicated salesforce. With a limited number of products, the salespeople can become product experts. With complete control of the product from development through delivery, division management can be held completely accountable for their business performance.

Taking a global view from the organizational perspective, however, uncovers some problems with this approach. First, the company may have salespeople from several divisions calling on the same customer. This is not only an inefficient use of resources, it runs counter to most customers' objective of reducing the number of salespeople calling on them. In addition, if there is an overlap in the product lines, the customer may receive competing proposals from the same company. When a single company submits multiple proposals, the message is clear. The company does not know the best solution, and it is up to the customer to figure it out. Also, unless the activities and processes of the divisions are coordinated, the customer may receive multiple billings and work under different contracts with different terms and conditions. From the customer's view, it is almost the same as dealing with different companies.

Consider the challenge facing GE chairman Jack Welch in 1987. He had just taken General Electric through a major restructuring, acquiring new businesses and selling off old ones. The result was a company made up of twelve major businesses in three groups. The businesses ranged from aircraft engines, medical systems imaging, and engineered materials in the high-technology group to major appliances, electric motors, power generation equipment, and lighting in the core group. The third and fastest-growing group was financial services. It included business such as insurance, leasing, brokerage, and the NBC network. Some of the businesses were new to the GE family and culture; others had been part of the organization for decades. Each of these widely diverse business units was highly independent.

As GE's former Western Area manager Gary Hessenauer explains: "We had twelve businesses operating independently of each other. It was conceivable that ten to twelve of them could be calling on the same customer. They would be calling at different levels and selling different products. They would be stumbling over each other, without regard for the impact that their actions and message might have on the other GE businesses. Each business unit was responsible for selling its product or service and was measured independently of the other businesses."

Although the business units operated independently, the customers viewed GE as a single company. This created a problem within GE when a customer had an issue with one of the business units. The customer would often leverage a purchase from one GE business unit against an unresolved issue with another. This led to contention between the two business units. Frequently the customer would get involved in the conflict as well. It was clear to Jack Welch that the company needed to find a new approach to ensure that company sales efforts were efficient and that the company presented a single image to its customers.

GE began by dividing the country into four geographical areas and assigning a manager to each one. These four area managers were charged with finding ways to coordinate sales activities, encourage communications, and leverage GE's resources across all twelve business units within their areas. These managers reported directly to GE headquarters. They had no line authority and only a small staff to accomplish their objectives. The salespeople continued to report to their respective business units where they were measured on traditional short-term sales goals.

The corporate area managers had the unenviable task of leading twelve independent businesses that initially did not want to be led. To accomplish the assignment, each corporate area manager formed a council. The council members were senior managers from each of the operating units within the twelve GE businesses. The councils began to meet periodically with the corporate area manager to identify and discuss common issues and opportunities. Although the individual operating units continued to be responsible for their short-term sales goals, they also learned to work together in a coordinated fashion for the best long-term interests of their customers and the corporation. When customer issues were raised, the deciding factor was, "What is best for the customer."

The area councils were emulating GE's corporate executive council. That council is made up of the chairman, the CEO, the business unit leaders, and the corporate staff. Its objective is to take a global view of the organization. Although in the past business units had focused on their individual issues without regard to the rest of the organization, that was not consistent with Jack Welch's vision for the company. He wants GE people to share processes and resources and work together as a team. The corporate council provides the structure for the business leaders to focus on what they need to do to fuel the overall GE engine.

Where the corporate executive council took a companywide view, the area councils were concerned about the sales and customer issues within their geographical boundaries. The corporation gave the area councils the vision, scope, and power to do what made sense to resolve issues and address opportunities. By creating the area councils in the image of the corporate executive council, GE demonstrated its commitment to the approach and objectives. This helped get the participation and cooperation of the area council members. It also helped that the corporate area managers had the ear of GE's senior leadership when they needed support and resources.

The Western Area council communicated the vision of GE as one company in several ways. They developed programs to take high-potential people from one business and move them to another business. They provided a forum for sharing tactical information across the business units and resolving inter-business-unit issues. Although the business units still paid their salespeople on the sale of unit products, the council developed ways to recognize and reward those salespeople who supported the single company vision. For example, if a salesperson in lighting saw an opportunity for leasing and passed the lead on to GE Capital, he or she could receive a cash award and be recognized by senior management. The message to the salespeople was clear. They did not have to support the vision; it wouldn't be a black mark against them, but the world would pass them by.

GE used two measurements to determine the success of the project: the rate of sales growth and the ability to achieve and sustain significant productivity gains. Gary Hessenauer reports that in the first five years, in his area alone, sales more than doubled. The annualized revenue growth rate was over three times the rate of the company as a whole. The productivity gains in the salesforce were more difficult to measure. However, a conservative estimate of the value of the time salespeople saved by sharing information was $5 million, and that was just in one of the four geographical areas. By the end of the first five years, the project was clearly a success.

Jack Welch's global view of GE's companywide organization and its twelve independent businesses led to this unique management system. Considered an experiment in the late 1980s, it continues to evolve and represents a change in GE's culture from the old silo mentality to a single company attitude. In the west, the area council is now fostering local councils organized in its own image. This makes the benefits of the global view approach available on a local level, reaching more salespeople and the smaller customers.

### Distribution System View

Most companies do not own the complete relationship with the end users or consumers of their products or services. They work in concert with some combination of agents, brokers, distributors, dealers, retailers, franchisees, manufacturers' representatives, and other service providers to create a system to market and sell and service their products. The global view reveals how all of these organizations relate to each other and work together. Take the simplest of examples, a two-tier distribution channel in the PC software industry. It includes a software developer, dealers, and customers. From the standpoint of the software developer, who is the customer—the dealer who sells the product or the end user who purchases the product? The answer is both. The dealer is a customer, receiving packaged copies of the PC programs, marketing materials, product support information, and invoices. However, the dealer is not the user of the PC software, at least not in any significant quantity. The end user is the ultimate customer. The user sets the functional requirements for the product and the system that sells it, makes it available, and supports it. The global view shows the dealer as a key part of the system, adding value by stocking and selling the product, collecting license fees, and possibly providing local training and support. As a part of the sales, delivery, and support system, the dealer must also be part of the improvement process.

In this example, the opportunities for improving the distribution system lie in three different organizations. As the number of entities in the channel increases, taking a global view becomes even more important. The complexity grows with each additional level, and the chances for suboptimizing parts of the system also increase. Obviously, many companies are taking a global view and realizing that an easy way to improve the distribution system is to reduce the number of organizations involved.

Companies that take a global view recognize that nothing really happens until their product or service is used. They see that they are partners with every other organization in the system sharing a common goal. Their goal is to create long-term mutually profitable relationships with satisfied and loyal end users or consumers. To do that, it is in their mutual best interest for these organizations to recognize that they are all part of a system and to work together to improve that system and the processes that make it up.

To take a distribution system view and understand the system, they begin by creating a high-level functional flowchart, or process map, to show how the company and its partners work together to develop, sell, deliver, and support products and services. As we saw in Chapter Four, the process map shows the steps that make up the processes within the system and the organization that carries out each one. It also reveals redundant activities and possible gaps, things that are not getting done but that should be. An analysis of each activity shows how much real value it adds.

By seeing how the system really works, the partners can identify what they can do together to achieve their common goals. The process map will highlight ways to streamline the processes. The partners can eliminate the duplicate and non-value-added steps and identify needed activities not being done by anyone. Just as companies improve their internal processes, the partners can work together to improve their system to reduce cycle time, take out cost, and better serve the real customer. They also realize that it is in their best interest to eliminate contention and to support each other to strengthen the system.

The Wheelabrator Corporation in LaGrange, Georgia, knows the value of viewing distributors as a key part of the product sales and delivery system. Wheelabrator gets its major distributors involved in the decision-making process, determining which products to offer and how to sell them. The forum used is a council made up of the largest distributors from around the country.

To make the decision process work, Wheelabrator opens its books to show the council members where the division stands, whether it is making or losing money, and what resources are available for new product development and marketing programs. With that information, the council members are in a position to give Wheelabrator input on which new products to pursue and how to allocate the marketing budget. Before the distributors had the financial information, they could not understand why the division did not want to or was not able to participate in a trade show or run an ad in a trade publication. Now that they are aware of the costs of each marketing activity, the distributors can weigh its benefits for themselves.

The members of the distributor council are even beginning to reach consensus on their decisions. According to Wheelabrator's Tom Warren, "They recognize that the council's decisions are for the organization as a whole, and the organization is not just Wheelabrator. They also know that for them to be successful, Wheelabrator must be successful." The council members may decide to support a certain product line, for example. One distributor may not have a place to sell that line but will support the decision because he or she recognizes that the decision is for the good of the overall organization. The process is based on trust. Wheelabrator has had to be willing to open the books to everyone from the janitor to the distributors to make it work. Doing that was a tough decision for the company, but the results have been worth it.

OSRAM SYLVANIA is another company that relies exclusively on distributors to bring its products to market. The company has long recognized that an effective distributor network is necessary for success. Like many leading companies, OSRAM SYLVANIA makes extensive industry and product training available to distributors and keeps them up to date on competitive products and marketing strategies. The distributors share in the training cost by paying tuition for the employees they send to OSRAM SYLVANIA's training center.

Like the Wheelabrator division, OSRAM SYLVANIA also uses a distributor council as a source of input. The council provides requirements for training, support, and marketing programs. The council members also help the company determine the value of each program. They operate in a very price-competitive market, where it is critical to match the benefits of each program against its impact on product pricing. OSRAM SYLVANIA clearly views its distributors as an integral part of its distribution system.

An independent company that relies on dealers is Agco Corporation. Agco sells tractors and farm equipment through a worldwide network of over 6,600 dealers. The company has developed its strong dealer network by recognizing that nothing really happens until a farmer buys the company's equipment and puts it to work. Selling equipment to a dealer and having it sit in inventory just increases the dealer's carrying costs. To ensure that Agco's salespeople focus on helping dealers sell equipment to the farmers, the company pays commissions to the salespeople when the dealer sells the product. This eliminates the temptation for salespeople to load the dealers' inventories.

The company's salespeople are dedicated to making the dealers successful in other ways. They help the dealers develop business plans and marketing strategies. They work together to identify the most effective sales and marketing approaches to keep the inventory moving. Each year, they sit down together to analyze the previous year's sales by product line and look for ways to increase sales of slower-moving equipment. Agco recognizes that its long-term growth and profits depend on the success of its dealers (Brewer, 1995b).

### Customer View

When organizations step back and take a global view, they can also see themselves as their customers see them. Recall how Eastman Chemical created a functional flowchart that showed what the international customers had to go through to do business with the company. The customer view will often reveal more opportunities for improvement in sales and marketing. Most of these opportunities lie in two areas: the number of points at which the customer contacts the company and the orientation of the company's salesforce.

One of the most frequent customer complaints is about the excessive number of contact points the customer has with its suppliers. The telecommunications company NYNEX provides a prime example. During its recent reengineering effort, NYNEX studied its small business segment, consisting of customers with from one to thirteen telephone lines. NYNEX found that these small customers could contact NYNEX at more than fifty different points. Imagine trying to maintain consistency and control the quality of the customer interface with that many contact points. IBM may be the champion of contact points, however. That company has more than 1,250 toll-free telephone numbers.

The problem of too many contact points is compounded in companies with multiple divisions when each one has its own salesforce. 3M has that challenge with its sixty-five divisions and eighty salesforces. Consider how it looked to a retail office supply chain like Office Max, Staples, or Office Depot. 3M has addressed the problem in two ways. First, the company set up separate salesforces to sell multiple product lines to its largest accounts. Second, it now allows cross-selling of products. For example, a salesperson representing the diskette division can take an order for Post-its, a product made by another division. To ensure that the salespeople do not compete with each other, 3M pays commissions to the salesperson who gets the order as well as to the one who normally sells the product in the account. This may increase sales costs slightly, but customers find it much more convenient.

At the Energy Services Division of Westinghouse, the nuclear and conventional power systems business units each had its own salesforce. This often resulted in two Westinghouse salespeople calling on customers that used both methods of power generation. According to Chuck Patrick, fossil program manager, the company has now established a single salesforce to represent both business units. Al Hendershot, vice president of marketing at AlliedSignal Aerospace, reports that Allied has reduced its divisions from twenty-six to fourteen, in part to reduce the number of contact points with customers. The company has also moved toward a single sales contact for each customer.

Square D Company's global view from the customer perspective identified another area for improvement. According to quality projects manager Bruce Kappel, customers told the company that its documentation did not have a "one company" look. A cross-functional team developed and implemented new documentation standards based on customer input. This resulted in the single company look the customers preferred.

The customer view also reflects an organization's orientation. Many companies are recognizing that their customers see them as product rather than customer focused. But as Bill Fightmaster, Square D's former vice president of quality, notes, "we know we cannot live in a product-focused world anymore." Pitney Bowes has reorganized its salesforce along account rather than geographical lines to provide better customer service. Many mainframe computer manufacturers are moving toward an industry orientation in their salesforces. When they organize by industry rather than geography or product, they are better able to identify and solve their customers' unique problems.

All the moves these companies have taken are based on what they saw when they took a global view from their customers' perspective. The results have been higher satisfaction and in many cases reduced sales costs.

## Systems Perspective

Although the global view of organizations and how their elements fit together is useful, it does not always reveal the way work really gets done. As described in Chapter Four, work gets done through processes, and these processes cross organizational boundaries. The global view makes this apparent. Taking a step back from individual tasks reveals the activities in processes. A second step back shows the complete process, from beginning to end. Viewing the complete process also shows that in many cases it reaches beyond company boundaries. For example, many companies subcontract activities such as advertising, market research, and sales lead generation. Even though they are done outside of company boundaries, however, these activities are still an integral part of the process.

Taking yet another step back shows how processes combine to work together as complete systems. In the search for increased effectiveness and efficiency, it is more useful to understand processes and systems than it is to understand organization structures. Examining systems shows the relationship between processes and how they work together across company lines. To understand this relationship, we need to know more about what systems are.

A *system* can be defined as a group of interacting, interrelated, and interdependent parts. None of those parts can function alone, but all of them are capable of affecting the characteristics or operation of the system. The system itself functions only as a complete entity. An example of a system is an automobile. Its battery, radiator, and steering mechanism are all interdependent parts and do not function alone. A human being is also a system. A person's heart, lungs, and brain are interdependent parts and cannot function by themselves. The same is true for a company. It is also made up of parts that do not stand alone.

The global view provides an understanding of the system as a whole and its interrelated parts. The system and its processes can only be improved when they are viewed as a whole without regard to the artificial boundaries created by internal departments and divisions and external suppliers and subcontractors. The traditional approach to improvement has been to take the system or process apart and examine tasks and activities at the individual or department level. That promotes suboptimization: improving one task or activity at the potential expense of others. The same thing is true when companies try to improve processes without understanding the systems of which they are a part. When this happens, the overall system may actually become less effective and efficient. To make real improvements, it is necessary to look at the whole system.

Take, for example, the sales and marketing processes. Companies continually look for ways to make them more effective and efficient. The most common approach is to try to break them down into separate activities such as generating leads, qualifying prospects, identifying requirements, writing proposals, making presentations, and closing orders. The company then tries to improve each activity and afterward puts the process back together again.

Taking a global view from the systems perspective provides a better way to improve. The global view reveals how the sales and marketing processes are linked to the customer's buying process. Whether the customer is a homemaker buying the week's groceries, a small business selecting a new copier, or a major corporation contracting health care coverage for its employees, that customer has a buying processes. That process is made up of activities for gathering and evaluating information and making a decision. The sales and marketing processes provide information to customers on which they make buying decisions. To improve these sales and marketing processes then, we need to understand the way customers make buying decisions.

Of course, buying processes vary widely from one customer to the next. They also differ by the type of product or service and the importance and size of the decision. A consumer uses a different decision process for an impulse buy at the supermarket checkout stand than he or she does in making a commitment for a new home. Corporations use different decision processes for buying major new computer systems than they do for buying office supplies. Nevertheless, all customers' processes have several things in common. Like every process, they have input, value-added activities, and output. The input includes the customer's requirements and information about the product or service being considered. The value-added activities analyze the information to determine how well the product or service meets the requirements. The output is a decision on whether or not to buy at all and, if so, which product or service to buy and where to buy it.

The functional flowchart in Figure 6.1 shows how a typical decision-making process might look for a PC word processing program. Note how this functional flowchart is a convenient way to show how the process flows across organizational boundaries. It effectively combines the organizational and process perspectives into a single global view.

This customer decision process may begin when the prospective customer recognizes an unsatisfied want or need. This is the case about half of the time. The other half of the time, a salesperson brings the requirement to the prospect's attention. In this first step, the prospect also defines the specifications for a product, in this case software, that will meet the requirements.

In the next step, the prospect identifies potential sources for the product. This includes determining which software developers have a product as well as where the product can be purchased. Step A in the marketing column represents all of the processes companies use to make prospects aware of their product and where to buy it. Examples of these processes include media advertising, point-of-sale displays, direct mail campaigns, and trade shows. The objective of these processes is to make potential buyers aware of the product and invite them to take the next step in their buying process.

## Figure 6.1. The Customer Buying Process.

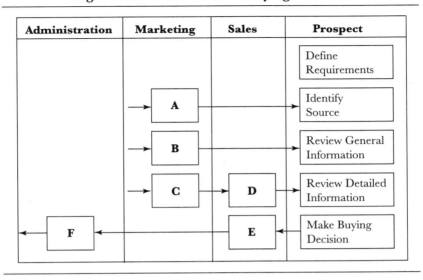

The prospect's third step is to gather more detailed information about the products that appear to meet the requirements. This information will be used to further narrow the field of alternatives. Marketing Step B includes all the processes software companies use to provide more detailed product information. These processes might include sending the prospect a manual with more complete product information or a demonstration copy of the word processing program.

After the prospect has reviewed the detailed product information, he or she may still have questions. In this case, the prospect may want to spend time with a product expert, a sales representative or systems person. In Step C, marketing supplies in-depth product information to the salesforce through manuals, demonstration programs, and product training. In Step D, the salesperson assimilates the product information, delivers it to the customer, and answers the customer's questions. Of course for the word processing program in this example, it is unlikely that a salesperson would make a face-to-face call. He or she would most likely deliver the information by telephone or in a sales office. If the prospect were a large company with a requirement for many copies of the software, the salesperson might make face-to-face sales calls and provide on-site product demonstrations.

The last step for the prospect is to reach a decision, place an order, and become a customer. In Step E, the salesperson receives the order, handles the paperwork, and sends it to an order entry department. In Step F, the order is entered into the fulfillment system. All of these steps seem obvious, and yet it is amazing how few companies are aware of how their customers make buying decisions or how their own processes must align with their customer's buying process to be effective.

Obviously Figure 6.1 is oversimplified. Even a customer decision process for selecting a single copy of a word processing program would have more than these five steps. A decision process to implement a major new computer system might have dozens of steps, involve several departments, and take years to complete. Also, the Steps A to F are all fairly complex processes, each requiring several major activities made up of many tasks.

The message is clear. Before trying to improve any of the marketing and sales processes, the seller needs to understand the customer's buying process. One large software development company found this out when it began listening to its customers. The company had twelve distinct channels for providing customers with product and service information. When a research firm was retained to find out how the company's customers made buying decisions and where they got their product information, the results were stunning. From the customers' perspectives, only four of the twelve channels provided the information they needed, when they wanted it, and in a form that met their requirements. The other eight were a waste of the customers' time and the company's resources.

This left the software company with several options. Given its new understanding of how customers make buying decisions, it could try to improve the eight ineffective channels and realign them with the customer decision process, or it could eliminate the eight channels and save time and money. The savings could be used to enhance the four valued channels of distribution, to develop new channels that better met customers' information requirements, or just to improve the company's bottom line. In any case, listening to customers provided the information the software company needed to become more effective and efficient in its sales and marketing processes.

ADC Telecommunications is another company that benefited from learning how their customers made buying decisions. ADC is a Minneapolis-based manufacturer and supplier to the telecommunications industry. The company opened for business before World War II and enjoyed steady and profitable growth for many years. During that period, they developed and made electromechanical devices sold primarily to telephone companies.

By 1988, the product line had matured, and telephone companies were beginning to shift their technology from electromechanical to electronic and fiber optic. ADC's growth flattened and profits dropped. The company was forced to close a plant and lay off workers for the first time in its history. The members of ADC's senior management recognized that to pursue their vision of being a leading supplier to the communications industry, ADC had to begin making the switch to the new technologies. They moved quickly to acquire several small companies with the engineering, design, and manufacturing experience and products they needed, and they set to work developing new products to meet customers' changing requirements.

ADC marketed to their major customers through a direct salesforce. These salespeople had matured along with the company's original product line. They had developed long-standing personal relationships with the customers' people who placed orders. These buyers were at a relatively low level in the customers' organizations. The old technology and products were a known quantity to them, and ADC was a proven supplier. The company fully expected that the existing salesforce could successfully sell these buyers the new products. That didn't happen. Although the salespeople continued to sell the old products, they were unable to penetrate the market with the new line. The company assigned three people to coach the direct salesforce on how to sell the new products. This approach also met with little success.

At the time, Dale Nelson was managing ADC's quality improvement effort and was familiar with the idea of the customer decision process. Nelson suggested that the sales department find out how customers were making their decisions to buy the new technology products. Mike Druar was an ADC marketing manager at the time. He picked up on Nelson's suggestion and began to study and document the customer decision process. He quickly uncovered several of the biggest barriers to selling the new product line.

First, the customers' decision makers were different. The people who bought ADC's old product line were not the same ones who made decisions about whole new technologies and the future direction of the customer's business. These decisions were being made by teams of people near the top of the organization, people who represented several of the key operating departments. Each of these departments had its own set of issues, concerns, and requirements. Because of the importance of the decisions and the number of people and departments involved, the decision process for the new technology products took longer, was much more complex, and required a consensus among the participants.

With the information Druar gathered, he was able to create a functional flowchart of the customer decision process. He also developed lists of the operating departments involved in making the decisions and checklists of their possible interests, objectives, and concerns. He documented a step-by-step selling strategy that aligned with the way customers were making decisions and took all of this information to the salesforce. However, the salespeople did not initially welcome these new ideas with great enthusiasm. The ideas were contrary to the strategy that the salespeople had used successfully with the old products, and those products still represented the greatest source of their commission earnings. Over time, however, most of the salespeople came to recognize the importance of the new products and the need to develop high-level contacts and understand their customers' buying processes. They aligned the way they sold with the way their customers wanted to buy. Today, ADC has regained their position of leadership. For the past five years, the company has grown faster than the industry and has had higher than average profits. Aligning their sales efforts with the customer buying process is not the only change the company has made since it expanded into the new product line, but the global view taken by Mike Druar was a major contributor to its success.

GE has also taken a global view from a systems perspective. This view has enabled the company to improve internal business processes by taking out redundant and unnecessary steps and shortening cycle times. GE is also sharing the company's process improvement techniques with customers to help make them more efficient. Here is how that approach worked with Kaiser Permanente.

Kaiser Permanente is one of the country's largest health maintenance organizations (HMOs), and as a trendsetter in managed care, it is one of the most important. This major HMO is also a significant GE customer. GE Medical Systems had been successful in selling magnetic resonance imaging (MRI) equipment by calling on purchasing people and radiologists and using traditional sales techniques. However, the health care industry was changing rapidly, looking for new ways to become more efficient, and GE was looking for better ways to serve this leading customer.

In early 1992, Gary Hessenauer and the GE Medical Systems team approached Bill Sheehy, then head of Kaiser Permanente's procurement and material department in the HMO's southern region. They offered to look for nontraditional ways to work together. GE would share some of the techniques and best practices they used to get costs out of their own processes. The two organizations would then work together to align their processes to make them more efficient. Sheehy accepted GE's offer. The processes that GE and Kaiser selected to work on were Kaiser's processes for capital equipment procurement, installation, and service and the GE processes that linked to them.

The two organizations formed teams and included the key decision makers in the improvement process, a move vital to its success. Their first step was to map their existing processes. They were horrified by the inefficiencies that they found. They identified duplicate and unnecessary steps in both organizations. As Gary Hessenauer reports, "GE would do something, and it would take six weeks. Then Kaiser would do the same thing, and it would take another six weeks. There were twelve weeks of unnecessary cycle time because those were precautionary steps. They were taken because neither side completely trusted the other." Once they built trust up between the two organizations, they could take steps like these and the associated costs out of the system.

Mapping the existing processes showed the two organizations how they currently worked together. The next step was to consider what the system would look like if they redesigned it, starting with a blank sheet of paper. They considered what they could do differently and more efficiently if there were no boundaries within or between the two organizations. The result was that both sides were able to take six to ten months of administrative time out of their cycle times, from order receipt to product delivery. That reduced cycle time translated to money saved for both Kaiser Permanente and GE Medical Systems. The process of working together on the project had additional benefits. The two organizations developed a greater degree of mutual trust. Although there are still problems from time to time, there is a process in place to resolve them.

The approach GE and Kaiser Permanente took was unusual, but it clearly demonstrates the value of taking a global view from a systems perspective. By looking beyond the artificial boundaries of the two organizations and their individual departments, even beyond their individual processes, they were able to learn how a major system worked. That enabled them to create a new way of doing business together, a way that was a win for both organizations. GE Medical Systems was able to strengthen a customer partnership and make both organizations stronger and more efficient. And it did this without sacrificing the attainment of traditional sales goals.

At GE, taking a global view resulted in organization and process improvements that went beyond the boundaries of sales and marketing. However, these changes resulted in significant increases in sales and customer satisfaction. These examples demonstrate that there are many factors that influence the customer buying decision, not all within the control of sales and marketing. The flowchart in Figure 6.2 demonstrates this idea. Part of the flowchart shows the customer buying process already described (Figure 6.1). The first-time buyer begins that process and relies on external information about the word processing software to reach a buying decision. Much of this information is provided through the marketing and sales channels. However, the process does not end there.

**Figure 6.2. The Complete Customer Cycle.**

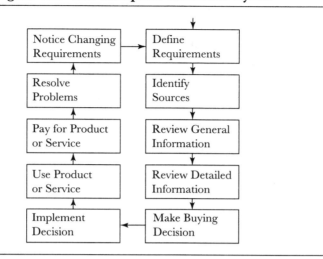

After ordering the software, the next step is to implement the decision. The customer installs the software and learns to use it. The product goes into productive use in the following step. At the end of the month, an invoice arrives, and the customer pays the bill. The customer also might need assistance in using a feature and have to refer to the help screens or read the manual. He or she might discover a defect and call the supplier's toll-free technical support number for help.

Over time the customer's requirements continue to change. He or she might need additional functions or the ability to connect to a network and share documents or possibly to move from a DOS environment to Windows 95 or OS/2 Warp. At this point, the customer is back in the market for a new version of the software or even an entirely new word processing program. The customer re-enters the buying process, but this time things are different. He or she brings personal experience with the current product and supporting services, documentation, billing procedures, and all the other factors that make up the relationship. Although in the second time through the process marketing and sales continue to provide input, the customer's previous experience heavily influences the buying decision. No amount of creative advertising or salesmanship can overcome a bad experience with a company or its products.

Obviously, the timing of this cycle is different for other kinds of products and services. A consumer decides where to buy groceries and which brands to purchase about once a week. The decision to buy a new car comes every four or five years. A manufacturing company may acquire raw materials weekly but select a health care plan for employees annually. However, in almost every case, there is a cycle similar to the one in Figure 6.2. By taking a global view, companies can identify the complete relationship, determine the points of contact, find out which are the most important to the customer, and focus improvement efforts on those areas.

Focusing on the complete relationship also helps determine a customer's total cost of doing business with the company. Customers are becoming more aware of and concerned about total cost, not just the initial price of the product or service. Many customers are realizing that the cost of acquisition of small items actually exceeds the cost of the product. A W.W. Grainger advertisement in the June 5, 1995, issue of *Forbes ASAP* (p. 21) highlighted the problem when it pictured seven people from one company involved in the purchase of a hammer. The cost of the hammer was $17. The cost of the people's time was $100. By taking a global view of the relationship between itself and its suppliers, a company can identify the total cost of a transaction. By reducing this cost, the company can often overcome a product price disadvantage.

## Question Everything

Organizations with an open culture are inquisitive; they question everything. They learn from listening to their customers, practicing awareness, and taking a global view. Then they ask why things are the way they are and how they can make these things better. They particularly recognize and question the assumptions and beliefs on which they base their business practices.

Recall from Chapter Three how successful GTE has been in raising customer satisfaction levels. In the process, GTE also reduced its new service installation staff by more than 40 percent. John Murphy was GTE's director of quality and executive education when the company began its effort. When asked how GTE was able to achieve such startling results, Murphy explained that in part, it was by questioning some of the company's 100-year-old assumptions. One such assumption was that when a customer called to get a new phone installed, he or she wanted it within forty-eight hours. GTE had a massive installation process in place to meet that standard.

As part of its quality initiative, GTE surveyed its retail customers. Someone proposed asking customers on this survey when they wanted new telephones installed. Several senior managers rejected the question. They already knew that the answer was forty-eight hours. However, the question survived and was asked. Much to the amazement of the senior managers, the answer was not forty-eight hours. It was "we want it when we want it." For some people, it might be twenty-four hours. For others, it might be two weeks. When GTE changed its policy to install new telephones at the time specified by the customer, it obviously improved customer satisfaction. However, the change had another startling effect. It cut new telephone installation costs in half. The system to install telephones in forty-eight hours required a massive distributed inventory of telephones, and installers had to be available to meet the standard during peak demands. When the policy changed, GTE no longer required much of that infrastructure.

TransCanada Gas Services had a similar experience. Its Toronto office was taking about a week to get sales contracts processed, approved, and back to customers. Company surveys revealed that this was not satisfactory to many customers. By applying business process improvement techniques, TransCanada reduced the cycle time to three days and planned to reduce that time to a single day when it completed an automation project. A year later, John Voss, former manager of market planning and development, answered, "Yes and no," when asked if TransCanada had achieved its objective. With its improved process and automation, it was capable of twenty-four turnaround. However, like GTE, it had learned that customers want it when they want it and that a twenty-four-hour standard was not the right measurement. Now when employees log a contract in, they note when the customer wants it back, and the new objective is to return contracts when the customers want them and to do that 100 percent of the time.

One of the things every organization with a direct salesforce should question is what its salespeople really do. Without knowing that, it is almost impossible to make meaningful improvements. To assume that the salespeople spend all of their time in face-to-face sales activities can be misleading. They are probably performing many other value-adding activities. It may also be a mistake to think that salespeople are the biggest direct influence on customer buying decisions.

Consider the example of Century Furniture, manufacturer of fine home furnishings. Its salespeople look for furniture chains and independent stores to carry the Century line. They consider store location, proximity to other Century dealers, and what other furniture lines a dealer already carries. When they sign up a new furniture dealer, the company sends a designer from its Hickory, North Carolina, headquarters to design a gallery to display the Century line. The store then orders furniture to fill the display.

That is the last order the salesperson takes. From then on, the retail dealer's salespeople show the furniture to potential buyers and place orders directly with the factory. What do the Century salespeople do? They provide information to the dealers about the product line, announce new products and promotions, and help train the dealer's salespeople. Their function is to deliver information, train and coach retail salespeople, and be an interface between the dealers and the company. An assumption that the salespeople spend their time closing orders would probably misdirect any efforts at improvement.

To achieve the company's vision of having a world-class salesforce, Century Furniture took a unique approach. It created a team of salespeople led by senior salesman Dick Carroll. The team's mission was to create its own improvement process. The team members went to their customers and asked them identify the characteristics they thought were most important in a salesperson. The next step was to ask every salesperson in the company to meet with several of his or her customers to review the list of characteristics and ask how he or she could improve in the key areas.

David Leffler, senior vice president of sales at Century, reports that the customers are receiving the idea very well and providing excellent feedback. They know better than anyone else what the salespeople really do and how they can improve it. When Leffler asked one salesman how he had gotten a $100,000 order from a store that had never bought much before, the salesperson explained that he did not really know. He did mention that he got the order shortly after he had sat down with the customer to discuss what was most important to him in a furniture sales representative. Today that customer has become one of Century's largest.

Zytec is another company that questioned how much influence salespeople had on short-term sales volume. Zytec's salespeople team up with the company's engineers to sell power supplies for copiers and computers to customers like Kodak and IBM. They work together to persuade their customers to use a Zytec power supply in a particular machine. However, the team has no influence on how many power supplies a customer will ultimately buy. That is a function of how many of the copiers and computers the customer sells. Like most companies, Zytec used to pay salespeople on commissions. However, after questioning how much influence the salespeople really had on the volumes sold, the company took another look at compensation. Zytec now pays its salespeople on salary only. Paying commissions for something beyond a salesperson's control did not make sense.

Some companies are questioning the value of having a direct salesforce at all. In both consumer and business-to-business sales, changing customer buying habits and advancing technology are causing companies to reexamine their need for a direct sales staff. They are looking for more effective and efficient ways to reach their customers.

One of the most highly regarded salesforces in consumer sales was recently disbanded as a result of this questioning. Until June 1996, Encyclopedia Britannica relied on the company's direct salesforce to sell its $1,400 sets of books. Declining sales, however, caused the company to rethink its position. Customers were beginning to shift their attention to encyclopedias on CD-ROM. They were also using direct mail, the telephone, and even on-line services to get information and place orders. In addition, the cost of generating leads and administering the salesforce continued to rise.

The salespeople were also finding it increasingly difficult to sell face-to-face in the home. An encyclopedia purchase generally involves both parents. With both parents working in many families, finding them at home at the same time was becoming more difficult. In addition, with the fear of crime increasing, many people were becoming reluctant to allow strangers into their homes at all. So for all these reasons, Encyclopedia Britannica has eliminated its direct salesforce and is concentrating its efforts on customer research, database marketing, direct mail, broadcast marketing, and on-line marketing (Corman, 1996).

Another company that has questioned the need for a direct salesforce is DuraTemp, a Holland, Ohio–based manufacturer of hot glass handling materials for the glass industry. The company has a limited number of customers across the country and initially sold their products through two in-house salespeople. Because the small number of potential customers was spread across the country, these salespeople spent more time traveling than selling. DuraTemp decided to partner with another company that sold lubricants to the same customer base. Although that approach was more efficient, the company soon learned that many of the lubricant salespeople were doing little more than picking up orders.

The company's next step was to try something very radical. They ended the sales agreement with the lubricant salesforce and now operate without any direct salespeople at all. They assigned the customer accounts to several headquarters people to cover by telephone. They also use videotape presentations and direct mail to deliver new product information. Due to downsizing in the glass container segment of the glass industry, the number of plants needing DuraTemp's products has dropped by one-third, making the new approach to covering customers even more effective. Sales volumes have remained essentially the same, and costs have dropped significantly. Eliminating the salesforce won't be the answer for most companies, but DuraTemp found that by questioning what salespeople really did, the company was able to make this strategy work.

Another thing that companies with an open organization culture question is how their salespeople spend their time. They realize that they cannot improve the sales process without knowing what their salespeople currently do and how much time they spend doing it. When a company finds out how its salespeople spend their time before it begins an improvement process, it also has a baseline against which to compare the results of the changes.

Recently, my firm and the Dartnell Corporation conducted a special survey. In addition to asking how salespeople spend their time, we wanted to know whether their companies had an improvement process and whether the salespeople participated in it. We also asked them how much time they spend fixing things gone wrong. The survey revealed that 60 percent of the companies that responded had some kind of improvement process, and in most cases the salespeople were involved. The startling revelation was the effect that an improvement process had on how salespeople spend their time. In the companies that had an improvement process, they spend an average of 16 percent of their time in fixing things gone wrong. In companies without an improvement process, the salespeople spend 28 percent of their time in that activity.

The survey results were confirmed by a number of the companies interviewed for this book. Eastman Chemical surveyed salespeople in two of the company's districts and found that they spent about 30 percent of their time fixing things. 3M got similar results when they asked their salespeople how much time they spent just handling customer complaints. The time salespeople spend fixing problems can be better invested in selling and adding value to the company's product or service. The companies that question how their salespeople spend their time have a big start toward knowing where to focus their improvement activities.

These are just a few examples of what companies with an open organization culture have questioned. The fields of sales and marketing are filled with myths and sacred cows. Challenging the status quo and gathering and analyzing facts helps companies make real improvements.

## Share Information

To question everything effectively, people need more and better information, something that has been closely held in most organizations. However, organizations with an open culture have awakened to the fact that the more people know, the more effective they can be. These companies share information, making it easily available to anyone who needs it. Many of them provide information to their distribution partners and their customers as well.

Recall General Electric's area councils. Part of their charter is to facilitate the sharing of customer information across the twelve GE businesses operating within the area. This information allows salespeople to recognize cross-business sales opportunities and to serve their customers more effectively. The salespeople are also aware of what the other GE businesses are doing. That enables them to understand the implications of their actions in relation to the other businesses and the total needs of their customers.

Cross-functional improvement teams benefit from sharing information and develop effective ways to do it. Remember how Eastman Chemical recognized the value of sharing information. They "link-in" their worldwide improvement teams, making improvements developed in one country office available to other offices around the world. Xerox has a similar process for sharing sales best practices across the company's district offices in the United States.

Companies with an open culture do not stop at their own boundaries either. As we have seen, General Electric shares its improvement techniques with many of its customers. The belief is that it is in the company's interest to have successful customers. Wheelabrator takes the same path when it opens its books to its distributors. That gives the distributors information they need to help the company make decisions about which new products to develop and the most effective ways to allocate limited marketing resources.

There are two major barriers to information sharing. The first is fear. In one company with several divisions, each with its own salesforce, many of the key accounts are being covered by salespeople from each division. These salespeople are not encouraged, or even allowed, to exchange information that would benefit themselves or their customers. They cannot sell as a team and sometimes find themselves competing with each other. The company's CEO is concerned that a salesperson might gather too much customer or product information and take it to a competitor. His fears are hobbling his company and its salespeople, making them less effective and efficient.

The second barrier is the old idea that information is power. Some people still believe that if they know more than their fellow employees, customers, or suppliers, they are in a position of power. Although this may be true in a political sense, withholding information actually drains power from the organization as a whole. It is the people who withhold vital information that company leadership should fear, not someone who might take information to a competitor.

## Take Informed Action

Anthony Robbins, respected author, speaker, and trainer, states that, "Information is not power, action is power" (1988). Action is the next attribute of organizations with an open culture. They share a sense of urgency and willingness to take action. They do not just gather information and study it forever; they use it to make decisions and accomplish objectives. Their actions are guided by the organization's mission, vision, and values, and they support the business's strategy, plans, goals, and objectives. Their actions are also founded on the combined knowledge and experience of the people and the organization.

If actions are to be founded on information, everyone in the organization must be keenly aware of this information. Companies cannot hide information in confidential documents or explain it in volumes of procedure manuals that attempt to cover every alternative, relegating decision making to a cookbook approach. Quite the opposite. Action founded on information is best typified by Nordstrom's simple statement that empowers employees to "Use your own best judgment at all times" (Peters, 1987, p. 378).

Companies with an open organization culture support and encourage action. People are recognized for taking risks. When they are successful, they are recognized and rewarded. When they fail, the experience is used as a way to learn, not an opportunity to punish. Both successes and failures provide input to the organization's improvement process. When they are willing to take informed and decisive action, companies become more flexible and responsive to their customers' changing requirements. They also attract people who are willing to take risks, make decisions, and get things done. This applies particularly in sales and marketing, where people can feel stifled by inaction, bureaucracy, and stagnation.

## Empower People and Teams

Some organizations reserve taking meaningful action for higher levels of management. However, those with an open culture empower people and teams at every level. They allow these individuals and teams to recognize and take advantage of opportunities, make decisions faster, and be more responsive to customers. The ability to take meaningful action is also a major morale booster for the people in sales and marketing.

Although it is easy to think of *empowerment* as just another way to describe delegation of authority, the idea of empowerment goes much further than that. It is true that like delegation, it is a decentralized management approach. However, to make effective decisions and take decisive and appropriate action, people need more than power. They need a clear understanding of the organization's mission, vision, and values. They also need to know the organization's strategy and goals and how their actions support them.

The leading organizations empower their people by giving them the authority, resources, and information they need. They also provide training and personal development activities necessary to build skills and knowledge. We have already noted that organizations with an open culture freely share information and knowledge. This is also a part of the empowerment process. To complete the cycle, empowered people get feedback on the action they take. This feedback comes from listening to customers and the organization's own measurement systems. Having information, taking informed action, and getting feedback on it—all of this results in building the experience that people need to be effective in making decisions and taking action.

Many organizations are giving their frontline employees more power and authority. One example is Stew Leonard's, the famous Norwalk and Danbury, Connecticut–based dairy stores. As part of their training, Stew Leonard, Jr., tells new cashiers that he wants them to let people take their purchases home without paying. Sound crazy? It turns out that about fifty people each week come to shop only to find that they have forgotten their wallet, checkbook, or credit card. The cashiers at Stew Leonard's stores are empowered to let customers leave with their purchases without paying. All the cashiers have to do is get the customer's name, address, and telephone number. Although it may sound like the risk of loss is high, Leonard reports that they have never had anyone fail to return later to pay for his or her groceries. Imagine the impact of this policy on customer satisfaction and loyalty.

Another company that has empowered people in the sales organization is Texaco Refining and Marketing. Until recently, Stu Crum was district marketing manager in the company's Overland Park, Kansas, field office. There he was responsible for the operation of over eighty Texaco retail outlets. One of the responsibilities shared by Crum, his zone managers, and his sales representatives was finding other vendors to participate in joint ventures in the Texaco convenience stores. They leased space to such other well-known companies as Subway and Dunkin' Donuts. With their knowledge of the territory, the members of Crum's sales team could tailor the services provided in each location to the needs and opportunities of the local community. Crum was empowered to make the deals without having to go "up the line" for approvals. He credits Texaco's quality improvement process with the enlightened approach to field sales management.

## Learn and Improve Continuously

Empowering people to take action and then giving them feedback on their results enables them to learn as individuals. A few leading companies are now going beyond this individual learning. They are beginning to focus on how they learn as organizations as well. Ray Stada, Chairman of the Board and CEO of Analog Devices, believes that "the rate at which organizations learn may become the only sustainable competitive advantage, especially in knowledge-intensive businesses" (Senge, 1990, p. 349).

One such company is Xerox, an organization already well recognized for its highly effective quality improvement process. Recently, Xerox commissioned a study to find out how it learns as a company. The survey revealed that in some cases the company had solved the same problem several times. It did a good job of solving problems, but not such a good job of learning to avoid the same problems in the future.

Many of the elements of the open culture contribute to the way organizations learn. The flowchart in Figure 6.3 shows how the

**Figure 6.3.  The Open Organization Culture Is a Learning Culture.**

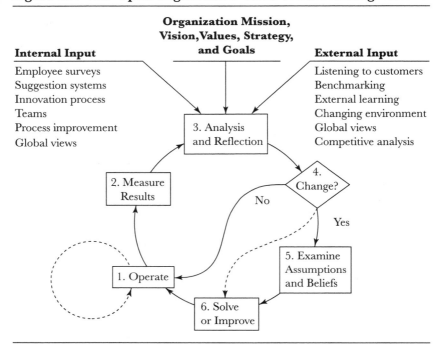

open culture pieces fit together. Once an organization is in place and doing things, the learning cycle of an open culture begins with the operate step. In a sales organization, this step includes processes such as identifying and qualifying prospects, preparing proposals, and taking orders. Processes in the marketing organization include conducting market research, identifying new product opportunities, and developing advertising campaigns.

Each of these processes in the operate step produces an output or result. It probably comes as no surprise that some organizations don't bother to measure the effectiveness of what they do in their operations, particularly in the areas of sales and marketing. They just keep doing what they always did, believing that it is producing the result they want. The dotted line around Step 1 represents what these companies do: the same thing over and over again.

Learning organizations measure the results of their operations at Step 2 in the cycle. Then, in Step 3, they analyze their measurements and reflect on whether they are getting what they want. If they are getting the result they want, they decide in Step Four not to make changes, and they go back to Step 1 from Step 4 and continue their activities.

If they are not getting the result that they want and decide to change, most companies go directly to Step 6. In this step, they may solve the problem that prevents them from getting the result they want. They may also choose to improve the process or even create a new process to get their desired outcome. In sales, this might mean improving the lead generation process or adding a telemarketing process to qualify leads. In marketing, it might mean switching advertising agencies, adding trade shows, or dropping print advertising. After Step 6, organizations go back to Step 1 and operate with the new or improved processes with the problems solved. They measure the results to determine the effectiveness of the changes they have made, and the cycle continues. Most organizations omit Step 5 in their problem-solving and process improvement activities yet this step is critical to sustaining long-term improvement. It is in Step 5 that organizations examine the underlying beliefs and assumptions upon which they have based decisions and designed their processes.

Consider Frederick Taylor's theory of scientific management. Taylor believed there was one best way to do any job and that industrial engineers were the best qualified to determine what that way was. He observed that the workers of the late 1800s and early 1900s were mostly poor uneducated immigrants and that they were best qualified to do simple repetitive tasks. Therefore it was up to the industrial engineer to study a job and break it down into its tiniest tasks. Companies then trained their workers to do some of these simple tasks and to pass the work on to the next person who did more simple tasks. When companies applied Taylor's theory, defects did go down and productivity increased.

Many organizations today still have processes based on Taylor's theory of scientific management. They have failed to realize that what was true of workers at the turn of the century is in most cases no longer true today. Most people are now well educated. They do not enjoy doing simple repetitive tasks all day. They are also capable of solving problems and helping design and improve the way they do their work. However, organizations that fail to examine and question the underlying beliefs upon which scientific management is based will continue to design processes by breaking them down into their simplest elements. They will also ignore the input from the people who know the work best, the people who are doing it. Clearly Step 5 is critical to the improvement process. Although organizations can solve problems and improve processes without Step 5, they will continue to design new processes using the old beliefs. Recall the example of GTE and that company's belief that customers wanted their new telephone service installed in forty-eight hours. Had GTE not questioned that belief, the company would still have a process in place that cost twice what was required, and customers would be less satisfied than they are today.

When an organization uses all six steps in the cycle, it is well on the road to becoming a learning organization. However, if the organization just analyzes and reflects on the measurement data, it is still operating in a vacuum. To be effective, the organization needs additional input to Step 3. This input comes from the internal and external sources shown in Figure 6.3. The organization also bases the analysis and reflection in Step 3 on the organization's mission, vision, values, strategy and goals.

All of the elements shown in Figure 6.3 combine to create a process for organization learning. The last piece, not shown on the figure, is some kind of corporate memory, a way to store what has been learned. Traditionally, this has been done through the culture of the organization. However, the organization culture is not a formal or necessarily reliable way to store and transmit what the organization has learned.

First, because culture is most often transmitted by word of mouth, it lacks accuracy. Over time people forget the details of why things are done the way they are or how problems were solved in the past. Even when management tries to record what it has learned, it does so in the form of policies and procedures. The underlying reasons, beliefs, and assumptions are lost, and the organization ends up with rigid, out-of-date processes documented in policy and procedure manuals that no one reads. Second, the past decade of corporate downsizing has performed a frontal lobotomy on the corporate memory. Often when people leave, they take knowledge and experience with them, leaving the organization to reinvent procedures and solve old problems all over again. Many companies have filled the gap with temporary or contract workers. This compounds the corporate memory problem. When temporary workers solve problems and then leave, they take their problem-solving logic, their underlying beliefs and assumptions, and even the solutions with them.

The answer to the need for corporate memory may lie in technology. By using computers to store and access what the company has learned through experience, organizations may be able to reach their full potential. However, only a few companies have begun to take advantage of computers' data storage and information search and retrieve capability to achieve this objective.

## Conclusion

To be effective, all the elements of the open organization culture must be used together. Gathering information by practicing awareness and taking a global view is of no value if the organization does not share the information or take informed action. Reserving action for the top of the business does not support fast response or take advantage of the skills of the people who really get the work done. Taking action without questioning the organization's underlying beliefs and assumptions may lead to repeating mistakes. It is when all the elements of an open culture work together that an organization becomes more effective and efficient, whether that organization is an entire company or a sales or marketing function.

Chapter Seven

# | Apply Technology

The application of technology is the most exciting and fastest growing of the six best practices. It is changing the ways that customers get information about products and services. It is providing new ways for companies to market, sell, and support their offerings. It is also increasing individual, team, and companywide effectiveness and productivity.

The *American Heritage Dictionary* defines *technology* as "the application of science, especially to industrial or commercial objectives." For our purposes, technology includes all of the equipment, software, and communication links that organizations use to enable or improve their processes. It includes the obvious mainframe and personal computers and the communication networks that organizations use to tie them together. However, it also goes beyond this. It includes everything from simple overhead transparency projectors to multimedia laptop computers, from fax machines to e-mail, from audiocassette and videocassette players to cellular phones and voice mail. Almost any device and its associated software comes under the heading of technology.

Unlike the other best practices, the application of technology does not stand by itself. It is an enabler, used by organizations in a variety of ways to support the other five best practices. Here is an outline of how that works:

*Manage for change.* One of the key elements of managing for change is measuring performance and improvement. Technology provides ways to gather and analyze measurement data and report the results quickly and easily.

*Listen to customers.* Technology provides faster and more efficient ways to collect, store, and analyze customer requirements and feedback. It can also make the customer information available to the people in the organization who need it, when they need it.

*Focus on process.* In the process equation of people, equipment, procedures, and information, technology is the equipment element. It is an integral part of almost every modern business process and makes many improvement and reengineering projects practical. It also makes possible new processes, ones that simply could not be done without it.

*Use teams.* Technology improves team productivity and provides team members with new ways to exchange information, manage projects, and solve problems.

*Practice an open organization culture.* Sharing information is a key part of the open culture. Technology helps make that possible, especially in large organizations and those with multiple remote sites. It also provides ways to gather and store the information that is a key part of organizational learning.

A common element in all these best practices is information. As we learned in Chapter One, information is also the product of sales and marketing. It is what flows through the sales and marketing processes. Customers need information to reach their buying decisions. Companies need information to understand their customers' requirements and how well they are meeting them. The sales and marketing processes discussed in Chapter Four take information input, add value, and create output that goes to customers. Customers provide requirements and feedback information to the organization.

Technology provides tools to make all these processes more effective and efficient. Some of the processes discussed later in this chapter would not even be possible without the use of technology.

## What Drives Technology

Although the application of technology is virtually exploding today, many of its capabilities have been available for years. However, it has just been within the past three to five years that companies have begun exploiting many of those capabilities in their sales and marketing functions. There are several forces at work.

## Customer Demands

Both business customers and individual consumers are driving the use of technology. They want their suppliers to respond to their unique requirements. In business-to-business sales, some customers will buy only from suppliers who can accept orders and confirm shipments through electronic data interchange. Other customers demand a single invoice from suppliers with multiple divisions, a task that can only be accomplished easily through information systems and communications technology.

Today's more sophisticated customers want hard facts on which to base their buying decisions, and they want that information to be available when they want it, not when sellers want to deliver it. They are also less influenced by traditional advertising and sales practices. Through the increasing use of the Internet and on-line service bulletin boards, word-of-mouth advertising is taking on new meaning.

Consumers also want to be treated as individuals. Large companies find they can meet that requirement only by using computer databases that make the customer information instantly available to frontline employees throughout the organization. Consumer products companies are responding by using computer databases to identify and communicate directly with their best customers.

## Cost Pressures

The drive to improve business process effectiveness and efficiency has also increased the focus on technology. Although many companies automated their processes in the past, they often failed to take full advantage of technology when they did so. They simply converted their existing tasks to computers. Will Ryan, president of the Systems Sales Support Company, refers to that approach as "paving cow paths." Today's leading companies are now improving or reengineering their processes as they apply the latest technology. They are building superhighways.

The corporate downsizing that began in the late 1980s has put pressure on salesforces to increase their productivity with fewer resources. Increasing productivity is the number one reason that sales managers give for today's flood of salesforce automation projects. The rapidly declining prices and increasing functions of personal computers and the availability of salesforce automation software is making this movement practical and affordable.

## Competition

As if customer demand and cost pressures were not enough, competition is also fueling the use of technology. Companies often find themselves at a disadvantage when a competitor can accept orders electronically, make product information and customer service available through the Internet, and provide its salespeople with up-to-date customer information and multimedia sales aids. Companies on the leading edge of technology are setting the standard for customer service.

In this chapter, we will see how companies are responding to customer demands, cost pressures, and competition by applying technology, including some of today's hottest applications: customer information systems, database marketing, communication, and salesforce automation. We will also look at sales and marketing's newest tool, the Internet.

## Customer Information Systems

Companies are beginning to recognize that their customers are a major asset, and they are looking for ways to manage that asset. Although the current term that describes the process is *customer asset management,* companies are not really *managing* their customers and probably do not want their customers thinking so. What they are actually attempting to do is manage information about the customer asset. This is true whether the customers are large multinational corporations or individual consumers.

Even at the level of the individual salesperson, the more that salesperson knows about his or her customer, the more effective he or she can be. Harvey Mackay brings this home in his book

*Swim with the Sharks Without Being Eaten Alive* (1988). He identifies sixty-six things that salespeople should know about every key customer contact. The success of his company, Mackay Envelope, and his personal accomplishments in such endeavors as helping get a new sports stadium built in Minneapolis and the 1996 Summer Olympics held in Atlanta attest to the value of knowing customer decision makers on a personal level. Most salespeople could improve their performance by following Mackay's lead. The same is true at the company level.

Actually most companies already know a lot about their customers. Chapter Three provided many examples of how they listen to customers to identify requirements and gather feedback. Most have extensive customer information that they have gathered through other sources as well. The problem is that all this customer information is buried in functional departments across the organization. The salesperson has a file of his or her contacts, including names, addresses, titles, and personal information. The marketing department has the latest customer satisfaction survey and market research data. Customer service has its list of customer contacts as well as information about complaints and open issues. The accounting department has accounts receivable and payment history data. The order entry department knows what is on order. Manufacturing is in control of the work in process for customers. The legal department has the customer contracts. The problem of having customer information spread all over the organization is multiplied when a company has more than one division selling to the same customers, and each division maintains its own set of files.

The problem of multiple functional files occurs in nonmanufacturing organizations as well. A typical bank may have ten or more distinct product lines, each with its own set of records for a customer, and no way to tie them together. My own bank has three complete sets of records for me. There are separate records for my personal checking account, business checking account, and personal credit card, and none of them seems to know about any of the others. A recent relocation of my office required three separate transactions with the bank just to make the address change.

Because customer information is kept in several departments, much of it is duplicated. This increases the cost of maintenance, and the files are frequently out of date and inconsistent. One address line in my company's bank account record was never changed. Although it does not prevent the Post Office from delivering the statement, the error reminds me every month that my bank cannot make a simple address change consistently across its records.

Few companies currently have a process to pull all the distributed information together quickly and easily and make it available to anyone who needs it. In several well-known and highly respected corporations, it takes weeks for a senior executive just to find out how much revenue the company gets from a major customer. In a few cases, it is virtually impossible.

To overcome these problems and support customer asset management efforts, some leading companies have created processes that enable them to access all their key information about their customers. The result of their efforts is a customer information system, or CIS. There are three approaches to a CIS. At the most basic level, a company can identify all the files that contain customer information and make those files available to anyone who needs them. Although it may still take time to pull information together, at least all the sources for it are identified. The next approach is to link the files electronically and create a process for pulling customer information together for processing and analysis. Some companies have gone further and adopted a third approach, creating large databases that consolidate all the important information about their customers in a single place.

## CIS Examples

Motorola is one company that has recognized the benefits of making relevant customer information available to salespeople. Although the company has not yet consolidated all its customer information into a single database, it does make much of that information available to its field salesforce. Salespeople can get customer information quickly and easily from three major processes. First, they can access the company's on-line Quality Response System, or QRS, to identify any outstanding customer problems or complaints. They can also get written reports from QRS. Second, the results of customer satisfaction surveys are given to field sales office on a PC disk, which is updated quarterly. Third, salespeople participate with Motorola executives in the Executive Customer

Advocate Program described in Chapter Three. This activity provides them with information on long-term customer requirements. The customer information available to Motorola salespeople from these three sources gives them a powerful competitive edge as they prepare for sales calls, develop account plans, and create proposals.

Although these information sources are not yet linked electronically, salespeople can access them easily from their sale branches. Motorola is currently considering ways to consolidate much of its customer information in a single system. The company refers to the location where it will store the information as a "data warehouse." This new approach will make access faster and easier for field salespeople and everyone else who needs access to complete customer information.

One company that uses a fully integrated customer database is Oxford Health Plans. This Norwalk, Connecticut–based firm has gone from being a new business to being a leader in the turbulent managed care industry in just ten years. It depends on its information systems to support the company's phenomenal growth rate—over 100 percent each year for the past four years. It also relies on technology and its customer database to meet its corporate objective of providing service excellence.

According to Jay Silverstein, vice president of marketing and communications, Oxford Health Plans understands that its customers and subscribers don't compare Oxford service levels to those of Oxford's competitors like Aetna or PruCare. Instead, Oxford customers' benchmarks for high-quality service are the companies with which they do business every day; companies like American Express, Nordstrom, and Lands' End. A corporate motto at Oxford is "Disdain bureaucracy," and the company backs it up by asking the question, "Whose life is this making easier?" of every process. To instill this culture of service quality, the CEO and other senior managers take part in the orientation training for every new employee.

Oxford has a completely open information environment. When customers or subscribers call, information about them and their health care plan is instantly available to the service representative taking the call. This is critical because Oxford tailors every plan to the specific employer on the basis of local doctors, coverages, and costs. This customer-focused approach has resulted in over 2,500 different plans. If a caller has a question, the computer prompts the person taking the call with the correct answer. This ensures that everyone answering the question will do so in the same way. In addition, every time the company "touches" a customer or subscriber in any way, the event is recorded in the database. It includes all transactions from simple inquiries by phone and mail to health care claims. This complete transaction history is available whenever a subscriber calls. When Oxford needs to contact a subscriber, the customer record shows the subscriber's preference for telephone or mail.

The customer database also provides Oxford with the ability to analyze transaction histories and improve operations. For example, if the company receives many subscriber calls with the same question about a particular coverage, it knows that its printed materials are not doing a good job of explaining that coverage, and it can take corrective action. Oxford can also analyze subscriber utilization to determine how to control costs. Analysis of claims history also enables the company to predict events. For example, when a woman stops submitting claims for birth control pills, Oxford sends a mailing on prenatal care and includes a suggestion that the subscriber take folic acid for prevention of birth defects. This may sound like a small thing, but in addition to the pain and anguish caused the parents, one baby with a birth defect can cost millions of dollars in claims.

Oxford continues to expand its use of its customer and subscriber database. The company recently hired an expert in fuzzy logic from IBM. He will be looking at new ways to analyze the subscriber database. Oxford is always seeking ways to improve health care, control costs, and improve customer service. None of what is described here would be possible had the company pursued the conventional approach of maintaining separate files in every functional area of the business.

Another company that has effectively used technology to support exceptional customer service is Amica Mutual Insurance Company. This Providence-based personal lines insurance company is well known for the way it takes care of its policyholders. The policyholders respond by consistently rating the company at the top of Consumer Reports' annual satisfaction survey of property and casualty companies. Policyholder satisfaction is so high, the company is able to rely on word-of-mouth recommendations as its primary form of marketing.

My personal experience shows how Amica uses technology and a customer information system to support customer service. When I relocated in 1990 and was looking for a new insurance company, I was already aware of Amica thorough the Consumer Reports surveys. I called Amica's toll-free number and provided the representative with all the information I had at hand. She told me what else Amica needed to know and invited me to call back when I had it ready. The next day, I called and asked for her by name. She was not available, but the person on the line said she could take care of me. All of the information from the previous day was stored in the company's database and available through her computer terminal.

By the time I had completed the application process for both automobile and homeowner policies, I had talked to at least four different people, but every time I called, it was as if I were talking to the same person. They always had all of the information at their fingertips. Since then, I have had two claims and have called frequently to ask questions about coverage. In every call, the first representative on the line has been able to answer my question or handle the transaction. The policy issue process was fast, flawless, and seamless. This level of service is possible because the Amica representatives have all the policyholder information instantly available. Because of their efficiency, they can offer this service at competitive rates and still operate profitably.

USAA is an insurance and financial services company that also rates high on Consumer Reports' annual satisfaction survey. This company also relies on customer information systems. USAA is about as close to paperless as a company can be in an industry that is recognized for the amount of paper it uses. USAA's paperless process begins for most of the company's areas in the mail room. As the day's incoming mail is opened, anything having to do with customer files and internal documents is immediately scanned into a computer system. These images are stored for retrieval by anyone in the company who needs the information and has the technology to access it, primarily the customer contact representatives. After that, the original document is returned to the customer if that has been requested. If it is not to be returned, it is shredded.

Like Amica, USAA stores everything in computer databases available to the employees who need it when they need it.

## The Customer Information System

Motorola, Oxford Health Plans, Amica Mutual Insurance, and USAA all enjoy the benefits of customer information systems. Each company has taken a different approach and tailored a system to its unique requirements. Because every company is different, it is not possible to define exactly what a customer information system might look like. The system design will depend on a number of factors including the size and organization of the company, the number of customers, the number of products and product lines, the customer information currently available and planned for the future, the company's information systems capability, and the resources available. However, some basic concepts are common to any system. These relate to the sources and types of information included and the ways in which it stored, accessed, processed, and maintained.

### *CIS Contents*

Here are some of the kinds of information the system might include:

- Basic customer data: the descriptive information every company has about its customers including company or individual name and shipping and billing addresses.
- Contracts: terms and conditions, coverages, and credit limits.
- Current transactions: on-order products, service projects in process, insurance or loan applications pending approval, billing and receivables, open inquiries and complaints.
- Transaction history: sales, projects, loans and policies, and revenue and payments.
- Salesforce: individual customer contact profiles (remember Mackay's sixty-six things to know about customers), sales call reports, and competitive products and services.
- Marketing: market research data and product requirements.
- Customer information: customer requirements and feedback from all of the methods used to listen to customers.

Note that much of this information is currently available somewhere in the typical organization, and a great deal of that available information is already stored and processed electronically. It is typically the "hard" information that is easily processed by computer: basic customer data, current and historical transactions, and financial history. However, there is an increasing need for "soft" information such as customer requirements and feedback, complaints and open issues, and executive and sales call reports. This information is stored in a text format. A CIS system can link hard and soft information and make both available for inquiry and analysis.

### Ownership

The CIS needs an owner just as the business processes described in Chapter Four do. That owner is responsible for developing, maintaining, and improving the processes and the computer software that makes up the system. He or she could be from any of several areas in the company including information systems, customer satisfaction, quality, or marketing.

Because the information in the CIS is drawn from many sources around the company, each major data element also needs an owner. The data owners will probably be the same executives or managers who own the business processes that enter and use the data. For example, in a manufacturing company the order entry process may be owned by an administrative executive. The same executive would logically be the owner of the on-order data as well. The data owners are responsible for maintaining the accuracy and currency of the information in the system. They are also responsible for determining who has access to the information. However, restricted access should be used sparingly. After all the whole purpose of the CIS is to make as much information as possible available to everyone who needs it, and sharing information is an integral part of the open organization culture described in Chapter Six.

Information in the system will eventually become out of date. The life expectancy of data will vary, but sooner or later data will have to be purged. The owner of each data segment decides when data have outlived their usefulness and provides for removing this information from the system. The data owner may select a purge date when the information is originally entered into the system or review the information periodically to decide when to remove it. In either case, provision for removing dated information is an important and necessary part of the system design.

### *CIS Customers*

Like the information systems department, the CIS is a service function. Its mission is to make customer information available to anyone in the company who needs it, quickly and easily. The end users are the customers of the CIS. It is up to them to measure and evaluate how well it meets their requirements for information availability and ease of access.

## CIS Barriers

Several barriers confront companies as they integrate customer information. Most are a result of company size, functional organization, and culture. Obviously it is more difficult for a large company with several divisions to tie together dozens of customer records and hundreds of sites than it is for a small company with one location and a single salesforce. Consider the information problems a company like 3M faces with its sixty-five divisions and eighty salesforces.

The problem is compounded by companies' functional organization structure. Each functional department owns its own customer files and processes for collecting, storing, and processing data. To make matters worse, the culture of most organizations does not encourage or reward sharing these data. The sales department gathers competitive information but does not share it with product development. The quality department gathers information on reliability but does not provide it to sales. Customer service may have a complaint-handling process but does not keep sales informed about open problems and issues.

The existing information systems in large companies are also a barrier to sharing and consolidating customer information. Although delegation and empowerment are important tools in the improvement process, they do have a downside when each division or department sets up its own system using computers and software that are incompatible with the technology used in other areas for the same purpose. The information systems department can also be a problem when it decides to create the ultimate customer information system. Like some of the information systems projects of old, this ultimate CIS takes years to develop and implement, and it is out of date the day it goes into use. It is better to find ways to make customer information available that are simple, quick, easy to use, and adaptable to the rapidly changing requirements of internal customers. In today's fast-paced sales and marketing environment, there is no place for more monuments to the information systems department.

Creating a customer information system requires the involvement of the CIS owner, the data owners, the internal customers, and the IS department. They all have to work together cooperatively to establish requirements, set priorities, design the system, accumulate the data, and train the end users. Although the job may seem overwhelming, especially in large companies, it is really like eating the proverbial elephant, taking one bite at a time. Begin by making the largest and most important chunks of data available. This might be existing customer master records or customer satisfaction survey data. Continue by adding the software linkage to bring in smaller pieces of information, like the customer complaint file. Then add electronic pointers to hard-copy records of surveys and research projects that are not stored in computer files.

## CIS Benefits

Clearly there are costs involved in creating a system like this. They include expenses for knowledge workers, computer hardware and software, communication networks, and end user training. However, in most cases offsetting savings and benefits far outweigh the challenges and costs. Here is a summary of the benefits that a CIS can provide.

First, a CIS helps the company present a single face to its customers. Whether customers are individual consumers or corporate decision makers, they tend to view each supplier as a single entity, not as a collection of businesses operating under a corporate logo. They are not concerned about their supplier's internal organization, and they expect to be treated as a customer of the company, not of various departments and divisions.

For example, a consumer thinks of a bank as a supplier of financial services, not as several separate businesses providing checking, savings, auto loans, and home mortgages, all conveniently located in the same place. Although it is not possible for everyone in a bank to know every customer personally, a CIS gives employees access to a complete profile whenever they need it. That enables them to recognize customers who may not have done business in their department yet but who are already good customers of other bank services.

Another benefit is that consolidating information often reduces the need for redundant records and files. This in turn cuts file maintenance costs and lowers the probability of errors and inconsistencies. In larger organizations, sharing customer survey results across the company may reduce the number of surveys needed. This also cuts costs and may reduce the number and frequency of customer contacts. Of course one of the primary reasons for customer surveys is to identify areas for improvement. Linking all the customer information provides a better foundation for analyzing processes and results and for setting priorities for continuous improvement projects.

Another benefit of the system is its usefulness in preparing company executives for calls on key customer contacts. Three of the large companies interviewed for this book revealed that it took them from two to three weeks just to find out how much total revenue a single large customer contributed to the company. And that information did not include all of the collective customer satisfaction information that would have been available through a CIS. Collective information is also important to product planning, finance, quality, and other departments. Any of these groups may need information on a single customer or cumulative data about a market segment or about all the company's customers.

Salespeople benefit from a CIS. It enables them to track all the elements of the relationship between a customer and the company. As they develop sales strategies, they can access information on customer satisfaction with current products and services, outstanding complaints and open issues, and the sales activities of other divisions. Having all this information better prepares them to develop sales proposals and manage customer partnerships.

The marketing department benefits from integrated customer information. They get a much clearer picture of each individual customer and of customer segments. They can identify trends and buying patterns and track customer loyalty. They can also cross-check customer information that comes from different sources within the company. By analyzing the more complete customer data and buying patterns on a CIS, the marketing department can develop profiles of lost customers and then create retention programs for the remaining customers with similar profiles.

There is one more major benefit to a CIS. The customer information in the system provides the core data for database marketing, the next major application of technology and the subject of the following section.

## Database Marketing

*Database marketing,* or DBM, is the application of technology to analyze customer information and use the results to create targeted marketing programs. Leading companies in telecommunications, banking, retail, insurance, and credit services are all creating massive customer files to take advantage of this high-leverage marketing approach. Business-to-business sellers are also getting into the action. They are all using their customer information to segment their markets, recognize trends, develop new products and to identify and communicate with their best customers. They are also ferreting out the unprofitable customers and customer segments and walking away from them.

The specific customer information needed for DBM will vary greatly by industry, but it is usually a subset of the data described in the previous section on the CIS. Companies that already have a large customer database have a head start in developing a DBM system, but even they will probably have to collect and enter additional data. Companies that have not consolidated their customer information can implement DBM without tying their operational customer databases together. All a company needs to get started is a database that includes descriptive information about its customers and their buying preferences and history. For most companies, this also means having a computer with sufficient data storage and processing capacity. However, database marketing concepts are simple enough that they have been implemented by very small companies using personal computers and even manual systems based on three-by-five-inch index cards.

In addition to the customer information, a DBM system of any size requires computer software to analyze that information. Like the contents of the marketing database, this software is specific to each industry, and its purpose is to identify buying patterns. In the past, companies divided customers into broad demographic and geographical segments. Using DBM, companies can now view consumers at the level of the postal route or the household or even the ultimate segment of one, the individual customer.

Once marketing identifies customer buying patterns, the company can take specific action directed at each segment based on segment buying patterns and preferences. For example, the marketing department may decide to restructure the product line, adding new items and deleting others. It may pinpoint direct mail or telemarketing efforts to selected customers to announce the changes or to highlight products or services for which they have shown a preference. Information in a DBM can also be used to create customer loyalty programs that recognize and reward the company's best customers.

## DBM Examples

At a recent American Marketing Association seminar, Karen Humphries Sallick of Harte-Hanks Direct Marketing reported the success of two of her clients with DBM. The first has over three million customers with an average annual value of $275 each. Analysis of the database revealed that the top 10 percent of the customers averaged $3,450 in purchases annually. It also revealed that 11 percent of those top customers were defecting each year. Sallick's client developed a retention program that included thank-you letters, gifts, and special services for the company's top clients. That program reduced attrition among the best customers by almost 10 percent, increased customer loyalty, and produced $10 million in additional annual revenue.

Another of Sallick's clients is a small regional specialty department store chain. The chain decided to target markdowns with a database marketing campaign. The first step was to profile active purchasing customers, identifying those that only bought during sales. The company then selected four products in three of the chain's stores to mark down. Using an $850 postcard mailing to customers who only bought on sale, the chain was able to increase sales 96 percent compared to the previous year while saving over $76,000 in unnecessary markdowns.

MCI Telecommunications is also using database marketing. One feature of MCI's program is its ability to identify customers the company refers to as "rate surfers." These are people who switch frequently from one long-distance carrier to the next based purely on a current promotion or the lowest rate. Anyone who has a history of frequent changes is marked in the database and is excluded from future telemarketing and direct mail efforts. After all, it takes months for a new customer to become profitable, and the rate surfers don't stay around long enough.

USAA also uses its customer information system for DBM. The company analyzed the database to create a profile of the policy-holders who are most likely to defect at renewal time and created a program to target and retain those customers. USAA knows that it is always less expensive to retain customers than to try to win them back after they have decided to leave. When policyholders send in an address change notice, USAA's system triggers a telephone call to offer assistance in setting up the move.

## DBM Implementation

Setting up a database marketing program is just like implementing any other improvement technique. The first step is to gain commitment from every part of the organization that is affected including sales, marketing, and information systems. The second step is to establish specific DBM goals, objectives, and measurements. These will help determine specifically what information is needed in the database and what software will be required to process it. An analysis of the existing customer information will show what additional data will have to be collected. This analysis will also determine the amount of computer data storage that will have to be available. As mentioned earlier, most companies will already have much of the data they need in customer and transaction history files. But some will have to begin collecting data as customers make purchases. After sufficient data have been collected, analysis of customer patterns can begin. These patterns will in turn suggest the kinds of marketing programs we have already discussed.

## Communications

So far, we have focused on how technology enables an organization to consolidate customer information in a single place or link it electronically to achieve the same end: to make the information available easily and quickly to everyone who needs it. In this section, we will shift our attention to the ways that companies are using technology to communicate information. They are linking people to information and people to people.

## Communication Tools

With all the focus on computers and telecommunications, it is easy to forget the simplest tools of technology, yet they can be responsible for sizable productivity gains. Just equipping salespeople with pagers and cellular telephones can make a big difference. Companies are learning that these two tools work well together as a cost-effective way to keep in touch with the salespeople active in their territories.

### Audiocassettes

Even more basic is the audiocassette. Companies are helping their salespeople make use of nonproductive driving time by providing sales and product training materials on audiocassettes to be listened to in the car. For example, the Baird Corporation in Bedford, Massachusetts, uses audiocassettes to deliver training to sales reps on the go. The tapes provide information on precall planning, presentations, product offerings, and a variety of other topics ("An Ear for Learning," 1995).

Interstate Batteries also uses audiocassettes as an effective way to deliver a newsletter to its more than one thousand route sales managers. According to Erin Cone, Interstate's public relations coordinator, the tapes "are a mixture of music, comments from management, and interviews with Interstate distributorship employees across the country." They are designed to entertain the salespeople while conveying information relevant to their jobs. The cassette format allows them to listen in their route trucks during the workday.

### Voice Mail

When effectively used, voice mail also improves communication among salespeople, their managers, and others in the organization by reducing "telephone tag." Most voice mail systems also allow messages to be sent to a list of selected users, making it easy for sales managers to broadcast information to their salespeople.

Obviously there is a downside to voice mail systems. When customers and colleagues use them as a fence or filter, they become a salesperson's worst enemy. Although the organization cannot control the way customers use voice mail, it can insist that its own telephones be answered by real people and that the voice mail box be used as a place to put messages. Customers appreciate hearing a real person answer the telephone. Recall from Chapter Three how IBM's voice mail system received the lowest ratings on the customer satisfaction surveys until a management emphasis program resolved the problem.

### Teleconferencing

Taking the use of the telephone a step further is audio teleconferencing. This technique is often overlooked, and yet it has proved very effective in bringing groups of remote people together. The format of the teleconference enforces good meeting behavior because it permits only one person to talk at a time and encourages each person to be concise in his or her comments. It also allows people to participate wherever they are—at home, in a car, in a telephone booth, or even on a commercial airliner.

Videoconferencing is also being used as a productivity booster in sales and marketing. At Federal Express, the top improvement teams from each division present their success stories to CEO Fred Smith and other company executives, often through a videoconference. The GE area councils described in Chapter Six use videoconferences to coordinate sales activities within their geographical areas.

### Telecommunications

Although linking people and information with low-technology approaches such as pagers, cassettes, and voice mail boosts productivity and improves processes, it is computers and telecommunications that are getting the attention. The earliest telecommunication efforts were based on the use of terminals connected to large mainframe computers. Originally located close to the mainframe, these "dumb" terminals were soon connected through computer networks to remote locations. Two early examples of remote terminals used for sales applications are the reservations systems at American Airlines and at Holiday Inns. These two systems revolutionized the way airline seats and hotel rooms were sold more than thirty years ago.

In the early 1980s, companies began to use electronic mail to speed communication between employees. At IBM, plant sites, administrative functions, headquarters locations, and remote sales and service branch offices were all linked by a computer network. Ultimately almost all of the employees were assigned computer IDs and passwords that allowed them to sign on to a terminal, send and receive messages with anyone else in the company, and share information files. In 1984, IBM's Home Terminal Program allowed some employees to have a terminal installed at their residences. The terminals were soon replaced with personal computers. Today many of IBM's salespeople work out of home offices completely equipped with personal computers and modems that connect on-line to the company's worldwide network.

Intracompany telecommunication networks do more than just transmit e-mail messages. The Cadillac Motor Division uses a network to transmit video programs with information and training to dealerships. Other companies send updated customer records, product information, and canned sales presentations to field salespeople. The availability of electronic communication of all types helps bring salespeople closer to the company and improves their productivity. With the advent of low-cost laptop computers and modems and the easy availability of telephone lines, salespeople anywhere can connect to their company's files to retrieve information and get and receive messages. If they have a cellular phone, they do not even need a local telephone connection to hook their laptop computer into their company's network.

### Electronic Data Interchange

In the mid-1980s, companies began to look for ways to expand their electronic networks and link themselves to customers and suppliers. The result of their search was electronic data interchange (EDI). EDI is defined as a standard structured method for the electronic exchange of business document information between a company and its trading partners.

By 1989, many of the largest companies had established a protocol and were linked with customers, suppliers, common carriers, and banks. They began by using one of several commercial networks to carry their data and maintain electronic mailboxes. These first applications transmitted purchase orders and processed financial transactions. They quickly grew to include

- Shipping schedules and releases
- Receiving advice
- Inventory data
- Order status and tracking
- Shipping information and freight bills
- Quality specifications, nonconformance information, and test results

General Electric viewed EDI as a way to extend continuous flow manufacturing to customers and suppliers. The company's early returns were impressive. Administrative cycle times were shortened by five to ten days. The company saved between $7 and $25 for every document it did not have to print. Data entry effort was reduced by 70 percent and input errors dropped by 90 percent.

The big three automakers were also early adopters of EDI. Today, even their smallest automotive parts suppliers have to use the EDI system to receive purchase orders and advise the automakers of schedules and parts shipments. The use of EDI has forced companies in general to reengineer many of their business processes. In many cases, EDI has also assumed functions once performed by salespeople.

Often EDI has profound side effects beyond the primary intent of the system. Texas Instruments' original interest in EDI was as a way to improve on-time delivery to customers. The company achieved that and more. The cycle time of the order entry process dropped from fourteen days to three. TI also gives the EDI system credit for reducing work in the sales offices. For example, the salespeople now handle 60 percent fewer customer inquiries about their order status.

Major retailers are also using technology to revolutionize the way they order products and manage their inventories. Chains like Wal-Mart, Kmart, and Target are linking electronically with their suppliers, making daily sales information available on a store-by-store basis. Each retailer is approaching the process a little differently, but generally these chains expect their suppliers to use the daily information to supply product when and where it is needed, managing their inventories, and being responsible for profitability of their product lines. In some cases, the supplier even takes responsibility for ordering the products and then fulfilling those orders.

When the major chains started looking for suppliers with whom to partner in about 1990, Bausch & Lomb Personal Products Division was one of the first to sign on. The objective of partnering was to take cost out of the distribution system and make it more efficient and responsive to customer needs at the store level. The bar code scanners at the checkout stands record sales data in each store. The data are transmitted by satellite to the retailer's computers daily. EDI links those computers with Bausch & Lomb, providing daily Bausch & Lomb sales information by store. This approach completely changes the way Bausch & Lomb works with the retailers. In effect, Bausch & Lomb owns the channel to the customer and gets direct customer feedback through product sales data. Marketing now focuses on creating consumer demand. For example, purchase of contact lens solution is 80 percent doctor driven, so marketing focuses on getting doctors to recommend the company's product. Of course Bausch & Lomb also advertises to consumers and conducts traditional promotional campaigns.

The bar scanner–satellite–EDI connection provides invaluable sales information to Bausch & Lomb. If the company wants to test a new product, package, price, or point-of-sale or advertising campaign, it can pick half a dozen retail stores in a target market and run a pilot. The chain retailers have detailed demographic information for each store location. By combining the geographical and demographic information with sales results, Bausch & Lomb gets the best possible customer feedback.

## Salesforce Automation

Salesforce automation, or SFA, is one of today's hottest application areas for technology. It is driven by sales management's need to improve salesforce productivity and desire to gain a competitive edge. The use of SFA has virtually exploded, spawning an industry of software developers, hardware manufacturers, consultants, and trainers. This section examines what salesforce automation is, how companies are using it, and what it takes for a successful SFA implementation.

### What Salesforce Automation Is

Salesforce automation is one of those improvement techniques that is not well defined. Ask sales managers what it is, and most will respond that SFA means giving salespeople laptop computers to help them in their day-to-day sales activities. Although this is frequently part of the SFA process, defining it this way runs counter to several of the best practices already covered in this book. It limits the productivity tools being considered to laptop computers, which eliminates even such mundane tools as fax machines, audiocassettes, voice mail systems, and pagers, all of which can contribute to improved sales processes. It may also exclude the broader use of technologies such as special purpose computers, companywide networks, and even the Internet. A more comprehensive definition of SFA is this: any use of technology to improve the sales process.

However, even this definition is limiting. It focuses the use of technology on a specific department—sales. And it does this at a time when companies are trying to break down functional barriers and improve cross-functional processes. It also ignores the value of aligning sales processes with the way customers make buying decisions. When companies make this alignment, they often find that many of sales processes need to be improved or reengineered or sometimes even discontinued. All these activities should come before applying technology to sales. Otherwise the company may be automating useless or dysfunctional processes or, as Will Ryan says, "paving cow paths."

However, given the current emphasis on the idea of salesforce automation, here are the ways companies are implementing it and integrating it into their overall improvement process.

## The Three Levels of SFA

There are three levels of SFA implementation: stand-alone, on-line, and advanced.

### *Stand-Alone Applications*

Most companies begin their salesforce automation projects by providing salespeople with stand-alone laptop computers, even if they plan to move to on-line and advanced applications later. Laptops are a way for salespeople to enjoy some productivity improvements and get comfortable with the operation and use of computers. Unfortunately many companies stop after they provide their salespeople with computers and some basic software. Today the most common SFA application remains word processing, even though many other stand-alone applications can help salespeople improve their effectiveness and efficiency.

Building on the standard word processing packages are programs that help salespeople write better letters, reports, and proposals and other programs that expand vocabulary and support correct grammar, punctuation, and spelling. Salespeople can also build their own files of standard documents such as form letters and proposals. Presentation programs such as Freelance Graphics, Power Point, and Harvard Graphics give salespeople the ability to create their own customer presentations or tailor those supplied by the company. Spreadsheet software and accounting packages help salespeople with travel and expense accounting.

One of the most popular computer-based productivity tools for salespeople is the contact manager. Programs like ACT, Maximizer, and Gold Mine help salespeople maintain their calendars, track sales projects, and establish automatic follow-up reminders. These programs can also keep customer name and address records and use them to generate letters automatically. With proper coding of customer master records, they can identify prospects based on specific selected criteria. Harvey Mackay's *Sharkware* even provides for recording the sixty-six things he believes every salesperson should know about his or her customers.

Besides the packaged programs, many companies provide their salespeople with software tailored to the specific business. Insurance agents need software to calculate client coverage and retirement needs. Manufacturing reps need pricing and proposal information. Financial salespeople need software to calculate loan and lease proposals. All these applications can run on stand-alone laptop computers.

### On-Line Applications

At the next level of SFA, the laptop computer is connected to a host system. This on-line connection usually employs a modem and a conventional telephone line direct to the host. However, it may also be made through a private communications network, an on-line service, or the Internet. In any case, the connection with the host allows real-time inquiry into company computer files. Salespeople can get the latest pricing information and delivery schedules, check on a customer's on-order position, and read the latest product announcements. They can also send messages to and receive responses from other people in the organization.

At this point, the process goes beyond the bounds of the sales department, even if in a limited way. Where most stand-alone applications simply enhance what the salesperson already does, the on-line applications invite cross-functional process improvement. They can fundamentally alter the way information flows, increasing its availability and the speed at which it can be accessed.

### Advanced Applications

Although many stand-alone and on-line applications increase sales productivity, it is the advanced applications that provide companies with the real benefits of applying technology to their sales processes. These benefits include expanded communication capability for salespeople and the use of new applications that are virtually impossible without the creative use of technology. Companies that reach this level of salesforce automation have overcome the limitations created by a narrow definition of SFA. They are taking a global view, looking at cross-functional processes. What is even more important, they are examining their customer relationships and finding ways to improve the processes that flow across company boundaries. Many are the marketing and sales processes that must align with the customer decision process to be effective.

Many of the advanced applications are made possible by the new category of PC software referred to as *groupware*. Susanna Opper, president of Susanna Opper & Associates and coauthor of *Technology for Teams* (Opper and Fersko-Weiss, 1992), defines groupware as "any information system designed to enable groups to work together electronically." To do this, the system must be able to manage communications among the group members and between group members and the databases that contain the information on which they are working. These sound like simple enough requirements to meet. The job becomes more difficult, however, when the group members are in different places, such as salespeople who are located in field sales branches. It becomes even more complex when the company's customers are added to the mix of users. They are remote and may not even have the same kind of computers or operating environments. The company headquarters might have a host computer or server running a UNIX operating system. The marketing department might use Macintoshes. The salespeople might be on IBM-compatible laptops with Windows 95, and the customers might be on still other platforms.

To make it tougher still, all of the users may have an interest in the same information at the same time. The system must be able to replicate the information and keep track of all of the copies. It also has to keep track of who can see each record, who can have a copy, and who can actually make changes to it. In addition to managing databases and the communication between the users, the system must also have computing capability. This capability may range from simple word processing to spreadsheet and presentation development software. It may also include a contact management system, as described earlier. Companies may also want to create their own unique applications or have them developed by the many consulting and service firms available.

Few software development companies have come close to providing all of the capability required for groupware. The acknowledged leader of this software category is Lotus Notes. Clearly IBM recognized the value of this product, having paid three and a half billion dollars to acquire the Lotus Development Company and its groupware technology in 1995.

It is easier to understand the function of groupware if we begin by looking at the databases in a hypothetical small manufacturing firm. Recall that at the first level of SFA, the salespeople have data about their customers stored in their laptop computers. They also have software to process the data: word processors, presentation programs, spreadsheets, and a personal information manager. The headquarters computer in our hypothetical company also has customer records used for order entry, shipping, customer service, and so on. Marketing also has customer files and leads generated through advertising and business shows.

At the third level of SFA, groupware provides an environment where all these data can be shared by those who need them. A master record for each customer is stored in the host computer or server. Every salesperson has an electronic copy of all of the master records for the customers in his or her territory. The salespeople use and update these records just as they would at the first level of SFA. Periodically they transfer the updated records to the server, so that others using the database will have current information.

The customer records in the server are available to everyone else in the organization who needs them. They can use them in the server or copy them to departmental systems for analysis or processing. If appropriate, the same record can support order confirmation, shipping, billing, customer service, and database marketing programs. This means one record to maintain, lower costs, fewer errors, and better service.

The marketing department can maintain current sales support materials such as catalogues, price lists, delivery schedules, standard proposal pages, and customer presentations in the server. Any salesperson can download these files into his or her laptop computer and modify them to fit a current customer situation. The result is faster response to salespeople, elimination of much of the paper flow to salespeople, and salespeople and others who have the most up-to-date information available whenever it is needed. The marketing department can also use the groupware system to distribute leads and track their progress through the sales process. Lotus Development Corporation itself uses Lotus Notes to assign sales leads to the company's value-added remarketers. The remarketers respond by communicating back to Lotus the status of the lead and the business closed as a result.

Salespeople can download more than just marketing information. The status of customer orders, open issues and complaints, accounts receivable, and customer satisfaction data can also be stored in the server and downloaded into the laptops. The remote salesperson can link up to the server each evening and download the most current information about his or her customers. Then he or she is ready to plan the next day's calls, write a proposal, or develop an account plan.

It is always a challenge to provide sales coverage for large customers with remote sites and divisions. Companies frequently assign each customer site to a local salesperson. To be most effective, however, they also need to coordinate sales activities and ensure consistent service levels, pricing, and terms. To accomplish these objectives, many companies use national account managers. Groupware systems are a natural support tool for national account managers, giving them easy access to customer information and sales activities in all of their customers' remote locations. These systems also give the managers and their sales team members the ability to participate in electronic discussions of common issues. They can work together to create account plans and companywide plans and proposals.

If groupware can support remote sales teams, it can do the same for improvement teams as well. One of the biggest problems with getting salespeople involved in teams is their remote locations. Groupware helps solve this problem by allowing team members to share information and discuss issues on-line. There are even software programs that support decision making for teams, products like Ventana Corporation's VisionQuest. These products help remote team members to participate effectively in problem-solving sessions—identifying problems and root causes, ranking them, then recommending solutions.

The discussion boards supported by groupware are among the software's most powerful features. When Santa Clara–based UB Networks, a supplier of networking hardware and software products and supporting services, first established its Lotus Notes system, the objective was to make headquarters information available to field salespeople. However, the company also set up a discussion board as a way for remote salespeople to communicate with each other. Although acceptance was slow at first, use of the discussion board soon exploded. For the first time, remote salespeople could communicate easily and freely. In the evening, they could link to the server and download the latest discussion information, read it, and respond or add a topic of their own.

If a UB Networks salesperson discovers a competitive situation in an account, he or she can post the circumstances to the discussion board. Salespeople in other parts of the country respond with their own experiences in similar situations. Now the full resources and experience of the whole salesforce can be brought to bear on situations in every territory. This capability is particularly useful and comforting to inexperienced salespeople who are in locations remote from their sales managers. It also has a profound team-building effect for the whole sales organization.

There is another advantage to the UB Networks sales discussion board. The company's senior management can also read the issues posted to the board. Managers now have the benefit of learning promptly what is on the salespeople's minds. What is the general attitude of the salesforce? Are there product function or quality problems, competitive pressures, or delivery or pricing issues? UB Networks has also made some files in the groupware system available to its customers, who can post questions or new product requirements to the system. UB Networks has assigned specific people the responsibility to watch the board, collect customer questions and ideas, and get answers back to them quickly. Of course this encourages customer participation in the new product development process.

DSSI, the software value-added remarketer, went a step further. Company president Ken Norland set up a discussion board for the company's customers where they could communicate with each other. They could ask questions and share ideas about their own experience with the Lotus Notes product. The discussion board virtually became an electronic users group. Of course, DSSI kept an eye on the discussions, using it as another way to listen to its customers. According to Lotus Development Corporation, of the companies that have had Notes installed for two years or more, about 60 percent use it in at least one intercompany application (Kirkpatrick, 1994).

The examples so far have focused on companies with a single product line and salesforce. A groupware system also has benefits for organizations that are in several businesses. Consider the major accounting and consulting organization Coopers & Lybrand. That firm's National Financial Advisory Services Group has adopted Lotus Notes as its groupware system. Each office tracks customer contacts and engagements for each of its own divisions.

A manager in Coopers & Lybrand's Chicago office litigation support division demonstrates how she uses the system for business development. She notices a newspaper article describing how a major manufacturing company is about to file suit against a competitor for patent infringement. Although her division has not done business with the company, she checks the firm's groupware database and finds that the company is a client of Coopers & Lybrand's audit and consulting divisions. A second database inquiry identifies the names and titles of the client contacts for each division. Database inquiry number three gives her the names of the Coopers & Lybrand account managers who support the client. Her next step is to call one of them and ask him or her to make an appointment with the client decision maker. Without the groupware database, she would have had only two choices: make a blind call on the company, without knowing whether it was already a client and if so what the situation was, or call every other Coopers & Lybrand division first.

All the groupware examples so far have been based on the use of Lotus Notes, but there are many other approaches that companies can take. For example, the Bank of Oklahoma has developed an application similar to the one that Coopers & Lybrand uses but using the bank's own software. Their system tracks customers of the bank's three divisions: personal lines, commercial lines, and trust. Salespeople in each division can easily check a customer's status in all three of the divisions to coordinate activities and prepare for sales calls, presentations, and proposals.

Many companies have demonstrated the value of salesforce automation, even those who have chosen to focus on the basic stand-alone applications. Those that have chosen to pursue advanced uses of technology have had even greater success. Their efforts go beyond the bounds of the sales organization as they use technology to improve existing cross-functional sales processes and implement new ones never before possible. Perhaps a new label for their efforts would be appropriate. Rather than salesforce automation, their programs might better be referred to as sales process automation.

Whatever the sales automation program is called, applying technology in sales needs to start out on the right foot. It is best to begin with the applications that have the most value for salespeople. Some companies begin by asking salespeople to enter huge amounts of customer information or make major changes in they way they do business. These companies usually meet resistance that sometimes borders on disaster.

The most effective way to begin any SFA project is to pick applications that have a direct positive benefit for the salespeople. Then select a few computer-literate salespeople, possibly those who have already invested in technology on their own. Use this group to conduct a pilot test of the proposed applications, working out the bugs and getting success stories to tell to the rest of the salesforce. Only then is it safe to roll out the first applications to the entire salesforce. Support the initial projects with intense training and technical assistance. Then recognize and reward the salespeople who accept and use the new tools. The companies that have taken this approach have generally been successful. Most salespeople will ultimately accept the use of technology as they recognize its benefits. As they become more comfortable with it, applications can be added that benefit other functional departments and customers.

## The Internet

The Internet is today's hottest new tool for sales and marketing. J. Paul Giroux, director of systems engineering at Sun Microsystems of Canada, reports that in January 1996, the Internet connected an estimated 40 million individual users. They are linked through almost 10 million computers and 250,000 networks at companies, universities and colleges, and governmental agencies around the world, and those numbers are growing daily. Giroux also notes that as many as 10 million people are active users of the World Wide Web. These users are sending messages to family members and friends; shopping from home; checking news, weather, sports, and financial reports; and chatting about common interests. Companies are using the Internet to communicate with suppliers and customers, advertise to prospects, and support their products and services. The Internet is spawning everything from romantic relationships to business partnerships.

## The Internet in Sales

The Internet has a variety of uses in a sales organization. Its simplest application is as a low-cost electronic communications link between the salespeople, their managers, and others in the company. Every member of the organization who subscribes to an on-line service or independent service provider gets the ability to send e-mail messages to anyone else with an Internet address. Salespeople can also use the Internet for two-way communications with any of their customers that have Internet addresses. The Internet can even become a company-wide e-mail system when people use security features such as passwords and software firewalls. Such systems are referred to as *intranets.* Many companies are already using them to link headquarters locations, sales offices, and remote salespeople together as if they had their own private networks. Intranets get electronic communication systems up and running quickly and avoid most of the cost of setting up and maintaining a private network. Using the Internet in this way enables many of the salesforce automation applications described earlier.

The World Wide Web can also be a rich source of easily available on-line information for salespeople on the go. They can sign on from home, the office, or many hotel rooms; read the latest business news; check their customers' web sites for up-to-date information and announcements; make hotel, airline, and rental car reservations; and check tomorrow's weather. They can also use the web for research or even to check up on the competition.

## The Internet in Marketing

The exploding use of the World Wide Web is providing companies with a whole new way to communicate with their customers. The web has become a virtual shopping mall where thousands of vendors display their products and services. The successful vendors in this mall are not just using the web as an electronic billboard with a flashy sign. They are taking advantage of the medium to make the buying process interactive.

Some companies are also using the web as a way for their customers to reach them more easily. Recall from Chapter One how Eastman Chemical uses its web site as a way for customers worldwide to reach technical support people. Other companies are using the Internet as a way to listen to their customers for requirements and feedback. For example, when Ford was designing the latest generation of the Mustang, management wanted input from loyal owners. Ford used e-mail as one way to get feedback on proposed models, designs, engines, and features. Computer software and hardware companies monitor Internet newsgroups and on-line services' bulletin boards to stay abreast of what their customers are saying about their products and services.

Michael D. Troiano, CEO of Ogilvy & Mather Interactive, recently described the agency's work in creating interactive marketing programs. One example was ExpressNet, a program that the agency developed for American Express in conjunction with America Online (AOL). American Express cardholders enroll in the program to get on-line access to their account information plus a cross-indexed database of travel-related information. Available through AOL, the program also allows users to make travel reservations, shop on-line, and learn about special offers and events. The program is targeted at what Troiano calls the "Wired Road Warrior." The objective of the program is to build customer loyalty and retention and increase "share-of-wallet" and average bill size. Launched January 30, 1995, the program has been an outstanding success. In its first year, it drew 220,000 enrollees and generated 31,000 new card applications for American Express.

The Internet is not limited to consumer marketing. CADIS, Inc., a Sun Microsystems business partner, worked with National Semiconductor to take advantage of a large business-to-business marketing opportunity at that company. Approximately one million engineers worldwide can specify National Semiconductor components, and the company needed a new way to reach more of these prospects with information about its 30,000-part product line. It estimated that its sales representatives, systems engineers, distributors, and database marketing efforts could only reach about 25 percent of these engineers. With the rapid changes in the product line, catalogues and CD-ROMs were too slow to reach the market.

The solution was the Internet. Customers can now locate information in the 30,000-part "haystack" through an easy-to-use search method built into National Semiconductor's web site. When customers locate the information they need, they can download product data sheets and application notes on-line. The Internet-based system has resulted in greater market penetration. It provides more current and accurate information at a reduced cost. Because the information is available twenty-four hours a day, it has increased the company's success in overseas marketing. For National Semiconductor, the Internet is an effective, low-cost marketing tool.

Companies don't have to be as large as American Express or National Semiconductor to take advantage of electronic communication with their customers and prospects. Even the smallest organizations can use the capability of the Internet. They can set up a homepage and open for business. With a little work and minimal cost, they can look just as good as their larger competitors. The company that gets there first can gain a real competitive advantage.

Consider the example of NeuroDimension, Inc., a small software start-up located in Gainesville, Florida. The company recently released its first product. Called NeuroSolutions, it is a program for developing artificial neural networks. This amazing new technology gives a personal computer the ability to learn from input data. Although its name sounds highly technical, many of its applications are really down to earth. They include financial forecasting, speech recognition, prediction of credit card default, machine maintenance scheduling, and a host of others.

As a small start-up company, NeuroDimension needed a way to reach prospects as quickly, easily, and efficiently as possible. The company identified the most likely early adopters and the best ways to reach them. Of course the company used ads in trade journals and demonstrated its product at business shows. However, its greatest success has been through its homepage on the Internet. Prospective customers searching the World Wide Web for neural network information are pointed to the NeuroDimension homepage. There they can get a description of what a neural network is and what it does. They can also download a demonstration program complete with a variety of examples they can run themselves. If they decide they like the program, the homepage also gives them ordering information. One of the company's founders, Gary Lynn, reports that the company is getting more than half of its new business as a direct result of the Internet marketing efforts, and is currently growing at the rate of 30 percent a month. It is the least-cost, most effective marketing tool the company has found.

## The Internet and the Customer

The Internet is changing more than the way companies sell, it is also changing the way customers buy. Recently a colleague, Jim Holland, was conducting a large research project. He decided he needed a 28.8-baud modem to speed up his search of Internet files. He wanted input from experienced users on performance, reliability, service, and cost. Holland signed on to an Internet Newsgroup and asked for information on the various brands of modems. Then he checked out the user forums on the manufacturers' web sites to find out what kind of problems their users were having. The information from these two Internet sources narrowed his search to two vendors. Only then did he check local dealers for the best price. Virtually none of his input came from traditional channels such as retail stores, 800 numbers, or catalogs.

## Web Site Implementation

Setting up a web site storefront is not just creating an on-line, electronic brochure with exciting graphics. Quite the contrary, it is a whole new way of reaching customers and prospects. The early users of the web have learned several lessons.

### *Make It Easy to Find*

No matter how well-designed, exciting, and informative a web site is, it is worthless if customers cannot find it. Be sure the site and its Internet address are shown predominantly in every other form of the company's marketing communications. Then get it into the popular on-line Internet search tools, and make sure it is referenced in as many other web sites as possible.

### Make It Interesting and Interactive

Many of today's buyers don't want advertising hype or high-pressure sales practices. They are looking for factual information delivered to them when and where they want it. They also want two-way interactive communication with vendors, making them active participants in the buying process. For example, when ITT Hartford Life Insurance Company set up its web site, it included the usual company and product information for browsers to read. One page was different, though. It contained an interactive capability that allowed users to calculate their estate tax liability and showed them ways to reduce the burden using products from the Hartford. Soon after the company opened its web site, it got the usage statistics that the World Wide Web provides automatically. These statistics show how often browsers visit each page and how long they stay. The reports revealed that the estate tax page was by far the most popular place on the company's web site.

### Change It Often and Keep It Up to Date

Make the web site easy to find, and interested customers and prospects will come. Make it informative and fun, and they will return again. However, if they return only to find that it does not have something new to offer, they are unlikely to come back again.

Last fall one of the major downhill ski manufacturers announced a radical new model. The manufacturer's web site had an enticing description, and the ski magazines gave the ski promising early reviews. The company expanded the line with several new variations of the ski. However, almost eight months later, the web site remained unchanged and had no reference to the new models. The company lost an opportunity to capitalize on the response generated by the ski press's interest in the initial product.

### Keep It Simple

There is a temptation to use the technical capability of the web to create fancy full-motion video graphics for the web site. It may look good, but unfortunately, given the current line speed limitations, being fancy takes too much user time. Web browsers will not wait for more than a few minutes for a fancy graphic to download. They go off to another site. Experienced web site developers have learned to keep sites simple, informative, and interactive.

### Maintain Marketing Ownership

One of the biggest mistakes a company can make is to let the information systems department own the web site. As Sun's Paul Giroux reports, do that and you will get "geekware." The web site is a marketing tool. To take full advantage of it, keep it in the marketing department. If IS attempts to own the effort, take it outside the company. There are plenty of independent service companies that can design an effective site, get it up on the web, and maintain it.

## The Internet in Sales and Marketing: Conclusion

The Internet is revolutionizing the sales and marketing processes for many companies. As Larry Weber, president of the Cambridge, Massachusetts–based Larry Weber Group says, "The Internet is big, it's cheap, and it's easy."

## More Technology Issues

There are two additional issues to be considered in the overall use of technology. First, do not view it as an end in itself. That is like finding a solution and then looking for a problem to solve with it. As I said in the beginning of this chapter, technology is just an enabler. It makes it possible to improve existing processes and to do things that could never be done before. The objective is to ensure that the things that technology can improve or do really need to be done at all. Throughout this chapter, we have seen examples of how companies use technology to support the other best practices. The defining question is, What are the opportunities and problems that the organization faces and how can the application of technology help address them?

The second issue concerns the traditional information systems department. Many of the companies interviewed for this book reported that their IS departments were, at best, reluctant supporters and, at worst, roadblocks to the use of technology in the sales and marketing organizations. Unfortunately many IS departments still regard themselves as the gatekeepers of technology rather than servants of their customers, the other functions in the company. Others are so involved in creating massive application monuments to the IS department that they don't have the time or resources available to support even minimal stand-alone salesforce automation applications. What is worse, they even try to prevent the sales department from moving ahead alone. They are concerned that sales might develop applications that are not compatible with the IS department's long-term plans.

Today the application of technology will not wait for massive two- and three-year IS projects. Only about one-third of these projects are fully successful anyway. The objective in technology today is to use flexible and adaptable computer and software platforms and employ package application programs where possible. This allows the sales and marketing functions to move quickly to gain and maintain a competitive advantage.

## Conclusion

Of all the best practices described in this book, applying technology is today's most visible. It has reached this status within the past five years, and it appears that it will continue to revolutionize the way customers buy and companies sell in the future. That makes it important to stay aware of changing technology, looking for ways to use it to address opportunities and resolve problems. It is the companies that find ways to use technology, frequently ways it was never intended to be used, that will create and maintain their competitive edge. The others will just be playing catch-up.

# Chapter Eight

# | **Making It Happen**

Over the past three years, people from dozens of companies across the United States and Canada have heard about the practices described in this book. They have read about them in magazine articles and newsletters; attended workshops, seminars, and conferences; and taken part in individual presentations. Their response has been almost universal. Virtually all of them have accepted the value of the six best practices and the critical need to implement them in the sales and marketing functions of their organizations.

Obviously, if accepting the ideas were all that was needed, everyone would already be using them, but most companies still have a long way to go. The most frequently asked questions by audiences and clients reveal the problem. As one vice president of reengineering asked, "How do we make this thing roll? How do we make it happen?" Even the companies that have implemented some of the ideas want to know how to maintain their momentum.

## Marriott's Formula for Continuous Improvement

Marriott International, Inc. has always focused on customer satisfaction and continuous improvement. Jim Burns, former vice president for Total Quality Management at Marriott, explains that the company uses a formula to explain what it takes to make change happen. He says the change effort succeeds when $D \times V \times F > R$. Here is how the formula works.

$D$ represents dissatisfaction. Without dissatisfaction with the way things are, there is little incentive for the organization to change. However, just being dissatisfied won't do the job. The organization also needs *V,* a compelling vision of the future, shared by everyone. Even these two won't make change happen unless people know what to do about *D* and *V.* People need to know how to take *F,* the first step. When all three factors are multiplied together, the result must be greater than *R,* the organization's resistance to change. As anyone with basic math skills knows, if any of the first three factors in the formula is zero, overcoming resistance will be impossible.

One internal company consultant expressed it this way: "We all look at the books, we all follow the steps, we have all of the bases covered, and then when it is time, the appetite just doesn't seem to be there." Clearly, in some organizations, there is not enough dissatisfaction with the present state or a compelling enough vision of the future to overcome the organization's resistance to change. A sales vice president at one of the world's largest pharmaceutical companies said, "We know we should do it, but there are ten other programs competing with it." At that company, the resistance comes from viewing the best practices as programs, additional things to do rather than more effective ways to get things done. Both these companies could benefit from Marriott's formula.

The formula is easy to turn into an effective improvement planning process. The process begins by identifying where the organization is today and understanding that staying there, or maintaining the status quo, is a going-out-of-business strategy. The next step is to create a compelling vision of the future. It is where the organization wants to go, but it is not going to be a comfortable new place. Rather it is a constant state of continuous improvement. The last step is to identify the best way to achieve the vision and the first step to take on the journey.

## The Four Phases of Implementation

Making it happen and keeping it going can be divided into four phases: commitment, planning, initial implementation, and continuous improvement. The first phase is a preliminary step but nonetheless important. It involves making or getting a solid management commitment to proceed. As described in Chapter Two, it is almost impossible to succeed without senior management commitment. The planning phase includes gathering information and developing an implementation plan. The third phase is taking the first steps, putting the plan to work. Phase four is continuous improvement, a continuation of the second and third phases.

To be successful, an improvement plan must be specific to the organization. It is a function of the degree of commitment, urgency of the need to change, and resources available, and no two companies are alike. This four-phase approach is very general and is intended to be a guide rather than a prescription. It can be applied within a functional area such as sales or marketing. However, it is more effective when carried out companywide.

## Phase I: Commitment

Senior management commitment begins with a triggering event. Next management takes a step toward institutionalizing improvement with the creation of an organization to manage the improvement effort.

### *The Trigger*

The commitment phase begins with a trigger, some happening that causes the organization's leadership to begin the improvement process. In those rare cases where change is initiated by a born-again CEO, the trigger may just be an awareness that the business could be managed more effectively. However, as described in Chapter Two, 95 percent of the time the trigger is an external event. Recall these examples:

At Xerox, the trigger for the company's Leadership Through Quality initiative came in the late 1970s. It was then that CEO David Kearns learned that Japanese competition could sell copiers at a price equal to Xerox's manufacturing cost and that the reason was not lower labor cost, it was higher product quality.

The trigger for Eastman Chemical's Make International Business Easy program was a finding from the company's customer satisfaction survey. When Eastman's U.S. customers rated satisfaction at the 75 percent level and international customers came in at 55 percent, company leaders knew they had to take action.

For GTE, the November 1982 *Business Week* article mentioned in Chapter Three that identified the company's low customer satisfaction was the wake-up call and led to that company's Quality, the Competitive Edge initiative.

Wal-Mart and Kmart announced to their major suppliers that they had to be able to link up to these retailers' computers and take orders through EDI. That was the trigger for companies like Bausch & Lomb to completely redesign the way they sell to and support these key retail customers.

These examples all show how an external trigger creates dissatisfaction with the present state. Ultimately these and the other companies referenced in this book have responded by implementing the six best practices. The triggers were so strong, there was no question about moving ahead.

Unfortunately the triggers that begin some efforts are not so strong. Often a CEO reads a book on a new technique like benchmarking or the sales vice president hears that the competition is giving laptop computers to its salespeople. These company leaders like what they hear and delegate the process to someone else to implement in the organization. The directive passes down through six layers of management and ends up in some staff department. No one quite knows why it is there, who will pay for it, how it ties into the organization's overall strategy, or how the results will be measured. In effect, the commitment phase has been omitted, and the initiative goes straight to the planning phase. The result is an unfair test at best and a recipe for disaster at worst. The objective of the commitment phase is to ensure that the leaders of the organization know what they are signing up for and what to expect. Without that knowledge, they often fail to support the effort with their personal involvement and adequate resources. When the outcome does not meet their uninformed expectations, and more often than not it does not, they blame the technique or people who implement it.

When the trigger is weak, it is critical that the organization go though the commitment phase. It is better for company leaders to reject an idea after closer examination than it is for them to go ahead without a full understanding of the effort's implications and their personal role in it. The commitment phase reduces the chance that the effort will not be successful.

To reach an enlightened decision to go ahead with any substantial organization-wide effort, senior leadership needs to clearly understand these two elements:

- *The need.* What is the problem this change will solve? In the Marriott formula, this is the dissatisfaction factor. It is what the organization is moving away from.
- *The benefits.* What will the organization get that it does not have (or have enough of) now? This is the vision factor, or what the organization is moving toward.

Just understanding the needs and benefits is not enough to sustain a commitment. As we saw in Chapter Two, commitment also requires the personal time and attention of the organization's leadership. Company leaders must revise the way they measure success. They must also recognize and reward a new and different set of personal behaviors and actions among the people in the organization.

Finally management must recognize the financial investment required to make improvement happen. Although Philip Crosby made popular the idea that "quality is free" (1979), many managers miss the point that quality still requires an up-front investment. Failure to fund improvement initiatives adequately is one major reason why many fail.

Getting a commitment from the organization's leadership is just like getting an order for a product or service. It begins by finding out who must make the commitment, who must support the commitment, and who influences the decision to commit. The next step is to find out what the decision makers, influencers, and supporters need to know to make a commitment, then to provide the information they need to make a decision. Sometimes it is important to give the customer more information than they request just to ensure that they know everything necessary to make a real commitment. It is usually better not to proceed than to do so with a commitment based on inadequate information. Most executives and managers do not like surprises.

If the leadership is not willing to commit to a major implementation of the best practices, consider conducting pilot projects. A pilot can often be conducted at small cost and risk while showing the value of one or more of the best practices. However, if the organization's leadership does agree to a pilot, be sure to get a commitment for additional action when the pilot is a success. This requires that management agree to the measurement of success and establish a baseline measurement of current performance before the pilot begins.

The information on which company leaders make a decision can come from many sources. They may get it through formal training in classes, workshops, seminars, and business conferences. Books and articles are also a good source of information. Customers and suppliers are often willing to provide input. After all, they have a vested interest in the organization's success.

### Establish an Organization

The next activity in the commitment phase is to establish an organization to manage the initiative or the pilot project. If the effort is companywide, the senior management committee is a logical choice to coordinate the overall activities. If it is within the sales or marketing function, the responsible senior executive and his or her direct reports are the logical group for the leadership team. Subgroups can be established to oversee the activities in departmental efforts or cross-functional process improvement projects. However, the senior management committee is in the best position to put together the initial organization-wide plan and tie it into the business strategy.

A prerequisite for steering committee or improvement team members is adequate time. They will need to meet fairly frequently, particularly during the planning and early implementation phases. They may also have individual assignments or lead subgroups that are carrying out planning activities and implementing projects.

Many companies also identify a champion for their effort. The champion is usually someone at a relatively high level in management with a strong interest in the success of the project and a belief in the effectiveness of the specific practices being applied. The champion should expect to spend a minimum of 35 percent of his or her time on the project.

This is also the time to identify any outside resources such as consultants, trainers, research firms, or computer software and hardware vendors needed for the project. It is useful to get them involved as early as possible in the effort, to get their input for the planning process.

## Phase II: Planning

After the organization's leadership makes a firm commitment, defines an organization, and identifies the players, the next step is to develop an implementation plan. Many of the companies that provided input for this book agreed on the importance of a sound plan, stating that if they had the process to do over, they would do a better job of planning and that they would base their plan on better information.

The objectives of the planning phase are to determine where the organization is today, where it wants to be in the future, and what steps it must take to get from here to there. As part of the planning process, the organization also identifies who is responsible for every activity, sets target dates for milestones and project completion, and estimates the financial and human resources required for each major project. Planning objectives also include setting specific goals for the overall improvement process and the specific projects within it. The last objective is to anticipate the barriers to implementing the plan and include specific actions to overcome them.

### Gathering Information

To achieve these objectives, the planning process needs to be based on sound information. The first step in the gathering information phase, then, is do an audit to identify the data that are necessary. The information audit answers the question, What does the organization already know and what additional information will be necessary? Some of this information may have been identified and gathered during the commitment phase. The rest will have to be gathered now.

### Qualitative Information

The information needed may be qualitative and include customer attitudes, industry trends, and competitive intelligence. Obviously the most important sources of information are customers. The company can gather customer input through the listening methods described in Chapter Two. Keep in mind that sales and marketing also have internal customers. Their qualitative input is also important to the planning process.

External and internal customers are not the only sources of information about where the organization is today and where it might want to go. Executives, managers, and staff can also provide information. In addition, input comes from employee opinion surveys and individual and focus group interviews. Employee exit interviews can provide particularly candid input on the current state of the organization. These interviews are a particularly good source of input if the organization is suffering from a high turnover in the salesforce. Suppliers, the trade press, industry analysts, associations, and consultants are also sources of useful information.

*Quantitative Information*

Information needed for the planning process may also be quantitative. Chapter Two includes information on management measurements, and Chapter Four describes ways to gather measurement data for business processes. Whatever its source, sound quantitative information provides the basis for creating an implementation plan and a benchmark for future improvements. Quantitative measures will tell the organization how well their improvement activities really work.

One possible finding of an information audit may be that the organization does not have enough data on which to base a sound plan. This is frequently the case. Many companies decide to go ahead on the limited data they have available. They begin their improvement efforts on a leap of faith and collect more information early in the implementation phase. Other companies stop to collect information through special surveys and one-time measurement projects. The decision on which course to take is up to the senior leadership of the organization.

However, having current external customer input is an absolute must. Companies that do not conduct regular customer surveys or do not have reasonably current customer input should consider a qualitative research study. Such a study can be conducted in eight to twelve weeks by a professional research firm using face-to-face or telephone interview techniques. The cost can be relatively low and the data invaluable to the planning process. It is amazing to learn how many companies get two to three years into an improvement process without ever having listened to their customers. When they finally get around to it, they often learn that they have been working on the wrong things or making changes that are not effective in the eyes of their external customers.

The last information needed for the planning process concerns the organization itself. Whether the improvement process is organization-wide or focuses on the sales and marketing functions, it should include the company's mission, vision, values, business strategy, goals, and objectives. To be effective, the plan must be based on the organization's core values and support its purpose and direction. Also required for the plan is an accurate assessment of any constraints such as budget and available head count.

### Create the Plan

When all the available input has been gathered, the next step is to create the plan. The organization's leadership is responsible for this step. If the plan is companywide, the senior management committee is in the best position to develop the plan. If this group is too large, a subcommittee may carry out the planning process. At a minimum, representatives of every key function in the organization should participate. This obviously includes sales and marketing.

If the scope of the improvement plan is a single major business process, the planning group should include representatives from every major activity in the process. If the improvement initiative is directed toward a single functional department such as sales or marketing, the senior leadership from that area is responsible for creating the plan. As has been pointed out many times in this book, however, the broader the scope of the improvement effort, the more effective it will be.

No matter what the scope of the effort is, one of the key functions to be included is information systems. As pointed out in Chapter Seven, technology is having a dramatic effect on the ways that companies process information and communicate with their customers. Virtually every major improvement effort will include some use of technology. In most companies, the information systems department is responsible for implementing any major technology projects. Unfortunately this group is frequently omitted from the planning process.

Most organizations have already adopted some kind of business planning approach that fits their culture and is familiar to the team developing the plan. However, there are some guidelines that will make the planning process more effective.

### Use External Facilitation

Use an external facilitator to guide the planning process. As we saw in Chapter Five, teams are more effective when they are guided by an outside facilitator. The role of the facilitator is to guide the group through both the task and relationship processes. In the case of the planning session, particularly one involving top management, the facilitator should come from outside the company. It is virtually impossible for a company employee to facilitate a group of top-level executives. It is an issue of that employee's job security.

### Meet in a Remote Location

Planning sessions are most effective when they are held away from the company's normal place of business. This does not necessarily mean taking the corporate jet to Aspen. A local hotel or conference center will do. Going off site reduces interruptions and makes it less likely that members of the planning group will try to conduct their normal activities during coffee breaks. Creating the improvement plan is important and deserves everyone's full attention. This also means allowing enough time to get the job done. Most groups find that an initial planning session will take from two to three days.

### Use an Agenda

Develop an agenda before the initial planning meeting and make it available to all participants ahead of time. Then follow the agenda. This seems so basic, and yet many groups attempt to do planning in a completely free-form environment. The agenda defines the planning process and helps the facilitator keep the meeting on track. Generally the agenda will begin with a review of the agenda and the planning process the group will follow. It will also include a discussion of the trigger, the event that precipitated the need for the improvement process. And it will review the information gathered in support of the plan.

### Define the Problems

The next step is to define the problems that the improvement process is intended to solve and the opportunities it will address. To the degree possible, assign some value to each potential project. The financial people will expect this value to be in dollar terms. However, not every improvement can be easily quantified. For example, what is the monetary value of giving remote salespeople the ability to communicate with each other, sharing information and ideas?

### Select Projects

The planning team can now select the specific projects on which to begin. In addition to considering economic value, the priorities can be based on estimated impact on customer satisfaction and loyalty, employee satisfaction, ease of implementation, or available resources. It is a good idea to establish the ranking scheme before the planning process begins and before considering the information about each proposed project. This approach helps take the emotion out of setting priorities.

Several years ago, one of General Electric's business units created a simple matrix that used baseball metaphors to identify which projects were most important (see Figure 8.1.). Projects that are easy to implement and have a high payoff are grand slams (often referred to in other organizations as the "low hanging fruit"). They are a logical place to start. And easy projects that have a low payoff are not ignored. Referred to as stolen bases, these projects show that change is possible and supported by the organization. Tough solutions with high return are labeled extra innings. They may have a high payoff but are also high risk. Like many of the information systems projects of the past, they tend to take a long time and often requirements have changed and opportunities have been lost by the time they are fully implemented. Obviously the low-payoff tough projects are to be avoided. They are strike outs.

### Assign Responsibilities

Once the planning team ranks the projects in priority sequence, the next step is to assign specific responsibility for each project to a man-

**Figure 8.1.  GE Project Selection Criteria.**

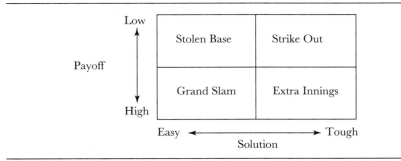

Source: General Electric (used by permission of Steve Kerr, 1996)

ager or implementation team. The planning team may also establish specific improvement goals and target dates for each activity.

*Select Improvement Techniques*

Creating and documenting the improvement plan as described here has an added benefit. It puts the focus on the problem or opportunity being addressed, not on the latest improvement technique or management fad. Once the projects have been identified and put in priority sequence, the next step is for the responsible manager or team to select the appropriate tools to use. Too often companies go about improvement the other way around. They become enamored with the latest tool and then look for ways to use it. Although it is useful to keep up on the latest thinking, it is more effective to add the new tools to the company toolbox and use them only when they fit.

Here is a summary of the functions of the formal improvement plan. It

- Identifies problems and opportunities
- Establishes priorities
- Identifies resources requirements
- Communicates intentions
- Demonstrates commitment
- Maintains focus on top-priority activities

*Learn from Experience*

Most organizations end their planning phase at this point and move on to implementation. The learning organizations are not through, however. They stop to evaluate their new plan in light of their own previous experiences and the experiences of other companies. As philosopher George Santayana said, "Those who cannot remember the past are condemned to repeat it." Learning organizations also identify the elements of the $R$ factor in the Marriott formula $(D \times V \times F > R)$, where $R$ is the organization's resistance to change.

If the organization is practicing awareness, improvement team members already know that approximately two-thirds of all major change efforts either fail or do not meet management's expectations. This is true of corporate downsizing, quality management, benchmarking, reengineering, and major information systems and technology projects. In most cases, management blames the approach and moves on to the next tool or technique. Careful examination usually reveals that the cause lies with management itself for all the reasons identified earlier in this book, including the following:

- An absence of real top management commitment
- Inadequate funding and staffing
- Unrealistic expectations
- Failure to involve all levels of management
- Not listening to customers
- Short planning horizon
- General resistance to change

According to Anthony Robbins (1988), "There are no failures, there are only outcomes." If something does not produce the outcome the organization wants, it can learn from the experience. When members of management examine the new improvement plan, they can look back at their experience and identify the causes of failure and the barriers to success. This requires an honest assessment of the root causes and a willingness to change whatever it takes to make the improvement plan work and the change effort a success. Remember, even though two-thirds of these efforts do not meet expectations, one-third do. It is also interesting that the one-third of efforts that do succeed are usually in the leading companies.

Implementing any kind of major change in the sales organization has some special challenges. Many companies locate their salespeople in remote sites. Some are clustered in sales offices; others work out of their homes or rented office space. This creates difficulties in getting the salespeople involved and in training, communication, and coordination. In addition, salespeople are usually measured on very short-term goals. As one frustrated internal organization development consultant once lamented to me, "Their planning horizon is next week." It is a problem that the organization must consider in the planning process.

Some sales organizations may also show particularly high levels of resistance to change. When this is the case, the improvement plan for sales needs to identify that resistance and the forms it takes and include ways to overcome or get around it.

*Move Quickly*

There is one last point to keep in mind while developing the improvement plan. About half the companies interviewed for this book said that if they had an improvement process to do over, they would have moved faster and involved more people. Although there were a few examples of organizations that took on too much, particularly in information systems projects, most took the opposite position. They would have been bolder in their efforts.

According to planner Daniel H. Burnham (Vitullo-Martin and Moskin, 1994, p. 217):

> Make no little plans;
> They have no magic to stir men's blood...
> Make big plans; aim high in hope and work...

With a sound plan in place, resources identified, responsibility and authority assigned, and barriers acknowledged, the organization is ready to begin implementation, the next phase.

## Phase III: Implementation

The third phase of making it happen is the initial implementation of the plan. Due to the wide variation in the scope and content of implementation plans, it is difficult to be specific here. However, a few elements are common to almost every change process, from a problem-solving project to a major reengineering effort. These elements include communication, skill development, behavioral change, and measurement.

### Communicate

The first common element in implementing improvement projects is communication about the plan. Recall that one of the features of the open organization culture is sharing information. If the organization has not practiced this in the past, now is the time to begin. All those touched by the plan need to be aware of it and how it will affect them and their jobs. This is true regardless of the scope of the project.

The leading companies begin their major improvement projects with a comprehensive announcement program. For companywide initiatives, the message comes straight from the CEO. If the effort is smaller in scope, the highest-level manager involved is the logical choice to announce the activity. The message may come through employee meetings, newsletters, bulletin board announcements, videoconferences, and any other mass communication technique.

One of the most critical elements of the announcement package is a forum for employee questions. People want the opportunity to ask questions about the effort and how it may affect them personally. Obviously in large companies and companywide efforts, middle- and lower-level managers are responsible for this activity. They have to be thoroughly prepared to answer the questions they will be getting.

Once the improvement process is under way, good communication must continue. People want to know what is going on and how well it is working. If a project meets its milestone and completion dates and performance objectives, they want to celebrate its success. If it does not, they want to know why and what the organization will do differently. This is all a part of the open organization culture and of the learning organization in particular.

### Develop Skills

The second common element of the implementation phase is making sure that everyone involved in executing the plan has the skills and knowledge he or she needs. This usually suggests some formal classroom training. For the training to be most effective, be sure it is designed around the way adults learn best. Research shows that they learn best through experience rather than lecture. Fortunately, most of the skills necessary to implement the best practices lend themselves to experiential training. Team exercises, process analysis, and the use of technology are all taught best using hands-on techniques.

People learn new skills best when they have a real need to use them. If they learn a skill in the classroom and then do not apply it, they quickly lose proficiency. Therefore the most effective way to transfer skills is to give people a general understanding of the tools and techniques involved. Then provide in-depth training on specific skills at the time people need and are ready to use them.

To provide skills just-in-time, experts must be available to individuals or team members fairly quickly. Managers and team facilitators usually fill this role for the team and process improvement skills. Technical support people or support centers provide the training for technology applications. In either case, people and teams that need to acquire a skill can do so when the requirement is present.

Classroom and on-the-job training are just two ways to build competency. Many skills can also be transferred through such technology as videotape and audiotape courses, computer-based training, and software tutorials.

Just providing skills training is not enough. Managers must also reinforce the desired new behaviors. Whether people are working on teams to solve problems or improve processes, gathering customer requirements, or using a salesforce automation system, it is up to the manager to communicate the desired new behaviors and how they will be measured.

Managers are also responsible for recognizing and rewarding the desired behaviors when they are observed. This activity itself may be a new skill for many managers. In the past, they spent much of their time looking for things that people did wrong and correcting them. Research shows that this is not the most effective way to reinforce new behaviors however. Positive recognition and reward are.

According to Dave Stockmal, director of bulk gas sales at Holox, "Don't wait two or three years to start recognizing people for their accomplishments." Based on his experience in implementing a quality process in a sales organization, he says recognition and reward for the new behaviors should start immediately. In a sales management job at another company, he took the lowest-ranked sales team in the company and took them to the top in a year.

### Measure

The last common element in the implementation phase is measurement. Although we have covered the importance of measuring performance and progress several times, it bears repeating. If an activity or process is not measured, it cannot be managed or improved.

To measure the success of each project, management needs a baseline against which to compare later data. The baseline measurements may already be part of the organization's management process, or they may have been gathered as part of the planning process. If not, now is the time to get them in place. Again, it is impossible to measure progress or success without a baseline against which to compare the results.

## Phase IV: Continuous Improvement

The objective of the fourth phase is to establish and maintain a state of continuous improvement. The organization seeks to accomplish this by focusing on customer satisfaction and loyalty, striving for world-class status in its core competencies, and responding quickly to change and opportunity.

The divisions between the first three phases are fairly distinct. However, the division between the third and fourth phases is less clear. As the organization completes the initial elements of the improvement plan, teams at all levels in the business identify new projects on which to work. They also review the results of their efforts and may go back to refine the processes that they have already improved.

If continuous improvement has become part of the culture of the organization, everyone is looking for new ways to do things. If the organization is successfully practicing an open culture, the members are maintaining an awareness of new technology and new improvement techniques. They are seeking new ways to solve problems, improve processes, and break down internal barriers. They are entering into partnerships with their best customers and trying to increase their understanding of customer requirements. They are employing today's best practices while constantly looking for new ways to do things.

The objective of having a separate improvement plan is to emphasize the importance of the effort. By now, this objective should have been fulfilled, and it is time to make continuous improvement an integral part of the organization's business strategy. Although there is no rule as to when this integration should happen, it probably should occur between one and three years after a major effort has begun. Keeping improvement processes separate from the business strategy sends the wrong message—that improvement is a separate activity and not part of the day-to-day course of business. To be successful, improvement must be part of the business strategy and the culture of the organization.

## Conclusion

Every company implements continuous improvement a little differently. The approach an organization takes has to fit its culture, its immediate requirements, and its available resources. This chapter identified some of the key elements in making continuous improvement happen. There are dozens of excellent books that provide detailed information on how to develop a plan and manage the projects that are part of it. That said, however, there are two things that are fundamental to making it happen. The first is informed commitment, and the second is taking action. Commitment is the foundation upon which the effort is built. And without action, the plan is just a dream.

# Chapter Nine

# Conclusion

This book began with four objectives in mind. The first was to identify and describe the best practices for improving the sales and marketing functions. There should have been no surprises when managing for change, listening to customers, focusing on processes, using teams, practicing an open organization culture, and applying technology made the list. As usual, there are no silver bullets, no deep dark corporate secrets, just good solid business practices. The same practices also lead the list for companywide improvement. The real message here is that they work as well in the sales and marketing functions as they do in any other area of the organization.

The second objective was to report specific examples of how companies are applying these practices in sales and marketing. This book has shared as many of these stories as space would allow and included examples from virtually every size company and every major industry. Dozens more just like them came out of my research and demonstrate the use of the six best practices.

The next objective was to support the design and implementation of an improvement process in sales and marketing. Clearly no one book can have all the answers for every organization and every situation. However, the company examples, the specific techniques and the planning process may help point the way.

The last objective was to show how sales and marketing can contribute to the companywide improvement process. Obviously it cannot be a companywide effort if it does not include the critical sales and marketing functions. They participate by taking part in cross-functional problem solving and process improvement teams. They contribute input on customer requirements and feedback. And they are aware of what is going on in the market and what the competition is doing.

The need to change, to implement the best practices, and to improve continuously is driven by customers, cost, and competition. Because sales and marketing are the company's primary contact points with the customers, they are often the first to recognize changing customer wants and needs and competitive pressures. Sales and marketing people are aware of the need for efficiency and productivity when their company shares expense and revenue information with them. Most professionals in sales and marketing already understand the need for continuous improvement, both companywide and within their own functions. All they need is the support of committed management and the tools to get the job done.

In the final analysis then, it comes back to management. According to consulting partner John Lawrence at Xerox, "The full context of Total Quality is beginning to be understood. It is not about the quality of products. It is about the quality of management. Get that right and the product quality follows." Yet in many companies, management is the biggest barrier to change. Many managers want to continue to run their business in the same way they always have, but the world has changed around them and the old ways no longer work. Lawrence has also shared a quotation attributed to Albert Einstein: "Doing the same thing over and over again and expecting a different result is the definition of idiocy." Those might be strong words but some psychologists have a similar view. One of their definitions of insanity is expecting new outcomes out of old behaviors.

Throughout, this book has focused on improving the processes owned by the sales and marketing functions and those in which sales and marketing play a major role. However, it is just as important to apply the improvement techniques to the management processes as well. For example, one of the most popular management techniques of the last ten years has been downsizing. Hardly a day goes by without some major corporation announcing more job cuts. However, almost never does a company announce that it is analyzing and improving the management processes that caused it to have more people than it needed in the first place. It is only the best companies that consider their management processes to be among their core competencies, and fewer still strive to improve these processes continuously.

The level of management commitment is another driver for successful improvement. According to Darrell Rigby at Bain & Company, the Boston-based international strategy consulting firm, his research shows that the level of a company's satisfaction with a management tool is in direct relationship to the degree of commitment to its use. He says, "Take Total Quality Management as an example. Users reporting the highest levels of satisfaction with TQM report that they used it in a major (versus limited or trial) effort, fully implemented the recommendations that resulted from the tool's usage, and belonged to organizations that focused heavily on increasing teamwork and managing cultural changes. Users who were least satisfied with Total Quality Management customarily used the tool on a more limited basis, received less top down support, and were less likely to have the entire organization focused on TQM at the same time." Figure 9.1, from the Bain & Company research results, demonstrates the relationship between satisfaction with the effort and level of commitment and support.

Most of the companies that contributed to this book have maintained their commitment to continuous improvement, both companywide and in sales and marketing. Sadly some have lost momentum, and a few have even gone backwards. In most cases, the cause was a lack of long-term commitment; in others, a change in the top management of the business. In none of these examples did company performance improve after they abandoned their continuous improvement process. In most cases, it deteriorated.

One company used process improvement to identify the need for a consolidated customer service department. They improved service levels and reduced costs. They also used an executive contact program, assigning top executives to key accounts. When a competitor acquired the company, the executive contact program died. The new management now responds to poor quarterly sales by reorganizing and downsizing.

Another company was using its successful quality process in sales and manufacturing as a sales tool. It held a seminar, bringing in its best customers to share the company's experience in quality management. Outside speakers from other companies that are leaders in the quality process added to the day-long program. One

**Figure 9.1.  TQM Satisfaction Is Linked to Usage Patterns.**

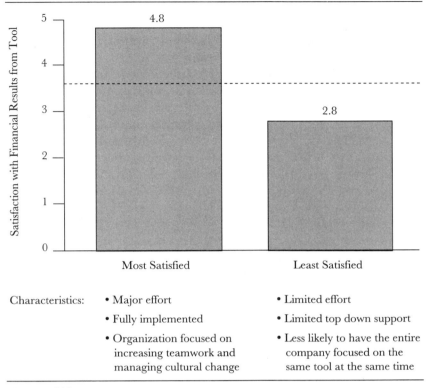

| Characteristics: | • Major effort | • Limited effort |
| --- | --- | --- |
| | • Fully implemented | • Limited top down support |
| | • Organization focused on increasing teamwork and managing cultural change | • Less likely to have the entire company focused on the same tool at the same time |

*Note: n* = 508.

*Source:* Bain & Company, "1994 U.S./Canada Survey," 1995.

order from one new customer paid for the whole event, but a change in top management put a stop to additional quality seminars. It was back to business as usual.

Fortunately these two companies are among the minority. Most of the leading companies mentioned in this book have stayed the course. They have maintained their commitment to continuous improvement, eliminating barriers, and knocking down the old organizational silos. They are identifying the new behaviors that support an open organization culture and reinforcing them. They are making decisions based on facts, not hunches, opinions, or company traditions.

The enlightened managers in these companies are role models for the behaviors they want. They understand that the old adage about raising children, "Do as I say, not as I do," does not work. They know that the message adults as well as children hear is "Say as I say; do as I do." They walk their talk.

This brings us to the end of our journey together. We have examined six best practices for continuous improvement in sales and marketing. The message is clear. Companies that have made a commitment and then managed for change, listened to their customers, focused on their processes, used teams, practiced an open organization culture, and applied technology have shown better bottom-line results than those that have not. The leading companies have applied all six of these practices successfully in their sales and marketing functions. They have increased customer loyalty and raised employee satisfaction while growing their revenues and profits. It is my sincere hope that this book will provide both an inspiration and a set of guidelines to help you do the same.

# References

"An Ear for Learning." *Sales & Marketing Management,* Aug. 1995, pp. 30–31.

Belasco, J. A., and Stayer, R. C. *Flight of the Buffalo.* New York: Warner Books, 1993.

Brewer, G. "Insuring Excellent Selling." *Sales & Marketing Management,* Oct. 1995a, pp. 53–54.

Brewer, G. "Wheeler Dealers." *Sales & Marketing Management,* June 1995b, 39–44.

*Business Week,* Oct. 18, 1993, pp. 7–8.

Camp, R. C. *Benchmarking, The Search for Industry Practices That Lead to Superior Performance.* Milwaukee, Wis.: Quality Press, 1989.

"Cigna Places a Premium on Being the Best." *Sales & Marketing Management,* Nov. 1993, p. 41.

Corman, L. "Closing the Book." *Sales & Marketing Management,* Sept. 1996, pp. 80–86.

Crosby, P. B. *Quality Is Free.* New York: New American Library, 1979.

Daniels, A. C. *Performance Management, Improving Quality Productivity Through Positive Reinforcement.* Tucker, Ga.: Performance Management, 1989.

Dartnell Corporation. *Dartnell's Annual Sales Force Compensation Survey.* Chicago: Dartnell Corporation, 1992.

Deming, W. E. *Out of the Crisis.* Cambridge, Mass.: MIT Center for Advanced Engineering Study, 1986.

"Follow the Leader." *Sales & Marketing Management,* Apr. 1994, p. 34.

"General Telephone of California: Trying to disconnect a bad image." *Business Week,* November 29, 1982, pp. 66–67.

Hammer, M., and Champy, J. *Reengineering the Corporation: A Manifesto for Business Revolution.* Harper Business, 1993.

Harrington, H. J. *Business Process Improvement.* New York: McGraw-Hill, 1991.

Herrington, G. M. "The Catch–22 of Total Quality Management." *Across the Board,* Sept. 1991, pp. 53–55.

The International Quality Study[SM]. *Best Practices Report.* Cleveland, Ohio: American Quality Foundation and Ernst & Young, 1992, p. 35.

Kirkpatrick, D. "Why Microsoft Can't Stop Lotus Notes." *Fortune,* Dec. 12, 1994, p. 154.

Korzybski, A. *Science and Sanity.* (4th ed.) Lakeville, Conn.: The International Non-Aristotelian Library Publishing Company, 1958.

Lawler, E. E., Mohrman, S. A., and Ledford, G. E. *Creating High-Performance Organizations.* San Francisco: Jossey-Bass, 1995.

Loeb, M. "Where Leaders Come From."*Fortune,* Sept. 19, 1994, p. 241.

MacKay, H. B. *Swim with the Sharks Without Being Eaten Alive.* New York: Morrow, 1988.

Nanus, B. *Visionary Leadership.* San Francisco: Jossey-Bass, 1992.

O'Guin, M. "Aerospace and Defense Contractors Learn How to Make Their Businesses Soar." *Quality Progress,* June 1995, 35–38.

Opper, S., and Fersko-Weiss, H. *Technology for Teams: Enhancing Productivity in Networked Organizations.* New York: Van Nostrand Reinhold, 1992.

Peters, T. J. *A Passion for Excellence.* New York: Warner Books, 1985.

Peters, T. J. *Thriving on Chaos: Handbook for a Management Revolution.* New York: Knopf, 1987.

*Profiles in Customer Loyalty, An Industry-by-Industry Examination of Buyer-Seller Relationships.* Stamford, Conn.: Learning International, 1989.

Ramirez, C., and Loney, T. "Baldrige Award Winners Identify the Essential Activities of a Successful Quality Process." *Quality Digest,* Jan. 1993, pp. 38–40.

Rice, F. "How to Make Diversity Pay." *Fortune,* Aug. 8, 1994, p. 79.

Robbins, A. *Unlimited Power.* New York: Ballentine, 1986.

Robbins, A. "The Mind Revolution: Three Steps to Personal Power." A public seminar, New York, Oct. 1988.

Royal, W. F. "Is He a Deal Maker?" *Sales & Marketing Management,* Sept. 1994, p. 90.

Senge, P. M. *The Fifth Discipline: The Art and Practice of the Learning Organization.* New York: Doubleday, Currency, 1990.

Seligman, D. "Keeping Up," *Fortune,* June 26, 1995, p. 175.

Sergesketter, B. F., and Roberts, H. V. *Quality Is Personal: A Foundation for Total Quality Management.* New York: Free Press, 1993.

U.S. General Accounting Office. *Management Practices: U.S. Companies Improve Performance Through Quality Efforts.* U.S. Government Accounting Office, 1991.

Vitullo-Martin, J., and Moskin, J. R. *Executive's Book of Quotations.* New York: Oxford Press, 1994.

# Index

**A**

Account teams, 145, 168–170, 173. *See also*
    Cross-functional teams; Sales teams; Teams
AccuRate, Inc., 58–59, 60, 160
ACT, 237
Action, taking informed, 207
Active awareness, 178–180
ADC Telecommunications, Inc., 195–196
Aerospace industry, 125, 127–128
Aetna, 220
Agco Corporation, 188
Agenda, for planning sessions, 261–262
Alexander Group, 142, 145
Alignment: of measurements with compen-
    sation and priorities, 41–42; of measure-
    ments with customers, 41; of
    measurements across departments, 39–41;
    of measurements with strategy, 39; of mea-
    surements with values, 42–44
Allen, J., 166–167
AlliedSignal Inc., 189
America Online (AOL), 246
American Airlines, 17, 233
American Compensation Association, 142
American Express, 220, 246
*American Heritage Dictionary*, 137, 214
American Marketing Association, 123, 229
American National Standards Institute (ANSI),
    128
American Quality Foundation, 26, 122, 134
Amica Mutual Insurance Company, 95,
    221–222
Analog Devices, 209
Arami, S., 85
Area councils, 183–185, 206, 232
Arendt, C. H., 103
Ashe, M. K., 29
Aspired-to-norms, 165–166
Associates for Improving Management, 50
Associations, 70, 80
Assumed requirements, 55–56. *See also* Cus-
    tomer requirements, 55
Assumptions, questioning of, 200–205
AT&T, 30–31, 74, 92, 147
AT&T Paradyne, 132
Audiocassettes, 231–232
Audits: information, 258–260; for ISO-9000
    registration, 129

Authority of teams, 141
Automakers, 234
Automobile dealership, 37–38
Awareness, 178–180
Awareness training, 36–37

**B**

Bain & Company, 51, 52, 272, 273
Baird Corporation, 231
Bank of Oklahoma, 243
Barksdale, J. L., 27
Basic process model, 53–55, 93, 97
Bausch & Lomb, Inc., 82, 87–88, 235
Belasco, J. A., 179–180
Bell Laboratories, 17
Benchmark groups, 124
Benchmarking, 17, 51; contraindications for,
    122; defined, 119; information sources for,
    122–123; imputing results of, 127–128; ob-
    jectives and uses of, 127–128; on-site visits
    for, 124, 126–127; organizational perfor-
    mance, 120; personal, 120; process, 109,
    119, 120–128; product, 120; steps in,
    122–128; surveying potential partners
    for, 123–125; types of, 119–121
*Benchmarking* (Camp), 119
Benchmarking partners, 121; on-site visits to,
    124, 126–127; quid pro quo for, 124; sur-
    veying potential, 123–125
Bennis, W., 28–29, 34
Best practices for improving sales and market-
    ing: basic concepts of, 17–22; defined,
    13–16; effectiveness of, 16–17; illustrated,
    in Eastman Chemical Company story,
    4–16; listed, 4; technology applied to,
    214–215. *See also* Customers, listening to;
    Improvement process; Management for
    change; Open organization culture;
    Process focus; Teams; Technology
Blackiston, G. H., 49
Blankemeier, B., 143–144
Blind surveys: benchmarking, 124, 125; cus-
    tomer satisfaction, 67
Boeing, 150
Born-again CEO, 49, 254
Boundaries: crossing, between organiza-
    tions, 197–198; process, 104, 106; team,
    161

Brainstorming, 17
Brewer, G., 37, 44, 188
Brooklyn Union Gas (BUG), 61
Budget, sales and marketing share of, 2
Bulletin boards, electronic, 241–242
Bureaucracy, 111–112
Burger King, 60
Burnham, D. H., 265
Burns, J., 252
Burzon, N., 89
Business process improvement (BPI), 98–115;
   benchmarking and, 109, 121–122; execu-
   tive improvement team for, 100; and
   reengineering, 117; Step 0 (Commit),
   94–100; Step 1 (Identify and Select
   Processes), 100–101; Step 2 (Select Process
   Owner and Team), 101–103; Step 3 (De-
   fine the Process), 103–106; Step 4 (Identify
   Process Requirements), 106–107; Step 5
   (Measure the Process), 107–109; Step 6
   (Benchmark the Process), 109, 121–122;
   Step 7 (Analyze the Process), 109–112, 117,
   127–128; Step 8 (Improve the Process),
   112–115; Step 9 (Operate the Process),
   115; steps in, 99; teams for, 173
*Business Process Improvement* (Harrington), 111
Business process management (BPM),
   115–116; and reengineering, 117
Business processes. *See* Processes
Business units, companywide organization ver-
   sus, 181–185
Business-value-added activities, 111
Business volume measure, 108
*Business Week*, 50, 89, 254
Buy-in, through use of teams, 138
Buying decision: bases of, 53; flowchart of, 192,
   193, 198–200; influences on, 22–23; the In-
   ternet and, 248; systems analysis of,
   192–196, 198–200

**C**

Cadillac Motor Car Division, 233
CADIS, Inc., 246–247
Caffey, J., 21, 24, 162
Calgon Corporation, 73–74, 91–92
California & Hawaiian Sugar Company, 72
Callahan, P. G., 127
Camp, R. C., 119, 121
Carroll, D., 202
Celebration, 11
Cellular phones, 231, 233
Center for Effective Organizations, 134
Century Furniture Industries, 29, 74, 202–203
Champion: improvement, 257; team, 156
Champy, J., 17, 116–117, 118
Change: drivers of, 1–2, 32, 48–49, 271; resis-
   tance to, 265; responses to, 2–4; training
   and, 162. *See also* Improvement process;
   Management for change
Change continuum, 117
Chief executive officers, 49, 254. *See also* Lead-
   ership; Management for change

Chrysler, 170
CIA, 179
Cigna Corporation, 121
"Cigna Places a Premium on Being the Best,"
   121
Classroom training, 267
"Clip, scan and review," 179–180
Coach, team facilitator as, 157–158
Code of conduct, 165–166
Colletti, J., 142
Command and control management model,
   31–32
Commitment, of managers: to business process
   improvement, 98–100; education for,
   36–37; eliciting, 48–51, 254–257; importance of, 24–28; and measurement and
   reward systems, 49–50; phase in improve-
   ment process, 253, 254–257; relationship
   of, to company satisfaction with management tool, 272, 273; sticking to, 34–35,
   272–274; triggers for, 48–51, 254–257
Commitment, of team members, 154
Committees, teams versus, 135–136
Communication: about improvement plan,
   266; management and, 47–48; with remote
   salespeople, 171, 241–242; about team
   progress, 10; in teams, 138; technology for,
   231–235. *See also* Information sharing;
   Technology
Companywide view, 181–185
Compensation: alignment of, 41–42, 46–47; for
   team members, 168–170. *See also* Recogni-
   tion; Rewards
Competition: and change, 2, 48–49; and team-
   work, 168; and technology use, 217
Competitors' customers, 59–60
Complaint system, 75, 81
Computer software. *See* Software
Cone, E., 231
Congruence, 29–32
Connors, J. J., Jr., 95
Consumer Reports, 90, 221
Contact points, 189
Continuous improvement, 209–213; manage-
   ment commitment and, 272–274; Marriott
   formula for, 252–253, 264; phase in im-
   provement process, 254, 268–269; in plan-
   ning phase, 264–265. *See also* Improvement
   process
Coopers & Lybrand, 243
Corman, L., 204
Corporate memory, 212–213
Corporate reengineering, 116. *See also* Reengi-
   neering
Corpuz, F., 150
Cost measurements, 108
Cost reduction, sales, 42
Cost-per-student measure, 40
Cost to customer, global view of, 200
Councils: area, 183–185, 206, 232; customer,
   69, 80; distributor, 187, 188
Crew, M., 24, 88

Critical success factors (CSFs), 27; management-owned, 158–164; team member-owned, 165–166; for teams, 158–166
Crosby, P. B., 5, 256
Cross-company teams, 149–150
Cross-functional focus, 96
Cross-functional teams: across business functions, 148–149; compensation for, 168–170; goal alignment in, 166–167; information sharing in, 206; in marketing, 147–148; in sales, 144–149, 168–170; staffing of, 159. *See also* Process improvement team; Teams
Cross-selling, 189
Crum, S., 209
Culture. *See* Open organization culture
Current customers, 58
Customer asset management, 217, 219
Customer buying decision. *See* Buying decision
Customer complaints, 75, 81, 189
Customer councils, 69, 80
Customer cycle, 198–200
Customer demand: as driver of change, 1, 49; as driver of technology use, 216
Customer feedback. *See* Customer information; Customers, listening to
Customer focus: and customer information systems, 220–221; in Eastman Chemical Company, 5–8; and measurement priorities, 44–45; popularity of, 52; in process improvement, 96; versus product focus, 190; and quality, 17–18
Customer information: analysis of, 86–88; content of, 53–57, 223–224; costs of gathering, comparative, 78–81; gathering, for improvement plan, 258–259; methods of gathering, 61–77; methods of gathering, applied to sales and marketing, 78–81; in multiple functional files, 218–219; pitfalls in gathering, 83–88; in process model, 53–55; and sales effectiveness, 217–218; sources of, 2, 57–60, 71–72, 84; technology for, 12–13, 216, 217–228
Customer information systems (CISs), 217–228; barriers to, 225–226; benefits of, 226–228; benefits of, examples of, 219–223; costs of, 226; customers of, 225; and database marketing, 230; development of, 223–228; information content of, 223–224; life expectancy of data in, 224–225; ownership of, 224–225; soft information in, 224
Customer interviews, face-to-face, 65–66, 79
Customer perspective, 188–190
Customer planning sessions, joint, 72–75, 81
Customer report cards, 76, 81, 90
Customer requirements: and aligning measurements, 41; categories of, 55–57; criteria for, 107; identifying, 55–57, 106–107; in process model, 53–55; and process requirements, 106–107, 110. *See also* Customer information; Customers, listening to

Customer retention, priority of versus incentive for, 42–43
Customer satisfaction: correlation of, to repeat business, 87, 88; and employee focus, 45; with goods versus services, 22
Customer satisfaction surveys, 2, 5; analysis of, 86–88; getting adequate response to, 85–86; in improvement planning phase, 259–260; periodic, 61; popularity of, 52; questions on, 84–85; scheduled, 61; telephone, 64–65, 77, 78; transaction-based, 62; written, 62–64, 77, 78. *See also* Surveys
Customer segment teams, 147. *See also* Cross-functional teams
Customer teams, 145, 173; cross-company, 149–150. *See also* Cross-functional teams
Customers: aligning measurements with, 41; competitors', 59–60; current, 58; defining, in sales and marketing, 18, 53; end user, 84, 185–186, 225; factors that influence, 22–23; indirect, 60; internal, 53, 60; international, 6–11; involving, in process implementation, 114; lost, 58–59; prospective, 59
Customers, listening to, 14, 51, 52–92; barriers to, 88–92; costs of, 90–91; followup to, 77, 82–83, 86–88; information content for, 53–57; information sources for, 57–60, 71–72, 84; methods of, 62–77; methods of, applied to sales and marketing, 78–81; objectives of, 53; pitfalls in, 83–88; rationale for, 52–53; technology and, 215; timing of, 60–62; workload created by, 91–92
Cycle time reduction, 197–198, 201–202; using electronic data interchange, 234–235

### D

Daniels, A. C., 5
Dartnell Corporation, 20, 42, 205
Data gathering, in team problem-solving process, 152. *See also Information headings*
Data owners, 224–225
Database marketing (DBM), 228–229; examples of, 229–231; implementation of, 230–231
Davenport, E., 6–7
Decision-making process: distributor involvement in, 187; team, 138, 151. *See also* Buying decision, customer
Defects: defining, in sales and marketing, 21–22; in personal quality process, 31
Defense industry, 125, 127–128
Deming, W. E., 5, 35
Departmental teams, 141–144, 150. *See also* Teams
Distribution partners, 60, 235
Distribution system view, 185–188
Distributor councils, 187, 188
Diversity, 137
Documentation, for single company look, 189–190
Dow Corning, 170

Downsizing, 15–16; and management processes, 271–272; and organizational culture, 213; and reengineering, 117–118; and self-managed teams, 135; and technology, 217
Druar, M., 196
DSSI, 168, 242
DuraTemp Corporation, 204
Duration of teams, 141
Dutkiewicz, K., 69

**E**

"Ear for Learning, An," 231
Eastman, G., 4
Eastman Chemical Corporation, 22–23, 160, 188, 205, 206, 246; customer communication, 83; executive contact responsibility, 71; improvement process, 4–13, 254; mission statement, 19–20; six best practices illustrated by, 13–16
Eastman Kodak Company, 4
Education, for eliciting commitment, 36–37. *See also* Training
Effectiveness process measure, 108, 113–114
Efficiency process measure, 108, 113–114
Einstein, A., 271
Eisner, M., 29
Electronic data interchange (EDI), 6, 234–235
Electronic mail (e-mail), 233, 245. *See also* Internet
Employee empowerment, 208–209. *See also* Teams
Employee feedback, 32–34, 259, 266
Employee focus, 45
Employee involvement, in process improvement, 97
Employee morale, and teams, 138–139
Employee satisfaction, in Eastman Chemical Company, 6
Empowerment: defined, 208; management for change and, 208; in open organization culture, 208–209
Encyclopedia Britannica, 203–204
End users, 84, 185–186, 225
Ernst & Young, 26, 122, 134, 168
Ethics, 44
Ethyl Corporation, 132
Executive contacts, 70–71, 81, 227
Executive improvement team (EIT), 100

**F**

Facilitator: as coach, 157–158; as leader, 158; for planning phase, 261; team, 156–158, 163
Fear, of information exchange, 206
Federal Express Corporation, 27, 30, 45, 49, 232
Feedback. *See* Customer information; Customers, listening to; Employee feedback; Performance feedback; Suppliers, feedback to
Fersko-Weiss, H., 239

Fightmaster, B., 190
Financial collapse, impending, 48–49
Financial measurements, 108
Flexibility, 166
*Flight of the Buffalo* (Belasco, Stayer), 179–180
Flowcharts, functional: of customer buying decision-making process, 192, 193, 198–200; for distribution system view, 186; of open organization culture as learning culture, 209–211; of order fulfillment process, 93, 94; of processes, 104–105, 110–111, 197–198
Focus groups, 66–67, 79
Follow the Leader, 71
*Forbes ASAP,* 200
Ford, 170, 246
*Fortune,* 28–29, 45
Foseco, Inc., 149–150
Fourteen Points for the Transformation of American Industry, 35
Freelance Graphics, 237
Frontline employees, 208–209
Functional organization, 181–185; customer information in, 218–219, 225–226

**G**

Gallup, 37
Garcia, P., 65
Gates, B., 29
General Electric Capital Corporation, 184
General Electric Company, 27, 29, 38, 74, 110, 150, 197–198; area councils, 182–185, 206, 232; EDI at, 234; project selection criteria, 262, 263
Gillmeister, E., 87–88
Giroux, J. P., 244, 250
Global view, 180–200; organizational perspective in, 180–190; systems perspective in, 190–200. *See also* Organizational perspective; Systems perspective
Globe Metallurgical, Inc., 72, 130, 149, 170
GM, 170
Goal alignment, 166–167
Gold Mine, 237
Groupware, 239–244
GTE Corporation, 35–36, 37, 38, 89, 147–148, 200–201, 212, 254
Guideposts, 99

**H**

Hammer, M., 17, 116–117, 118
Harrington, H. J., 26, 53, 111, 122
Harte-Hanks Direct Marketing, 229–230
Harvard Graphics, 237
Health care claim processing, 220–221
Hendershot, A., 189
Herrington, G. M., 20, 48, 49
Hessenauer, G., 27, 28, 150, 183, 185, 197
Heublein, Inc., 41
Hewlett Packard Company, 21, 24, 121, 132, 162

High-performing organizations, 3; customer focus in, 52; formal improvement plans in, 36–38; measurement priorities of, 44–45; open organization culture in, 175–176; qualities of, 25–26; six best practices illustrated in, 4–13
Holiday Inns, 233
Holland, J., 248
Holox, 268
Howard, J., 36

**I**

IBM Corporation, 24, 47, 68, 84, 88, 104, 160, 162, 189, 203, 232, 233, 239–240
Implementation phase, 254, 265–268
Improvement plan, 35–38, 260–265; communication of, 266
Improvement process: best practices and, 4; commitment phase in, 253, 254–257; communication and, 47–48; continuous improvement phase in, 254, 268–269; duration of, 34; at Eastman Chemical Company, 4–13; evaluating the need for, 255–256; initial implementation phase in, 254, 265–268; and management for change, 24–25; management commitment to, 25–28, 48–51; managers' roles in, 28–48; Marriott formula for, 252–253, 264; measurements and, 38–47; organizational learning and, 209–213; pilot projects for, 256–257; planning phase in, 253–254, 258–265; and responses to change, 2–4; sales and marketing functions and, 1–2; salespeople's involvement in, 205; and self-managed teams, 148–149; skill development for, 266–268; systems approach to, 191–192; triggers for implementing, 48–51, 254–257. See also Best practices
Improvement teams: goal alignment in, 167; information sharing in, 206; mission of, 141; remote salespeople in, 171, 241–242; resources for, 161, 257; staffing of, 159, 160, 257; task skills needed in, 152. See also Cross-functional teams; Process improvement team
Improvement techniques, selection of, 263
Incentives, and priorities, 41–42
Indirect customers, 60
Information: action founded on, 207; and active awareness, 178–180; in best practices, 215; gathering, for improvement plan, 258–260; and power, 206–207; qualitative, 258–259; quantitative, 259–260; as sales and marketing product, 19, 53, 215; soft, 224. See also Customer information; Customer information systems; Database marketing; Technology
Information content, about customers, 53–57, 223–224
Information sharing: barriers to, 206–207; with customers, 48, 77, 82–83, 206; in open organization culture, 205–207, 208. See also

Communication; Customer information systems; Technology
Information sources: for benchmarking, 123–127; about customers, 57–60, 71–72, 84
Information systems. See Customer information systems; Database marketing; Internet; Salesforce automation; Technology
Information systems (IS) departments, 225–226, 250–251
Information systems (IS) improvement team member, 103
Insurance policy change process, 95
Internal customers, 53, 60; of customer information system, 225
International customer satisfaction, 6–9
International Quality Study$^{SM}$, 26, 122, 134
International Standards Organization (ISO), 128–133
Internet, 12–13, 244–250; and the customer, 248; in marketing, 245–250; in sales, 245, 250; size of, 244–245
Interstate Batteries, 231–232
Interviews, face-to-face: benchmarking, 125; customer, 65–66, 79. See also Site visits, 125; Surveys; Telephone surveys
Intranets, 245
ISO-9000 standards, 128–133
ISO-9001, 129
ISO-9002, 129
ISO-9003, 129
ITT Fluid Transmission Corporation, 143–144
ITT Hartford Life Insurance Company, 249

**J**

James River Corporation, 33
Jennings, N., 72, 130, 149
Job satisfaction, 138–139
Johnsonville Sausage, 49
Joint customer planning sessions, 72–75, 81
J. P. Morgan Bank, 121
Juran, J., 5, 50
Juran Institute, 49
Just-in-time training, 267

**K**

Kaiser Permanente, 197
Kappel, B., 131, 189
Karmilovich, S., 73, 91–92
Kearns, D., 49, 50, 254
KFC, 60
Kirkpatrick, D., 242
Kmart, 118, 235, 255
Knowledge-based professions, 32
Kocher, J., 160
Kodak, 203
Korzybski, A., 105

**L**

LaMontagne, R. J., 41
Lands' End, 220
Laptop computers, for salesforce automation, 238, 240, 241. See also Salesforce automation

Large companies, information systems in, 225–226

Larry Weber Group, 250

Lawler, E. E., 134

Lawrence, J., 16, 45, 87, 271

Leadership, 28–35, 48–51; of teams, 155, 158; and values, 42–43

Learning International, 53

Learning organization, 209–213, 264–265, 268–269

Leffler, D., 29, 202–203

Leonard, S., Jr., 208

Listening. See Customers, listening to

Literature request fulfillment process, 95

L. L. Bean, 121

Loeb, M., 28–29, 34, 35

Loney, T., 25–26

Lost customers, 58–59

Lotus Development Corporation, 240–241, 242

Lotus Notes, 239–243

Lynn, G., 248

**M**

Mackay Envelope, 218

Mackay, H. B., 217–218, 237–238

Mail surveys, 63. See also Surveys

Major accounts sales, priority versus incentive for, 42

Make International Business Easy (MIBE), 6–9, 254

Malcolm Baldrige National Quality Award, studies of contestants/winners, 16–17, 34, 52, 175–176

Malcolm Baldrige National Quality Award winners, 13, 36, 76, 85–86, 89, 146; learning from, 50; potential return on investment in, 50

Management bureaucracy, 111–112

Management by Objectives (MBO), 5

Management for change: as best practice, 13–14; in business process improvement, 98–100; communication in, 47–48; and empowerment, 32; improvement techniques applied to, 271–274; managers' commitment to, 24–28, 34–35, 36–37, 48–51, 98–100, 253, 254–257, 272–274; managers' leadership role in, 28–35; managers' management role in, 35–38; measurement systems and, 38–47; role of, in team success, 158–164; technology and, 214; versus traditional management, 31–32

Manager: as process owner, 101–102; as role model, 14, 29–32, 274; as team leader, 155

Manion, P., 24

Market research, 2. See also Database marketing

Marketing function: best practices for improving, 4–16; cross-functional teams for, 147–148; customer information systems and, 228; customers of, 18, 53; database, 228–231; defects in, 21–22; drivers for change in, 1–2; groupware for, 240–241; Internet in, 245–250; ISO-9000 standards

in, 130–133; mission of, 20; process improvement results in, 95–96; processes of, 20–21, 94–95; product of, 19; quality and, 17–18; responses to change in, 2–4; team issues in, 166–171; vision in, 29. See also Best practices

Marketing teams, 173–174; issues of, 166–171; measurements for, 164. See also Teams

Marlow, R., 49

Marlow Industries, Inc., 49, 85–86, 146

Marriott formula for continuous improvement, 252–253, 264

Marriott International, Inc., 252

Martin, A., 87

Maximizer, 237

McDonald's, 60

MCI Telecommunications, 230

McNamara, D., 114

Measurements, 38; aligning, with compensation and priorities, 41–42, 169–170; aligning, with customers, 41; aligning, across departments, 39–41; aligning, with strategy, 39; aligning, with values, 42–44; business process, 107–109, 113–114, 115; and commitment, 49–50; in improvement implementation, 259, 268; number of, 47; and organizational learning, 210–211; prioritizing, 44–45; for teams, 163–164, 169–170; unintended consequences of, 45–47

Medicus Systems Corporation, 95

Merton, R. K., 45

Mission: of marketing, 20; process, 104; of sales, 19–20; of teams, 140–141, 158–159, 165; and vision, 29

Mission measurements for teams, 164

Moskin, J. R., 265

Motivation: for listening to customers, 89–90; for management commitment, 48–51, 254–257

Motorola, Inc., 30, 60, 70–71, 85, 219–220

Murphy, J., 201

Mutual Life Insurance Company of New York (MONY), 36–37, 38, 44

Mystery shoppers, 68–69, 79

**N**

Naisbitt, J., 179

Nanus, B., 28

National account managers, 241

National Cash Register, 16–17

National Semiconductor, 246–247

Nelson, D., 195–196

Nelson, J., 85–86, 146

NeuroDimension, Inc., 247–248

New accounts sales, priority of versus incentive for, 42

NeXT Computer, Inc., 69

Nordstrom, 207, 220

Norland, K., 168, 242

Northrop Grumman Norden Systems, 127

"Not invented here" (NIH) syndrome, 128

No-value-added activities, 111
NYNEX Corporation, 189

**O**

Office Depot, 189
Office Max, 189
Ogilvy & Mather Interactive, 246
O'Guin, M., 125
On-line SFA applications, 238. *See also* Sales-force automation
On-the-job training, 267
Open organization culture, 15, 48, 175–213; awareness in, 178–180; background of, 175–176; versus closed organization culture, 176–178; continuous learning in, 209–213, 268–269; elements of, 176–178; empowerment in, 208–209; global view in, 180–200; information sharing in, 205–207; informed action in, 207; organizational perspective in, 180–190; questioning in, 200–205; systems perspective in, 190–200; technology and, 215
Operating guidelines for teams, 165–166
Opper, S., 239
Order fulfillment process, 93, 94, 96, 104
Organizational culture: as barrier to listening to customers, 89–90; change of, 34, 89; unreliability of, 212–213. *See also* Open organization culture
Organizational learning, 209–213, 264–265, 268–269
Organizational performance benchmarking, 120
Organizational perspective, 181–190; company-wide view in, 181–185; customer view in, 188–190; distribution system view in, 185–188
Osborn, A., 17
OSRAM SYLVANIA, 69, 187–188
Ownership: of customer information system, 224–225; of process, 101–103; of web sites, 250
Oxford Health Plans, 220

**P**

Pagers, 231
Park Place Motorcars, 37–38, 142–143, 144
Parliamentarian, team, 156
*Passion for Excellence, A* (Peters), 26
Patrick, C., 189
PC software industry, 185–186
Peer group evaluation, 164
People's Bank, 24, 27
Performance feedback, 48, 120, 164, 266
Performance improvement, through use of teams, 137
Performance measurements, for teams, 164, 169–170
Periodic surveys, 62. *See also* Customer satisfaction surveys
Personal development, 139–140
Personal quality checklist, 30–31

Peters, T. J., 26, 28, 207
Pilot projects, 51, 256–257
Pitney Bowes Inc., 62, 87, 106, 114, 166–167, 190
Pizza Hut, 60
Planning phase, 253–254, 258–265; assigning responsibilities in, 262–263; creating the plan in, 260–265; information gathering for, 258–260; learning from experience in, 264–265
Planning sessions, 261–262
Power Point, 237
Price Waterhouse, 125
Priorities: compensation and, 41–43; of measurements, 44–45
Problem definition, in planning phase, 262
Problem-solving process, team, 151–152
Process activities, 104–105; categories of, 111–112; review of, 110–111
Process analysis, 109–112, 117, 127
Process benchmarking, 109, 119, 120–121; as part of process improvement, 121–122; steps in, 122–128. *See also* Benchmarking
Process boundaries, 104, 106
Process dimensions of teams, 151–153
Process flow: documentation of, 104–105; review of, 110–111
Process focus, 14, 93–133; technology and, 215
Process improvement: benchmarking and, 121–128; characteristics of, 96–97; commitment to, 98–100; implementation of, 112–115; ISO-9000 and, 128–133; labels applied to, 96; of management processes, 271–274; objectives of, 98; ongoing management of, 115–116; operation of, 115; people to involve in, 114; process of, 98–115; relationship to profitability, 125; results of, in sales and marketing examples, 95–96; systems approach to, 190–200; technology and, 216–217. *See also* Business process improvement; Business process management
Process improvement team (PIT): charter for, 103; measurements for, 164; mission of, 141; in process implementation, 114; selecting members of, 102–103, 159; tasks of, 103–115; training of, 103. *See also* Teams
Process management, 115–116
Process mapping, 197–198. *See also* Flowcharts
Process measurements, 107–109, 115; building-in, 113–114; types of, 108
Process mission, 104
Process owner: selection of, 101–102; training of, 103
Process reengineering, 116–119
Process requirements, 106–107, 110
Process walk-through, 105, 106
Processes: basic model of, 53–55, 93, 97; defining, in business process improvement process, 103–106; defining, in sales and marketing, 20–21, 94–95; elements in, 97; identifying and selecting, 100–101; order

fulfillment, 93, 94, 96, 104; systems perspective on, 190–200. *See also* Business process improvement; Business process management
Procter & Gamble, 121, 122
Product, of sales and marketing, 19, 215. *See also* Information
Product launch process, 106
Product launch team, 174
Product teams, 147–148. *See also* Teams
Productivity: through teams, 136–137; and technology use, 217
Productivity process measure, 108
*Profiles in Customer Loyalty* (Learning International), 53
Profit contribution, 42
Profitability: relationship of continuous process improvement to, 125; of sales, 46
Profits, focus on, 45
Project selection, in planning phase, 262, 263
Proposal preparation process, 95
Prospects, 59
PruCare, 220
Public rating, 90

**Q**

Quality: defining of, 17–18; of management, 271
Quality circles, 159
Quality management process: and commitment, 24–26, 36–37; in Eastman Chemical Company, 5–6; and improvement plan, 35–37; personal, for managers, 29–32. *See also* Benchmarking; Improvement process; ISO-9000 standards; Process improvement
Quality revolution, drivers of, 48–49
Questioning, in open organization culture, 200–205

**R**

Ramirez, C., 25–26
Real-value-added activities, 111
Recognition, 32–34; alignment of, 41–42; in improvement process, 267–268; of teamwork, 33–34, 167–168; timeliness of, 268
Redundancy, data, 218–219, 227
Reengineering, 17, 116–119; corporate versus process, 116–117; need for, 118
*Reengineering the Corporation* (Hammer, Champy), 116–117
Regression analysis, 87–88
Relationship processes of teams, 150, 151, 152–153, 154; and facilitator's role, 156, 157; operating guidelines for, 165–166; training for, 162
Report cards, customer, 76, 81, 90
Retail chains, 118, 235
Rewards, 32–34; alignment of, 41–42; and commitment, 49–50; in improvement process, 267–268; for teamwork, 33–34, 167–168
Rice, F., 137
Rigby, D., 52, 272

Risk taking, 207
Robbins, A., 3, 207, 264
Robbins, V. A., Jr., 6, 12
Roberts, H. V., 31
Role models, managers as, 14, 29–32, 274
Royal, W. F., 61
Ryan, W., 216, 236

**S**

*Sales, Marketing, and Continuous Improvement* survey, 3–4
*Sales & Marketing Management*, 37
Sales contact points, 189
Sales contests, 168
Sales function: best practices for improving, 4–16; cross-functional teams for, 144–149; customers of, 18, 53, 57–60; defects in, 21–22; departmental teams for, 141–144; drivers for change in, 1–2; ethics in, 44; functional versus companywide organization for, 181–185; Internet in, 245; ISO-9000 standards in, 130–133; measurements in, 41–42, 46–47; mission of, 19–20; open versus closed culture in, 176–178; process improvement results in, 95–96; processes of, 20–21, 94–95; product of, 19; quality and, 17–18; recognition and rewards for, 33–34, 167–168; responses to change in, 2–4; team issues in, 166–171; vision in, 29. *See also* Best practices
Sales priorities, and sales incentives, 41–42
Sales quotas, 34, 46
Sales teams: benefits of, 173; cross-company, 149–150; departmental, 141–144; issues of, 166–171; measurements for, 164; staffing of, 159. *See also* Teams
Sales training measurements, 40–41
Salesforce automation (SFA), 236–244; advanced applications for, 238–244; defined, 236–237; implementation of, 244; on-line applications for, 238; stand-alone applications for, 237–238
Salespeople: communications technology for, 231–235; customer information systems and, 217–218, 219–223, 227; disbanding of, 203–204; and distributors, 188; in improvement teams, 160; influence of, 202–204; involvement of, in improvement process, 205; remote, 170–171, 241–242; as source of customer information, 71–72, 80; in teams, 141–144, 149–150; in teams, special issues of, 166–171; time spent by, analysis of, 204–205
Sallick, K. H., 229–230
Santayana, G., 264
Saturn, 149
Scandals, 44
Scientific management, 31–32, 211–212
Scoggin, D., 86
Scope of Registration, 129
Scope of team, 140
Scoreboards, 10

Scribe, team, 155
Sears Automotive Centers, 44, 46
Secura Insurance Companies,
Segmented marketing, 228–231
Self-managed teams, 135, 144, 148–149. *See also* Teams
Seligman, D., 45–46
Senge, P. M., 209
Sergesketter, B. F., 30–31
*Sharkware,* 237–238
Sheehe, B., 197
Shewhart, W. A., 17
Shute, J., 33
Silverstein, J., 220
Simplicity, 47
Single-face presentation: customer information service for, 226–227; documentation for, 189–190
Site visits, benchmarking, 124, 126–127
Size: of company, and information systems, 225–226; team, 140
Smith, F., 49, 232
Software: for database marketing, 229; groupware, for advanced SFA implementation, 239–244; for on-line SFA implementation, 238; for stand-alone SFA implementation, 237–238
Software buying decision-making process, 192–195, 198–200
Software industry, 185–186
Sony, 178–179
Special purpose teams, 141. *See also* Teams
Specialists, on teams, 156
Sponsors, team, 156
Square D Company, 60, 67, 131, 189–190
Stada, R., 209
Staffing, of teams, 153–154, 159–161
Stand-alone SFA applications, 237–238. *See also* Salesforce automation
Standards, ISO-9000, 128–133
Staples, 189
Stated requirements, 55. *See also* Customer requirements, 55
Stay the Course, 34–35
Stayer, R. C., 49, 179–180
Steal Shamelessly, 128
Steel, J., 76
Steelcase, Inc., 69, 136, 139–140, 147, 164, 174
Steering committee, 257. *See also* Improvement teams
Stew Leonard's, 208–209
Stockmal, D., 268
Strategic Leadership Forum, 52
Strategy: aligning values and, 43–44; measurements and, 38, 41–42
Student evaluations, 40–41
Success, celebrating, 11
Sun Microsystems, 244–245, 246, 250
Suppliers: electronic data interchange with, 235; feedback to, 97; involving, in process implementation, 114
Support people, 167–168

Surveys: analysis of, 86–88; benchmarking, 123–125; blind, 67; company versus independent, 125; in customer information systems, 227; design of, pitfalls of, 83–85; getting adequate response to, 85–86; giving feedback of, to customers, 77, 82; questions on, 84–85; source of contacts for, 84; telephone, 64–65, 77, 78; written, 62–64, 77, 78. *See also* Customer satisfaction surveys
Susanna Opper & Associates, 239
*Swim with the Sharks without Being Eaten Alive* (Mackay), 217–218
Synergy, 137
*System,* defined, 191
Systems perspective, 181, 190–200
Systems Sales Support Company, 216

**T**

Target, 118, 235
Task forces, teams versus, 135–136
Task processes of teams, 150, 151–152, 153; and facilitator's role, 156, 157; operating guidelines for, 165–166; training for, 162
Taylor, F., 31, 211–212
Team leader, 155, 158
Team members: compensation for, 168–170; critical success factors owned by, 165–166; full-time versus part-time, 159–160; performance measurement of, 164; selection of, 153–154, 159–161; selection of, for process improvement team, 102–103; roles of, 155–158; voluntary versus required, 160–161
Teams: attributes of, 140–141; attributes of, in sales and marketing, 141–150; authority of, 141; barriers to, 163; benefits of, 134–135, 136–140; as best practice, 14–15; boundaries of, 161; buy-in of, 138; categories of, 140–141; categories of, in sales and marketing, 141–150; circumstances that preclude use of, 172; communication in, 138; content dimension of, 150–151, 156, 157, 165; critical success factors for, 158–166; decision making in, 138; definition of, 135–136; duration of, 141; in Eastman Chemical Company, 8–11, 14–15; employee morale and, 138–139; empowerment of, 208–209; flexibility in, 166; goal alignment in, 166–167; guidelines for deciding whether to use, 171–174; issues of, in sales and marketing, 166–171; management support for, 158–164; measurements for, 163–164; members of, 153–158, 159–161; mission of, 140–141, 158–159, 165; operating guidelines for, 165–166; performance and, 137; personal development in, 139–140; popularity of, 134; processes of, 150–153, 165–166; productivity and, 136–137; recognition and rewards for, 33–34, 167–168; relationship processes of, 150, 151, 152–153, 156, 165–166; resources for, 161; roles in, 155–158; scope

of, 140; size of, 140; structure of, 153–158; task processes of, 150, 151–152, 153, 156, 157, 165–166; technology and, 215; tools of, 150–153; training for, 9–10, 162. *See also* Process improvement team

Technology: applying, as best practice, 15, 214–251; for communications, 231–235; defined, 214; for customer information systems, 217–228; for database marketing, 228–231; drivers of, 215–217; in Eastman Chemical Company, 6, 12–13, 15; for electronic data interchange, 6, 234–235; enabling role of, 214–215, 250; and implementation plan, 260–261; and information systems departments, 250–251; the Internet and, 244–250; ownership of, 250–251; and process reengineering, 118–119; and process review, 112; and quality improvement, 17–18; for salesforce automation, 236–244; for team communication, 171. *See also* Customer information systems; Database marketing; Internet; Salesforce automation; Software

*Technology for Teams* (Opper, Fersko-Weiss), 239

Telecommunications, 233

Teleconferencing, 171, 232

Telephone surveys: benchmarking, 123, 124; customer satisfaction, 64–65, 77, 78

Texaco, Inc., 209

Texas Instruments, Inc. (TI), 74, 95, 96, 234–235

3M, 189, 205, 225

*Thriving on Chaos* (Peters), 26

Timekeeper, team, 156

Timing: of listening to customers, 60–62; of recognition, 268

Total Quality Management (TQM), 271, 272, 273

Trabue, G. O., Jr., 7–8, 9, 11

Training: with audiocassettes, 231; distributor, 187–188; in improvement implementation phase, 266–268; process owner, 103; process team, 103; for remote salespeople, 170–171; sales, measurements of, 40–41; team, 9–10, 162, 170–171

Transaction-based surveys, 61. *See also* Customer satisfaction surveys

TransCanada Gas Services, Ltd., 111–112, 201–202

Travelers Insurance Asset Management and Pension Services, 27

Troiano, M. D., 246

Turner, T., 29

**U**

Ungerman Bass (UB) Networks, Inc., 241–242

Unintended consequences, law of, 45–46

Unisys Corporation, 86, 95

Unknown requirements, 57. *See also* Customer requirements, 55

USAA, 222–223, 230

User groups, 70, 80

U. S. General Accounting Office (GAO), 16, 25, 34, 52, 175–176

**V**

Value-added process activities, 111

Values, measurements and, 42–44

Ventana Corporation, 241

Videoconferencing, 232

Vision: aligning values and, 43–44; development of, 28–29

*Visionary Leadership* (Nanus), 28

VisionQuest, 241

Vitullo-Martin, J., 265

Voice mail, 232

Voss, J., 201

**W**

Wachovia Bank, 121

Wal-Mart, 49, 118, 235, 255

Walk the talk, 14, 29–32, 274

Walk-through, process, 105, 106

Walton, S., 29, 83

Warren, T., 148, 187

Watson, T., Sr., 16–17

Weber, L., 250

Welch, J., 29, 182–183, 184, 185

Westinghouse Electric Corporation, 34, 103, 132, 147, 189

Wheelabrator Corporation, 86, 119, 148–149, 187, 206

Withheld requirements, 56–57. *See also* Customer requirements, 55

WMX, 149

Woollcott, A., 110

Work teams: cross-functional, across business functions, 148–149; cross-functional, in marketing, 147–148; cross-functional, in sales, 144, 145–147; mission of, 140; task skills needed in, 152. *See also* Teams

World Color, Inc., 48

World Wide Web, 12–13, 244–250; in marketing, 245–250; web site design for, 248–250

Written surveys: benchmarking, 123, 124; customer satisfaction, 62–64, 77, 78

W. W. Grainger, 200

**X**

Xerox Corporation, 16, 33–34, 44–45, 49–50, 64–65, 206, 209, 254, 271; benchmarking, 87, 119, 121

**Z**

Zummo, P. J., 27

Zytec Corporation, 76, 147, 203